Architect's Essentials of Starting, Assessing, and Transitioning a Design Firm

Peter Piven, FAIA
and Bradford Perkins, FAIA

with William Mandel

WILEY

John Wiley & Sons, Inc.

This book is printed on acid-free paper. ∞

Published by John Wiley & Sons, Inc., Hoboken, New Jersey
Published simultaneously in Canada

For general information about our other products and services, please contact our Customer Care Department within the United States at (800) 762-2974, outside the United States at (317) 572-3993 or fax (317) 572-4002.

Wiley also publishes its books in a variety of electronic formats. Some content that appears in print may not be available in electronic books. For more information about Wiley products, visit our Web site at www.wiley.com.

Library of Congress Cataloging-in-Publication Data:

ISBN 978-0-470-26106-4
ISBN 978-0-470-33973-2 (AIA Edition)

PRINTED IN THE UNITED STATES OF AMERICA
10 9 8 7 6 5 4 3 2 1

Dedication from the original edition of Architect's Essentials of Starting a Design Firm:

To Alf Werolin and Weld Coxe, who taught each of us to be effective advisers to others

To Lawrence Perkins, who passed on his wisdom and experience about starting a firm

and

To our wives, Phyllis Friedman Perkins and Caroline Piven, who supported us with this project even when it got in the way of family obligations

Dedication from the original edition of Architect's Essentials of Ownership Transition:

THIS BOOK IS DEDICATED

to the design professionals whose inventiveness and dedication to improving the built environment has inspired our work with them,

and

to our wives, Caroline Piven and Christine Mandel, whose continued encouragement and support have contributed immeasurably to our writing this book.

—Peter Piven and Bill Mandel

Contents

Part 2: Ownership Transition

Introduction to the New Edition

Brad Perkins and Peter Piven

This book combines two earlier books, *Architect's Essentials of Starting a Design Firm* and *Architect's Essentials of Ownership Transition*, on issues that architects and other design professionals face, first at the beginning and then later in their careers. The first covers the issues that one faces when starting a new design firm, and the other covers the issues surrounding the transition of the firm's leadership and ownership, either when the founders decide to expand ownership in the firm, generally driven by growth, or when they begin looking toward their own retirement. In between is a professional lifetime full of challenges.

Other books in the Architect's Essentials series cover many of the issues encountered along the way: marketing, presentation skills, winning proposals, contract negotiation, cost management, and professional development. One group of issues that is not yet covered in the series, however, is how to evaluate and make course corrections after the start-up period is over and a practice is established. This is the "what do we want to be when we grow up?" period that a firm's leadership faces when it is no longer dealing with the survival issues of a start-up. These are also the issues that a firm's leadership faces when they are contemplating the remaining years of their careers.

For some, these issues generate a professional midlife crisis. For others, a thoughtful analysis and action plan redirects the firm toward the leadership's most important long-term goals. In this introduction to the combined book, we suggest how to determine when it is time for a midcareer review. What are the essentials of such a review, and how have some other successful firms used this review as the platform for a period of positive growth and change?

The Start-Up Phase

The start-up phase is frequently characterized by a generally unplanned, "hand-to-mouth" existence. The founder or founders focus on the projects on hand and begin worrying about new work when the work on current projects nears completion. More thoughtful founders consider their capabilities, desires, and objectives and develop plans that include marketing for the kind of clients and projects they would like to work on and believe they have the ability to get.

If they choose to stay small, or are unable to secure a sufficient quantity of work that enables growth, that remains the pattern of their professional careers and future ownership transition becomes very difficult or impossible. If they want to grow and are able to secure work that allows them to grow, they typically add staff as volume increases, first professional/technical and then administrative. If growth continues, and the principal-to-staff ratio increases to approximately 1:11, founding principals generally find that the firm's marketing, management, client satisfaction, and project team leadership needs have outstripped their ability to do all that must be done to run the firm successfully. They start looking for partners.

The "Too-Small" Firm

The firm has reached the point where it has steady work for a staff of 12 to 15. In spite of good work and a lot of marketing effort, the owners find that they cannot get the next scale of projects, nor can they successfully sell their core areas of expertise beyond a limited geographic area because they are viewed as too small.

These owners have a critical decision ahead of them: To grow or not to grow, that is the question. If they opt to grow, then how can they do it? They are unlikely to be able to do it without some essentially different direction. One might be to elevate or bring in an owner who adds expertise in a different market sector, which might allow growth within the same geographic area. Another is to merge with a firm of relatively equal size, immediately creating a larger firm with similar or added capabilities. And still another is to establish an office in a new geographic location, either by starting one from scratch by sending an emissary or by merging with (or possibly acquiring, although that may be less likely) another firm. Each of these conditions implies an ownership transition of some kind.

The Stable, Midsize Firm

The firm is established in a limited area in or near a midsize city and has grown to 30 people; its workload and staff size are relatively stable. Sometimes the owners of such a firm opt to coast—to continue along the same path that got them where they are. However, the midlevel professionals who have become key to the firm's operations want the opportunity to grow and become owners, but the "pie" is too small to divide. If they do not see a future, they threaten to move on.

The owners can risk the loss of key midlevel professionals, which will inhibit their ability to continue to run the firm successfully *and* deplete the ranks of potential future successors. On the other hand, they could choose to begin transferring ownership interests to others. Although "dividing the pie" into smaller slices may be uncomfortable at the beginning, it keeps key professionals, preserves future retirement opportunities, and may create new energy that could lead to growth and/or success in new areas. If the owners proceed in this way, the most important thing for them to consider is identifying those "rising stars" that they see as having the best potential to lead the firm successfully in the future.

The Project Opportunity Elsewhere

The firm gets a major, high-profile project in another region. Is this project the platform to open a second office serving a second region, or should it be treated as a one-time event?

Here, the owners are faced with a critical decision about the essential nature of their firm: Will they remain a one-location firm, or take the first step toward a multioffice practice? If the latter, then the same questions arise about how to achieve it, albeit with beneficial new conditions that are driven by the project itself. Project fees will fund the start-up, either partially or entirely, and there will be a need for the staff necessary to execute the project, to whatever degree and at whatever level the firm decides.

Even so, if the new office is to be successful beyond the initial project that created the opportunity to open it, the owners must be mindful of putting a leader in place—an emissary from headquarters, a leader recruited in the new location, or a leader in a firm identified as a potential merger candidate. All these conditions imply ownership transitions.

Investment in the Future

The firm has been doing well and cash flow has improved to the point where the principals have the choice to take some excess money out for their personal use or to use the firm's reserves for an investment in growing the firm. The temptation may be to buy the country house or some other long-desired purchase that was deferred by the demands of a young firm. But will an investment in developing a new market, a new office, a new principal, an aggressive public relations effort, an acquisition, additional technology, or a stronger staff offer the opportunity to achieve more of the firm's long-term goals?

Ambitious firms often continue to defer the principals' personal interests in order to pursue their professional ambitions. The gamble of a firm's financial reserves often complicates the eventual issue of ownership transition by depleting the cash necessary to fund the founding principals' retirement. Nevertheless, ambitious plans usually require the willingness to invest.

Self-Assessment vs. Professional Goals

The firm has prospered but has not reached the position in the profession that the founders once dreamed of.

In a principal retreat at a resort that helped create a relaxed atmosphere for introspection, the founders were able to be candid enough with each other to agree that they could not get to the first tier on their own. They were missing some of the skills—particularly in design—necessary to achieve their goals for the firm. How do they fill this hole in their firm's leadership?

One way is to recruit and develop younger staff until they can provide the necessary new leadership. Another is to merge with a firm or to acquire the necessary leadership. The first brings up strategic, long-term transition issues, while the latter makes these issues a tactical, short-term concern.

Divergence of Interests and Goals

The firm has become established, but the founding principals are finding it increasingly difficult to agree on fundamental aspects of the practice—for example, design, their respective roles, promotions, and the long-term goals of the firm. The problems have become so serious that they are hurting the firm's performance.

The leaders of a firm do not have to be close friends (although it helps), nor do they have to have the same personal goals, but it is important that they share values and agree on the core vision for the firm and on their respective roles. Mutual respect is also critical. Shared ownership of a design firm can be an inherently unstable relationship. It has many of the stresses of a marriage without some of the glue (such as children) to keep the leaders focused on common goals.

Unfortunately, it is quite common for the founding principals' interests, energy level, and vision for the firm to diverge over time and for this to lead to conflict. If the conflict cannot be resolved, it may be necessary for one or more members of the firm's leadership to leave. This, too, brings forward many of the issues on ownership transition covered in this book.

Crisis

The firm suddenly runs into a very bad patch. The firm is losing money, the cash reserves are depleted, key people want to leave, new work is slow in coming in, construction problems have resulted in serious lawsuits. The future looks grim.

All firms have bad moments, but the best ones find a way to get through them. Firms, and their leadership, usually get along fine while things are going well, but the real test is a crisis. Well-managed firms know that one or more bad periods are inevitable and plan for them. Some parts of the plan may include building financial reserves, pursuing marketing efforts in building types that are less vulnerable to economic cycles, and conducting an open discussion of how the firm will respond to a severe problem.

Crises in professional organizations always impact the owners/leaders and frequently foment ownership transition issues. Crises start people thinking about retiring, selling the firm, getting rid of partners, and so on.

Practice Abroad

A foreign-born employee decides to return his native country and soon calls a principal to see if she will work with him to pursue and do projects in his home city. Does the firm stay local or does it take on the additional challenges of association with others and international practice?

This opportunity adds new wrinkles to the fabric of opportunities. Should the former employee simply be an independent representative, possibly with a consultant contract of some kind? Should he join the firm as a principal in order to properly represent the firm, have the firm's needs at heart, and have a stake in the future rewards he or she helps makes possible? If the employee has developed a firm of his or her own, should that firm be merged or acquired? Or should a joint venture be created so that each firm's interests are respected without encumbering either's current ownership or future obligations?

Some of these have important ownership transition implications, others not.

Merger Consideration

The principal is approached by a principal in another firm of comparable size to discuss the possibility of merging. Merger means loss of absolute control and working with another (likely) strong partner or partners. Does this move the firm closer to its long-term goals, or does it just complicate life? Possibly both!

If the principals want to grow their firms, then merger is a transaction that creates a larger firm—instantly, and with little or no cash required. The important distinction between a merger and an acquisition is that a typical "merger of interests" is accomplished without cash changing hands. The two firms pool their assets and liabilities. The owners own the increased value of the merged firm proportionally; each owner owns the same value the day after the merger as he or she did the day before.

Although the predominate reason for merging is to create a larger firm that is more competitive in the marketplace, there are others, including market and staff diversification. Also, for a firm with principals who are beginning to think about their own retirement but who do not feel they have potential successors in their firm—younger professionals who they believe have what it takes to run the firm successfully—merger with another firm that has potential successors provides an exit strategy they would not otherwise have.

Loss of Clients or Market Share

Firms that have grown and prospered can still lose clients or market share in many ways. Clients can get into financial trouble. They can be acquired by larger firms in which facilities' decisions are made by a different group of people. They can have fulfilled their capital expansion programs. Their facilities decisions may have been made by people with whom you had solid relationships but who have retired. They can choose to seek other design professionals, for good reasons (e.g., different capabilities or proximity) or not. Regardless, firms can lose access to clients they have depended upon and need to replace. What can be done?

Of course, the principals can apply their knowledge, experience, and energy to pursue new clients that might consider them. But suppose the principals have lost touch with the marketplace. Perhaps they've rested on their laurels—relied on the clients with whom they had relationships. Perhaps they're tired. Perhaps they're not age-contemporaneous with the current client decision-makers. What then? They can transfer ownership to professionals who are experienced, eager, and energetic and who are more likely to be successful in connecting with prospective clients.

Death, Disability, and Retirement

Although design professionals tend to love what they do, sooner or later they either choose, or are required by their agreements, to retire from ownership, or they become disabled or die. If they consider such eventualities sufficiently early in the life of the firm, they can provide for a gradual transition of ownership to others who will acquire their ownership interests and continue the firm. If they haven't, then an ownership transition of another kind will occur. Either the deceased owner's estate will sell the firm to others, possibly others in the firm, or the firm will be liquidated—a less desirable and less effective solution for all.

The scenarios introduced above are just some of the more common issues that leaders of a design firm face over the life of a practice. This is not intended to be a comprehensive list of these issues, but they do highlight many of the most serious, as well as many of the most common.

As the material covered in this book illustrates, except for unanticipated opportunities, most of these issues are best approached with a plan. The same argument that we make to our clients about the need to begin with a plan before building also applies to starting, building, and managing a practice. Chapter 9 of *Starting a Design Firm* outlines our recommendations for the major elements of such a plan.

You will know where you are going and you will be better able to measure your progress in getting there if you have a road map—a destination and a route. A plan will help clarify how you want to start and how you want to grow (that is, *if* you want to grow). Planning implies envisioning and articulating a desired future, and then identifying the action steps you will take to achieve it, along with the responsibilities and milestones that will help you actually take the steps you believe necessary. You don't need to look 30 years into the future; 3 to 5 years will do just fine.

We wish you much good luck as you proceed!

PART I

Starting a Design Firm

Introduction to Starting a Design Firm

So you're thinking about starting your own design firm. You are not the first to have this desire, nor will you be the last. It is a common dream for many—if not most—design professionals. In fact, hundreds of design professionals start new firms each year for various reasons, and many others plan for the day when they can take the same initiative. Some start their own firms because they want to pursue their own ideas and interests, others because they see it as an opportunity to make a better living, and still others because they do not want to work for someone else. For each individual, there are different factors that lead to this common dream.

This book was written to help those who have this dream decide whether, and when, to start their firm, as well as to guide them through the steps necessary to achieve a successful launch and get them through the challenging first years of operation. As in any field, a significant number of new design firms never get off the ground or achieve the founders' major goals. But for many professionals, having their own firm is a satisfying, challenging, and rewarding experience.

There is no one formula to follow to guarantee success, but most founders of new firms who achieve their goals observe the basics of creating a successful practice. One of the most important basics is to have a plan. This book was written for design professionals (including architects, engineers, graphic designers, interior designers, landscape architects, and others involved in planning and designing the built environment) who are considering starting, or have already started, a new firm. Most of the material is also relevant to smaller design firms whose founders are interested in growing and/or changing their current practice. It focuses on the basic financial, marketing, and other necessary tools and puts them all within the framework of a plan for operating the new firm.

Most of the examples used in the book are drawn from firsthand experience and are relevant to the issues facing any design professional building a new or working in a small firm. Some of this material was first developed to support a course on the same topic given by the two of us each summer at the Harvard Graduate School of Design, but the bulk of the book is based on our personal experience as principals of architectural firms and as advisers to others in the field.

Part 1 of this book is organized into 12 chapters and 2 appendices:

- Chapter 2 discusses the motivations and analysis that often precede the start-up of a new firm. Most design professionals have some, but not all, of the skills, capabilities, and resources needed to start and build a successful practice. For some this means they should consider a career in an existing firm. For others, this initial analysis helps clarify why having their own firm is important and identifies what steps—such as finding partners with complementary capabilities—they must take to have a realistic chance of success.

- Chapter 3 addresses the essential task of obtaining clients. Without a steady flow of new work, any design firm will fail. All successful firms find a way to achieve this essential goal, and most of the techniques they use can be learned. To that end, the first part of the chapter discusses the strategic techniques involved in establishing a marketing plan; the second part outlines some of the most important tactical aspects of a successful sales program.
- Chapter 4 explains the financial management of a design practice. It does not try to teach design professionals how to be accountants, but it does describe the basic tools and techniques used to plan, build, and guide the financial health of a young design firm.
- Chapter 5 investigates two of the most challenging tasks faced by even the most experienced heads of successful firms: setting fees and negotiating contracts.
- Chapter 6 introduces some of the central organizational and personnel management tools and options that a young firm should consider.
- Chapter 7 outlines some of the legal and ethical basics that should be considered.
- Chapter 8 lists a number of the available resources that will help a new firm both in its early years and once it has become established.
- Chapter 9 coordinates the material presented in Chapters 2–8 and describes how these

techniques can be used to create a comprehensive plan for your firm's future.

- Chapter 10 confronts one aspect that should be—but rarely is—included in the firm's plan: a structured approach to achieving design excellence.
- Chapter 11 provides some cautionary advice for avoiding pitfalls of starting a new firm.
- Chapter 12 outlines the major first steps in launching your firm.
- Appendices to Part 1 include a Study Guide that contains a number of supplemental projects intended for use by both readers and schools, the latter of which may choose to incorporate this material in their practice courses. Appendix B, "Charting Your Course," provides a widely recognized guide to understanding how firms can be organized and managed.

Even for someone with a great deal of self-confidence, starting a new design firm is a daunting task. Part 1 and the techniques and examples it contains are intended to make the task seem less overwhelming. As you read, keep in mind that the firms that you admire and consider successful today were once fragile start-ups. They launched, survived, and then prospered, and so can you.

Deciding to "Go on Your Own"

2

As stated in Chapter 1, having their own practice is the goal of many design professionals. A new firm that is successful and achieves its founders' basic goals can be a very satisfying way to pursue a career in the field. But while the rewards (in self-expression, if not income) can be significant, so too can the risks. Most new businesses—whether architectural, engineering, and interior design firms or restaurants—never get off the ground. Some manage to launch and survive, but never really achieve much more than a modest success. A few, however, manage to surmount the inherent problems and achieve success as a business, as well as become what most professionals hope for: a respected firm that is both professionally and financially successful.

Have a Good Reason for Starting Your Own Firm

Assuming you are considering "going on your own" (otherwise why would you be reading this book), the first question to ask yourself is: Why do you think that having your own firm is the right thing for you?

We have spoken to hundreds of people who have started their own firms and no two cite exactly the same motivations. Nevertheless, we've found the answers can be placed into 10 categories, which share a central theme: the desire for greater control over one's future. These categories are:

1. Ability to realize one's own goals and follow one's own interests.
2. Greater ability to balance one's personal and professional lives.
3. More direct relationship between effort and recognition for one's professional accomplishments.
4. More direct relationship between effort and financial reward (the opportunity to make more money than is possible as an employee of someone else).
5. Greater control over one's own destiny, design, and other issues of personal importance.
6. Survival during bad economic times.
7. Satisfaction of building one's own practice.
8. Ability to be involved in everything.
9. Failure to "fit" into an established organization.
10. Desire to work with friends, a spouse, or others of one's own choosing.

It's important to point out that in some ways the concept of greater control is illusory because the founder of a new firm soon finds out that he or she has exchanged the control by a boss for the pressures exerted by demanding clients, making payroll, and carrying out the greater range of tasks expected of the head of even a small firm. Nevertheless, when you have your own firm and face these issues, you usually feel that you are in control because they are yours to deal with.

The new pressures on the individual starting his or her own firm, however, are usually more than balanced by the benefits of one—or all—of the reasons listed for starting a firm. Few people who have started their own firm and reached the point at which its survival is no longer in question would ever go back to working for someone else.

Having a strong reason to go out on your own is a prerequisite, because the risks, effort, and initial financial investment can be significant. Without a strong reason, most design professionals decide that they are better off having a career within an existing organization. Your reason might be as simple as the prospect of having one or two interesting clients that could help launch a practice or, as for Thom Mayne of Morphosis, it can be recognizing that your personality and work habits are ill-suited to a large corporate practice. As Mayne put it, there was "no other way." The point is, not everyone is cut out to run his or her own firm, but if you feel you have compelling reasons for doing so, there are a number of steps to take before you make the final decision:

1. Be clear as to why you are doing it.
2. Define the type of firm you want to have.
3. Set goals for the first year and for the long term.
4. Look at successful models and research how they succeeded.
5. Define what special services or abilities you will offer that potential clients need.
6. Decide if you have all the basic capabilities necessary to succeed, or if you will need partners and/or colleagues.
7. Decide how you will support yourself until the firm is generating an adequate income to pay you.

Know the Type of Firm You Want

Part of your motivation should be that you have a specific concept of the type of firm you want to launch. David Grumman began his successful mechanical engineering firm, Grumman/Butkus Associates, in 1973, because he wanted to work directly for owners involved in the rapidly emerging energy conservation arena. He explained, "I wanted to have a different kind of consulting firm, and I did not want to work for architects."

It is not enough to just hang out a shingle that says "architect," "engineer," or "interior designer," and announce, "Hello, world, here I am!" It is very important to define what your practice will offer, why it is special or unique, and why people should hire you. The answers to these questions may evolve over time as the firm matures, but it is important to have clear answers in your own mind from day one.

One way to help clarify what you want your firm to be is to define goals that will help measure progress or success. In the first year, some of the goals can be pretty basic, for example:

- To survive.
- To successfully complete three or four assignments.
- To secure enough work for the next year.

Even though it may seem impossible to set goals for 7 to 10 years out (the minimum time it takes most firms to mature from a start-up to an established firm), the exercise can help establish priorities for your efforts.

If, for example, your goal is to have a practice that is considered a leader in three or four building types, this should help focus your marketing and other efforts of the early years. Or if your goal is to run a firm of choice for a wide variety of assignments in a particular community, this will focus your efforts in a different way. (These choices are discussed in more detail in Chapter 3.)

Firm Types

Every firm is the result of its people and its circumstances, so in that sense each firm is unique. It is possible, however, to develop a general understanding of design firm typologies so that you can make an informed choice about the type of firm you want.

Two key driving forces shape the operation, management, and organization of every architecture firm:

- Choice of technology, defined as the system or process the firm employs to do its work
- Collective values of the firm's principals

Technology shapes the firm's delivery process. Examination of the marketplace reveals three major categories of design firm technologies:

- *Strong-idea* firms, which are organized to deliver singular expertise or innovation on unique projects
- *Strong-service* firms, which are organized to deliver experience and reliability, especially on complex assignments
- *Strong-delivery* firms, which are organized to provide highly efficient service on similar or more routine assignments

Values shape management styles. *Practice-centered* professionals, who see their calling as a way of life, typically have as their major goal the opportunity to serve others and produce examples of their discipline. Their bottom line is qualitative: How do we feel about what we are doing? How did the job come out?

Business-centered professionals, who practice their calling as a means of livelihood, more likely have as their personal objective a quantitative bottom line that is more focused on the tangible rewards of their efforts: How did we do? (A further explanation of this typology can be found in Appendix B.)

Model Types

In clarifying the type of firm you want to have, and defining a path to get there, it can be very helpful to look at how other firms became successful. Success, of course, should be measured against one's own goals, but for most professionals success includes achieving professional respect, producing interesting work, earning an adequate income, and other basic objectives.

In our experience, 10 common models can be used to launch a successful firm, and there is something to be learned from each. These models are:

1. Major client as "booster rocket"
2. House for mother
3. Academic incubator
4. Better mousetrap
5. Supersalesperson
6. Sponsor
7. Golden handshake
8. Spin-off
9. Rebuild of an existing firm (the phoenix)
10. Starting small in a good market

Some feel that achieving distinction as a successful new design firm is as much about public relations and salesmanship as it is about substance, but generally this is not true. Most design professionals accomplish their goals the old-fashioned way: They achieve them by creating a firm with distinctive capabilities and consistently high-quality work. For young firms, achieving success without compromising on other goals (such as making payroll) requires both talent and commitment, especially since they typically must build their practices on a foundation of small projects with limited fees.

Let's review the model types one by one.

Major Client as First-Stage Booster Rocket

The firm is founded or taken beyond the start-up with the support of a single client willing to gamble on a young firm. The combination of the client and the work of the firm acts as a booster rocket that lifts the firm above the crowd to where it can be seen. Most successful firms can trace their success back to one or two important early clients or projects. For architects, a rare variation on this is the firm that wins a major open competition.

House for Mother

For some new firms, the booster rocket comes in the form of a project for a family member or one completed using family money. Charles Gwathmey, Robert Venturi, and Philip Johnson are only a few examples of well-known architects who became visible thanks to such projects.

Academic Incubator

Many of the best-known design firm principals have relied on their teaching positions to provide them with the basic income, time, credibility, and exposure to lay the foundations of a practice. Only when their practice becomes too demanding do they cut their academic ties. Thom Mayne of Morphosis relied on his Southern California Institute of Architecture teaching salary until his practice finally took off.

Finding a Need and Filling It (the Better Mousetrap)

Some firms see an unmet need and set out to fill it. In past years, this has included firms that first focused on specialties, such as recycling historic structures, or smaller projects in communities not served by enough strong local designers, or, currently, sustainable design.

Supersalesperson

A few firms—Kohn Pedersen Fox being one of the best known—got off the ground due in large part to the exceptional sales skills and client relationships of one or more of the founders. All successful architects have some sales skills, but only a handful can convince clients to hire a new firm for major projects over the established competition.

Sponsor

A few firms—among them some of the best known—have had other established professionals act as their booster rockets. This takes various forms. Well-known architects, Charles Moore being the most prolific, have lent their names and skills to young firms. In a few cases, elder statesmen, among them Philip Johnson, promote emerging stars. Philip Johnson's role in winning Michael Graves his first major commission, the Portlandia Building competition, is a well-known example.

Golden Handshake

Sometimes the architect's former employer provides the new firm's initial work. When Brad's grandfather had to leave his position as head of the drafting room of Burnham and Root in the contraction after the 1893 Columbia Exposition, Daniel Burnham helped get him his first commission. A short time after they started, Voorsanger & Mills (later reorganized into two firms, Voorsanger & Associates and Edward I. Mills & Associates) received a major subcontract from I. M. Pei, their former employer, which sustained their start-up.

Spin-Off

Among the most common models are the spin-offs—firms that break away from established ones where the new-firm members have built their reputations, skills, and potential client base. In some cases, the spin-offs are led by senior partners of major firms. Kohn Pederson Fox, founded by the former leadership of John Carl Warnecke's New York office; Elkus/Manfredi, founded by a former partner of The Architects Collaborative; and Brennan Beer Gorman, founded by the former leadership of Welton Becket's New York office, are three major examples. More typically, the founders of a new firm spend their early years rising to senior positions below partner level in their former firms, and while there build strong personal reputations and reference lists, as well as a modest base of "moonlight" clients too small for their former employers. Then they break away.

Phoenix

The converse of the spin-off is the takeover. In a few cases, a new young leadership takes over a declining or moribund existing organization and revives and reshapes it into a new, vibrant firm. Johnson, Fain and Pereira Associates (JFPA, now Johnson Fain) is a well-known example of this model. This model is very complex because—as at JFPA—it involves assuming substantial financial liabilities, an established image, and an established senior organizational structure. Scott Johnson and Bill Fain had to deal with all these while reshaping the design direction of a large practice.

Starting Small

Some firms are content to begin by doing small projects and building on that base. For Tod Williams, Billie Tsien and Associates, a small dormitory at Princeton gave them credibility at an institutional level. After several smaller projects had been published, Princeton included them on a list of alumni architects to be interviewed for what was to be a small addition. Instead, it became a new building, which won several awards and was widely published.

Conclusion

What one learns from the success stories (and sometimes from failures as well) is that most successful firms find a way to define their unique position in the marketplace, to obtain good clients, and to serve these clients well.

On rare occasions, a firm's founder has the right personality, plus all of the requisite skills and capabilities, to make a success of a new launch. More often, though, professionals find that an objective self-analysis identifies one or more key gaps in the experience and skills required. This is when it's time to look for a partner or partners. Whether provided by a single person or a partnership, the two skills that the firm's leadership must provide are the ability to get the work and the ability to do it well. The first of these is the subject of the next chapter; the second is unique to each profession, firm, and individual.

3 Marketing and Sales

To develop a steady or growing volume of interesting projects, all design professionals launching firms have to seek clients and convince them to commission the new firm. Even "over the transom" clients will expect a presentation of previous work before they agree to work with a new firm, and this requires knowing how to market your firm and make project presentations.

Some firms refer to the efforts they make to obtain the clients they want as "business development," which in general can be categorized as *marketing* (the strategic approach to a market) and *sales* (the tactical steps taken to secure clients). This chapter provides an introduction to both of these essential tasks, and the box titled "Elements of a Business Development Program" summarizes them.

Molding a Business Development Program

The importance of a successful business development effort was memorably summarized by H. H. Richardson in response to a wide-eyed mother who implored him one day to advise her son who aspired to be an architect. "What," she asked, "is the most

Elements of a Business Development Program

Markets: Where you will seek work—client base that needs what you have to offer.

Capability: What you offer to the marketplace—the firm's qualifications to serve a market.

Message: What you tell prospective clients— your "distinctive competence" or "distinguishing benefit."

Process and methods: How you will pursue the work.

Marketing organization: Roles and budget.

Image: How you are perceived in the marketplace.

Public relations and promotion: Information that describes and enhances your image.

Marketing plan: Documents targets, desired and projected yields, responsibilities and costs.

Marketing: Process of seeking prospective clients.

Sales: Efforts focused on specific prospective clients.

important thing in architectural practice?" "Getting the first job!" Richardson replied. "Of course that is important," she agreed, "but after that what is most important?" "Getting the next job!" was Richardson's gruff response.

As this oft-told story implies, obtaining work is an essential first step for any practice. The *how* of business development is not something that can be taught as a series of tricks and pitches. Professionals are selling a service, not encyclopedias or vacuum cleaners. Each firm has to be extremely creative in developing the approach that is exactly right for it, that is molded to the unique personality of the firm.

The first steps in this molding process are to, one, formulate an internally consistent statement of the firm's goals and, two, conduct an objective analysis of the firm's strengths and weaknesses, as compared to those of the competition. Certain offices, for example, may want to pursue only prestige projects, the lion's share of which are obtained by what architect Morris Lapidus labeled in his book on building a practice, *Architecture: A Profession and a Business* (Reinhold Publishing, 1967), the "ivory tower" firms. If that is the firm's objective, then the architect must chart a realistic business course that will eventually bring his or her office to a point at which it is the logical choice for these commissions. A firm's members cannot expect to be chosen until they know how much and what type of work they want, as well as how to maximize the strengths and minimize the weaknesses that will affect the firm's selection.

The most important guide in this process is what is known in other businesses as the *marketing concept*. This concept, if it is well developed, can be used effectively not only to help sell professional services but also to improve the quality of the services sold. This concept was defined simply by Henry Kaiser as "finding a need and filling it." All clients have needs, which they expect the architect, engineer, or other design professional they commission to understand and to fill.

Finding a need and filling it is, of course, only one part of a successful marketing and sales program. There are at least 10 other issues that every professional should understand while undertaking his or her business development efforts:

1. Good projects can (with time, skill, and effort) be obtained, but doing so is easiest when you have a plan to begin with.
2. The core of most successful plans is identifying an unmet need and organizing to meet it.

3. No matter how you set out to get work, a thorough understanding of your potential clients' issues, concerns, and specific needs is always important.
4. Your firm's best salespeople are: satisfied clients, third parties with a client's ear, a good image, and a strong reputation for providing the service being sought.
5. Few individuals are natural salespeople. For most, it is a learned skill.
6. Marketing should be continuous, focused, and broadly based—even in a small firm. It's as important to sell when you are busy as when you are slow and think you have the time.
7. Many people have advance knowledge of most potential projects long before the client begins seeking a design professional and it's important to find out who these people are.
8. Each client is important and each early project should be seen as part of the foundation upon which to build the firm's long-term practice.
9. All design professionals should learn basic marketing and sales skills, including doing market research, writing proposals, and making presentations.
10. Some projects are not worth pursuing or doing. Sometimes there are bad projects for good clients. There are no good projects for bad clients.

The Marketing Plan

Twenty years ago, it was unusual to find a design firm that had a formal plan to guide its marketing and sales efforts. Today, a rapidly growing number of professionals have learned that a clear plan can dramatically improve their chances for success.

What is in a typical plan? Most firms that have plans have evolved their own approach, but it typically covers at least the following:

- Understanding of the market
- Analysis of the competition
- Objective view of your strengths
- Objective analysis of your weaknesses
- A plan to continually build strengths and minimize or eliminate weaknesses
- Market research and other techniques to identify and generate leads in the target market
- Outline of the materials that will be needed to support an effective sales process
- Image-building ideas
- Specific short-term (one-year) and long-term goals

Note: A sample market analysis and plan for a new firm is given at the end of this section.

An essential first step is to understand the market. A "market" in this case means a type of client or project that the firm wants. A market, however, is not synonymous with clients since a single market may include several different types of clients. For one firm, the primary market might be schools; for another, it might be luxury apartments and homes; and for still another, it might be municipal work in a particular region. Many firms are interested in more than one market sector, and in these cases there should be a plan for each.

To understand a market, a design professional should try to learn all he or she can about:

- The clients' primary concerns and issues
- Those with advance knowledge about the project before the selection process begins

- The process the clients typically use to select their design professionals
- References clients call on when choosing professionals
- Trends in project types, volume of work, and so on
- Clients to pursue and clients to avoid
- Prevailing fee levels
- Other complementary (noncompetitive) professional firms serving this market

Addressing Client Concerns

One of the most effective ways to become successful within a market is to attempt to "get inside the potential clients' minds," in order to understand how they perceive what you have to offer. Among the first things to understand is that most clients approach a building program with significant concern and trepidation. They are about to spend a great deal of money on something that they do not really understand. When viewed in this light, you realize that the firm they select will be the one that demonstrates the clearest understanding of their concerns and that provides the evidence that it can and will successfully address every major client issue.

For example, a school board that requires a design for a major addition or renovation will typically want to find a firm or team of firms that:

- Know school planning and design
- Understand how to help sell the need to the community and the design to the state education department
- Will keep the project within budget and on schedule

- Will be able to create an attractive community asset that is a good learning environment for the children
- Are likeable and easy to work with
- Can deal with particular challenges of the project—a tight budget or schedule, a difficult site, and so on

In such situations, for many clients, the safe choice is often a local firm that has performed well for other nearby school districts on similar assignments. That said, a new firm led by a principal who has worked successfully for the school district in question or other nearby districts while employed by another firm might still have a chance. To be successful, however, the new firm has to be prepared to deal with the conservative nature of committee decisions. Most committees vote for the "safe" choice, and a new firm, understandably, is often not regarded as such because its capabilities are untested and its name is unknown. Therefore, it is common for new firms to associate with an established firm to overcome this problem and begin to establish its reputation.

For an interior designer seeking to do a medium-size office renovation, the issues may be different. In many cases, the broker, the owner's rep, or an in-house real estate professional may be the decision maker. Because these decision makers may feel that any experienced interior designer can do the project, the decision may hinge on personal chemistry or a past working relationship that convinces this decision maker that the designer will make him or her look good to the ultimate users of the space.

For a mechanical engineer seeking to be involved in school projects, the decision maker may be the architect for the school, who will need to be confident that the engineer:

- Will be responsive, will meet the schedule, and will correct any problem as soon as it arises
- Will be easy to work with
- Understands the building type
- Will be able to accommodate the architect's contractual and fee arrangement with the owner

The point of these examples is to illustrate that, initially, to be selected as the design professional on a given project hinges on your making the decision makers believe that you and your firm are the most likely to satisfy their needs and assuage their major concerns. Research of a market or specific client can clarify what these concerns are likely to be, thus giving the professional seeking to serve that market a significant advantage.

Insider Information

A second key issue is to identify those who know about a project before the selection of design professionals begins. In most cases, a number of people know about a potential project—sometimes many months or even years before the client begins selecting a design professional.

For some building types, anyone involved in defining the need and scope of a project (the board or senior management, planning consultants, feasibility consultants, etc.) are the first to know.On other projects, "those in the know" might include anyone involved in finding the space or site for a project (real estate brokers, site selection consultants, local public officials, etc.). On still other projects, family and/or friends of the potential client might have foreknowledge of the project.

Finding out who has advance knowledge of a project can help to guide a design professional early in the process. For example, firms interested in designing lab facilities cultivate relationships with lab planners, as well as with the staff of research organizations. Firms interested in working on corporate interiors projects cultivate relationships with real estate brokers, owners' representatives, and the facilities staff of major corporations. The point is, for every project type, there is a network of contacts that can provide early intelligence.

Client Selection Process

The third topic to research and understand is the selection process. Though there are no standard selection procedures, for most building types, there are typical steps to take and typical hurdles to cross in the selection process. After you have been through 20 or 30 interviews, you will have taken most of the typical steps and heard most of the standard questions. Therefore, it is helpful to gain experience in interviews while working for others and before your own firm's survival depends upon your skill in this process. However, even if the process is not familiar to you, much of it can be learned from other design professionals who have been through it.

In its basic outline, most selections go through the following steps, either formally or informally:

1. The potential client decides that it needs assistance.
2. The client asks others for help in generating a list of firms to consider.
3. The client contacts the firms and asks them if they are interested and, if so, requests material detailing their capabilities and experience.

4. Based on the information received, the client draws up a short list of firms to interview.
5. The client interviews and requests written fee proposals.
6. The client checks references and/or visits select projects completed by the firms under consideration.
7. The client selects a firm.

Of course, there are variations on these steps. Public agencies, large institutions and corporations, and clients using professional advisers may formalize the process, whereas an individual homeowner or a developer used to making his or her own choices may handle these steps very informally.

References Clients Use

As can be seen from the description of the selection process, there are at least two ways in which third parties can be very influential: helping assemble the list of firms to be considered, and providing references. As will be discussed again later in this chapter, these third-party endorsements are often more important than the interview or proposal. Therefore, knowing whom potential clients might ask for referrals (e.g., real estate brokers for houses or office interiors, lab consultants for research facilities, school superintendents for schools, etc.) can help define for you who you want to know, like, and respect you.

Identifying Trends

It is, of course, easier to win projects when there is more work in a given area than the local competition can handle. For that reason, some architects and interior designers even move their practices to follow a trend—for example, to growing resort areas like Jackson Hole. In most markets, it's not necessary to take such a drastic step; instead, become adept at spotting trends that could generate a need for projects in the future (e.g., new medical technology that hospitals will need to implement; new educational initiatives such as mandatory early childhood programs, which will require expansion of schools; or new concerns about meeting sustainable design requirements). Many firms owe their success to their ability to spot trends and to position themselves to respond to emerging needs.

Recognizing the Good Clients

Of course there are clients who respect their design professionals, are fun to work with, pay their bills, and help the designers get future work. Unfortunately, there are also many who are abusive, litigious, and unlikely to pay what they owe. A common mistake on the part of new firms (and many experienced firms as well) is to ignore the warning signs of the latter type. Usually, a little research, such as calling other design professionals or people familiar with the community, can give an indication of what a client is like and whether working for them is likely to be a positive or negative experience.

Prevailing Fee Levels

Conversations with other design professionals and others can also help new firms define the current fee levels they can and should charge for various project types. There is a "going rate" for most projects, and most clients take the fee proposal into consideration during the selection process.

Tapping Complementary Firms

Other complementary (noncompetitive) disciplines and firms that serve the same market you are targeting can be valuable sources of leads, advice on fees, background on clients, information on trends, and proposal partners, as well as offer other important assistance.

Typical Market Analysis and Plan for a New Firm

Market: *Private Residence.* Forty-five custom homes were built in the county last year, and local realtors believe this number will increase this year and next. Most of these homes were built by five construction firms, and the land was purchased through four different realtors. The prevailing fees appear to fall in the 10 to 15 percent range, depending on the project size and complexity.

Lead Sources: Realtors and builders are the major source of leads.

Competition: About half of clients come with their own architects; but, reportedly, because they are new to the area, the other half ask for advice. At this time, two architectural firms are viewed as offering little in the way of either design or service, and two others are generally respected but very busy. Most people believe there is room for another strong design firm that offers quality design and good service.

Strengths and Weaknesses: We have designed three houses for family and friends and have strong references from these and several other jobs. Our main weakness is that we are unknown to the key referral sources.

Plan: Over the next six months, we must meet all of the realtors and builders and present our credentials. We have to get at least one of our first houses featured in a local or regional publication or write one or more articles on home design advice for the local newspaper. We also need to become involved in community activities supported by the real estate industry.

Goals: *Year One:* One new house and two major house additions, with architectural fees totaling at least $175,000. *Year Two:* Five new houses with architectural fees totaling $400,000.

Identifying Competitors and Competitive Position

The second part of the marketing plan is to understand the competition. You need to answer these questions:

- How have our competitors become successful?
- How are they viewed by our potential clients?
- What are their strengths and what are their weaknesses?

Then you need to analyze your own position in the same way. Even a new firm has strengths as well as weaknesses. The strengths may include clients, friends, or family members willing to help introduce you to potential clients; strong experience in a particular building type or geographic area; the time to work more exclusively for a new client; and the willingness to offer a more competitive fee or more service for the same fee.

Writing Targeted Market Plans

With this analysis complete, it is a worthwhile exercise to write out a plan for each target group of clients. This plan should summarize what you know:

- Market and primary client targets
- Sources of leads
- Your competitive strengths and weaknesses
- One- and five-year plans
- One- and five-year goals

In addition, even in the first year of a firm's existence, it is important to begin creating the support materials that can be important to both marketing and sales. These materials may include:

- Brochure
- Web site

- Reprints of material published on the firm or its principals
- Graphic, technical, and photographic records of projects

We'll discuss each of these promotional materials in turn.

Brochures

Obviously, your first brochure will be short of completed buildings. (A reviewer of our first brochure commented, "What a good model shop you have.") To address this shortcoming, *if appropriate and acceptable*, you can use projects completed for a previous employer. A word of caution here: Be sure to credit your former employer and to be accurate about your role and responsibilities. Typical wording in such a case might be, for example, "Project architect while a senior associate at Able & Baker Architects." Failure to properly credit your former employer can lead to negative publicity, claims of unethical conduct, and even legal action. That is not the right foot to start from.

In general, brochures should be designed for maximum flexibility, so that you can update or customize them as required. Most firms develop their brochure materials using a desktop publishing program or some other computer-based system. This allows you to continually update the brochure and adapt it to respond to each client's specific issues.

Typical sections you'll want to include in your brochure are:

- Description of the firm and its basic approach or philosophy (Remember you're writing for clients, not other architects, so use client-appropriate language.)

- Description of the firm's services
- Resume(s) for key personnel
- Client listing
- Project sheets with good graphics and descriptive materials for each of the firm's projects
- Reprints of articles, lists of awards, and other supplemental materials

Web Site

An ever-increasing number of potential clients, potential employees, and others use the Web as an initial screening tool in their selection process, so launching a Web site has become increasingly important for design firms. In fact, in the future, Web sites may replace traditional brochures. A new firm's site does not have to be elaborate, as long as it's well presented. To determine what to include on yours, look at how other smaller firms have set up their sites.

Article Reprints and Other Materials

Like awards, appearing in print gives third-party credibility. It is important to look for opportunities to get your firm's name or the names of its principals in print, whether in articles you or other team members write or those written about your work. Such exposure not only helps build your reputation, but reprints or copies of the articles can remain useful for a long time as marketing tools.

If you have something interesting to say or something good to show, you'll find it is not that difficult to get published. Though fewer design magazines exist today, there are hundreds of other magazines, newspapers, and other venues that need interesting content. Publications read by potential clients are particularly useful, but publication in the design press is also important since design professionals often sit on building committees or advise on who should be considered. Always remember that publications are in the business of selling newspapers and magazines, and most are constantly searching for interesting sources to help them increase readership. We both wrote articles, book chapters, and other material early in our careers, and doing so helped establish our professional reputations and credibility. And once you have been published, it becomes easier to be published again in the future.

Project Records

For many reasons, it is important to be meticulous about creating project files, and one of the most important is that they become resources for future marketing materials. And keep in mind that most firms trying to establish their design reputations supplement basic material created for each project with extra drawings, professional-quality photographs, and other content.

Building an Image

From the beginning, all marketing is part of building an image that complements and supports the type of firm you want to have. (This issue is discussed further in Chapter 10.) The quality of your work and service is, of course, the core of your firm's image, but it can be significantly enhanced by your marketing program, community activities, personal conduct, and many other factors. Building and protecting a strong, positive reputation can be critical to success because, often, "image is substance."

Generating Leads

Once you have the framework of your plan outlined, it's time to focus on generating leads. Most new firms think that this task will be more difficult than it is. In practice, you'll find that identifying potential clients and specific projects is one of the easier steps in your marketing and sales program.

There are three typical sources of leads for a new or small firm:

- Research
- Networking
- Proactive lead generation

Research can be as basic as reading local newspapers; obtaining lists of school superintendents, directors of facilities for local hospitals and corporations, and other clients with frequent need for design services; and identifying individuals who are likely to have advance knowledge of projects.

Identifying individuals who may know of projects in advance is one part of building and maintaining a network of contacts, sources of information, and people who will even help seek out leads for a young firm. For most successful firms, the network begins with school friends and family and is then aggressively expanded by active participation in community activities. In Brad's case, for example, one of the most productive sources of contacts came as the result of his coaching soccer for his three daughters. Over the last 15 years, each of his co-coaches identified a major project for his firm and referred them to still others.

Table 3.1 lists typical project types along with potential sources of advance knowledge and/or influence.

One of Brad's favorite pieces of advice came from his father. He said: "Everything leads somewhere." If you actively build and maintain a network of contacts, as it grows and matures, leads will appear from surprising sources. For example, in one recession year, Brad's firm interviewed three potential employees who later referred work to them. Though not in a position to offer them jobs at the time, the firm tried to help connect them with other potential

Table 3.1
Architectural Projects and Sources of Information

Market	Project Type	Those with Advance Knowledge	Those with Influence
Housing	Single-Family Houses	Past clients Homebuilders Real estate brokers	Past clients Homebuilders Real estate brokers
Education	Public Elementary/ Secondary Schools	School administration School board Local newspaper Educational planners	Other school district leaders Influential members of the community Noncompeting architects
Healthcare	Hospital Clinics and Specialized Facilities	Hospital boards and administrators Medical staff Health facility planners	Administrators and board members of other healthcare facilities
Interior Design	Office Interiors	Corporate management Corporate facility staff Moving consultants Furniture dealers Owners' representatives Interior construction companies	Other clients in the same industry Brokers Owners' representatives

employers. All three went to work for clients and later recommended the firm for projects, which were subsequently won.

But indirect methods will only go so far. Successful firms also take proactive lead-generation steps. No one likes making "cold calls," but often there are people in your network who will make introductions that lead to "warmed-up" calls. Some firms have even hired retired former clients to introduce them to their friends and colleagues (e.g., retired school superintendents and former nursing home administrators). In other cases, firm principals have simply asked friends to introduce them to a potential client over lunch.

Thus, by combining research, networking, and proactive efforts, you will be able to generate more than enough leads to keep a new firm busy with the next steps in the marketing and sales program, lead qualification and courting, and RFPs, RFQs, and responses.

Lead Qualification and Courting

Most firms find that they must generate a large number of leads to get one assignment. The traditional rule of thumb is that 10 to 12 "qualified" leads generate 3 to 4 interviews and 1 new job.

Any lead generation effort will identify those prospects that are worth pursuing and those that are not. Thus, it is important to try to evaluate, or "qualify," leads before spending time and energy following up. The qualification process, which may be as simple as a phone call to the client or a conversation with someone who knows them, should answer the following, and similar, screening questions:

- Is the project "real"?
- Is the selection process open or has it already been narrowed to a short list?
- Do the skills and experience required match yours?

The leads that remain after the qualification process should be the ones worth pursuing (sometimes referred to as "courting"). This effort, if successful, will turn a lead into a request for a proposal or presentation.

Often it takes personal contact to get a client to agree to include your firm on the list for consideration. In one case, Brad's firm avoided being eliminated from the interview short list when the client's key decision maker met him and realized Brad was his daughter's soccer coach. Again, it is very important

Marketing Process or "Funnel"

Market research: Determine that a market exists; find out where the work is.

List-building: Compile names and addresses of potential prospects.

Lead-finding: Contact people to find actual prospects.

Courting: Maintain contact with prospective clients and continue to express interest.

Strategy research: Interview prospective clients to determine needs, preferences, project details, selection criteria and methods, and competition.

Strategy decisions: Determine whether to pursue a lead, as well as the specific selling message(s) and tactics for getting the job.

Proposals and paperwork: Make formal written presentations of the firm's credentials.

Interviews: Make formal personal presentations of the firm's key people and approach.

Closing: Convince the prospective client to choose you; sign the contract.

Debriefing: Find out why the successful firm won the job, even if you are the successful firm.

to find a way to make personal contact and create a personal relationship with the client before the formal selection process begins.

RFQs, RFPs, and the Responses

The formal steps in the selection process often begin with a verbal or written *request for qualifications* (RFQ) or a *request for proposal* (RFP).

- The RFQ is typically used when a client wants to screen potential firms based on their capabilities and experience. Often an RFQ precedes an interview or an RFP.
- The RFP is used when the client wants to know—in addition to the firm's experience and capabilities—how the firm plans to approach the project, on what schedule, and for what compensation.

The most important questions you want answers to when responding to an RFQ include:

- Who else is getting the RFQ and how do they compare to you?
- What capabilities and areas of experience are likely to be of greatest interest to the client?
- Who is the client likely to ask for references?
- If there is a gap in your qualifications, is there a way to fill it?

The last question raises the question of *teaming*. One of the most common ways for a young firm to respond effectively to an RFQ or RFP is to join with another firm with greater and/or complementary experience and capabilities. Even established firms are often willing to team with a younger firm if it has developed a lead and received an RFQ or RFP that the more established firm missed.

It's Who You Know

When Brad's father's firm was brand-new in the late 1930s, they heard that a leading suburban school system near Chicago was planning to build a new, state-of-the-art elementary school. Brad's father called on the superintendent, a friend of his father, to ask to be considered. The superintendent was polite, but said the project needed a team with more experience (Brad's father's team consisted of three men in their thirties).

Brad's father refused to give up and asked the superintendent if they might be considered if they had a senior advisor. The superintendent replied, "Such as?" Thinking on his feet and mentally reviewing a list of his father's friends, he said, "Eliel Saarinen." This naturally impressed the superintendent, who responded, "If you can get Eliel Saarinen, we will consider you." Brad's father immediately drove to Cranbrook, asked Saarinen to act as their adviser, and with Saarinen's (and Saarinen's son Eero's) acceptance, secured the commission. The school—Crow Island in Winnetka—became the foundation for Perkins & Will's national practice in educational facility design.

Your response to an RFQ or RFP should, of course, be structured to directly answer all questions asked, as well as to address the issues you believe are the central concerns of the client. "Boilerplate" responses that are not tailored to these issues are not usually successful.

You should also be sensitive to the fact that most clients will not take the time to read every word of an RFQ or RFP, therefore your responses should include graphics, repetition of salient points, and other techniques to guarantee that your firm's important strengths are impossible to miss. The cover letter, for example, is one place where it is appropriate to reiterate the major points of your response.

The logical sequence of a response is also important. While many clients dictate how they want you to respond, a typical proposal—and the underlying logic of the sequence of proposal sections—has many common elements. The sidebar titled "Typical Proposal Format" lists these elements, and each is discussed in turn below.

To reiterate, the *cover letter* should be more than a transmittal; it should reinforce the key points of the proposal.

The *cover* should be graphically attractive and illustrate something about your interest in the project, even if it is merely a picture of the client's site.

The *table of contents* should make it easy for the reader to find the responses to the RFP questions. This can be reinforced by a clear introduction and executive summary of the proposal's key points.

The *proposal* itself often begins with a statement describing the design issues to be resolved. This is an important section because it speaks directly to the client's concerns and sets up the reasoning for the proposed approach, team, and schedule.

The *approach* should be more than a listing of the phases and tasks. It should include elements that reflect how you plan to deal with the unique challenges of the project. Include such topics as: special techniques to create an efficient program, cost management tools that will keep the project on budget, quality-control procedures to minimize change orders, communications techniques to keep the client informed and involved, a sustainable design focus to address a client's environmental goals, and so on.

The approach section is usually followed by a *description of the key personnel* who will make up the design team, followed by an explanation of the role each member of the core project team will play, and their resumes. This section may also include

Typical Proposal Format

1. Cover letter
2. Attractive cover
3. Table of contents
4. Introduction and executive summary
5. Understanding of the issues
6. Proposed approach
7. Proposed design team:
    - Component firms
    - Key personnel, organization of the project team, and each person's role
    - Resumes
8. Proposed schedule
9. Proposed compensation
10. Relevant experience
11. References
12. Appendices of other relevant material

statements about the availability and commitment of the key personnel. In all proposals, the proposing firm should be able to offer a great deal of capacity and the willingness to commit the best-qualified personnel to the project at hand. Being able to commit principals to a project may be more credible from, and thus, an advantage for, a smaller firm.

A page outlining the proposed *compensation* typically follows these sections. Many clients expect a definitive fee estimate even when the scope, schedule, and many other areas are as yet undefined. In these cases, try to point out the issues that need further definition and then propose tying the fee estimate to some assumptions (such as an immediate start date, few meetings during the public approval process, an early construction start, etc.) that are likely to change. It's also a good idea to list consultant fees separately so that a high number on one consultant line does not make the entire proposal noncompetitive. (Chapter 5 has more on setting fees.)

The final sections contain the material that *demonstrates your qualifications*: past experience that is relevant, strong references (from whom you have secured permission to use their names and who are reliable), and other supplemental materials (article reprints, reference letters, lists of awards, etc.) that support the argument that you are the best-qualified team for the job.

Presentations

Typically, the next phase is an interview. Though there are many things to learn about presentations, 10 of the most important lessons are summarized here for the purposes of this discussion:

1. Though most jobs are won before the presentation, in some cases the presentation will be the deciding factor.
2. The best presentations are usually those that engage the client in an interesting discussion of the project at hand.
3. Memorable props help draw the client into the discussion. These may include: site models with multiple inserts, site analyses, lists of key issues to be resolved, and so on.
4. In a standard 30-minute formal presentation, it is best to limit the content to express only five or six clear messages.
5. Committees have a hard time making a selection and usually begin by eliminating firms with an apparent weakness.
6. Selection committees typically aren't "warmed up" for the first interview, have trouble remembering or distinguishing the middle ones, and are often impatient with the last, so most firms prefer to be one of the later—but not last—interviews.
7. Presentations are theater, meaning that rehearsal always improves your performance.
8. Slide shows can be deadly unless they are concise, directly relevant, attractive, and interesting.
9. Keep the typical introductory, formal part of a presentation to less than 30 minutes, and finish with a lively "first-act closer."
10. The question-and-answer period is often the most important part of a presentation. A lively, intelligent, and friendly Q&A period can end a presentation on the right note.

It is unfortunate how much weight clients give to a presentation when you consider that most presentations are limited to one hour or less, with half devoted to the formal presentation by the firm and the remainder allocated to questions and answers. And because the principals of most new firms do not have the experience to make a compelling case for their firm in such a short time frame, they are at a disadvantage, especially if they are up against more established and experienced firms.

The new firms that succeed in surmounting the disadvantages of youth, inexperience, size, and/or a less established image usually do so by expending greater effort, by preparing carefully, and, simply, by being charming. For example, in the early years at Brad's firm, they went out of their way to meet the client *before* the interview. Not only did this give them insights as to how best develop their presentation, it also allowed them to create a personal connection with one or more of the interview committee members. We've said it before, but it bears repeating: In most cases, relationships trump experience in a client's mind.

In preparing for a presentation, several points are particularly relevant to keep in mind:

- *Clients are more interested in their project than in your firm*. Therefore, build most presentations to demonstrate your understanding of the client's issues and how you and your capabilities and experience can help them successfully address each of those issues.
- *Never underestimate chemistry*. Most people prefer to hire someone they like, trust, and can envision spending time with over the life of the project. Thus, it is important to be (or at least appear to be) at ease, friendly, and engaging.
- *Do not assume that a client will absorb every message you intend to deliver*. As noted previously, pick out the five or six you think will be most

important—for example, your ideas for their project, your analysis of the site, your approach to cost control, your sustainable design concepts, and so on. If you try to cram too much information into a brief presentation, the client may miss the relevant parts.

- *Many selections are made by committees, which tend to make conservative and "safe" choices.* After each firm interview, many committees look for weaknesses to shorten the list. Thus, it is not uncommon for a committee to start by eliminating firms with a perceived weakness (even if they gave—on balance—a strong presentation). Therefore, to survive the first cut, you must give the committee positive reasons to choose you. This is where working harder than the competition can make the difference. For a new firm, it is important to convey that you will work hard and bring more creativity to the project than the competition. Thus, it is important to have done enough project analysis to be able to talk intelligently about the project.
- *It is important to finish the formal presentation on a high note.* Concluding by describing how you will manage the project, for example, is usually a downer. A better choice is to use a model, a site analysis, or some other prop as the aforementioned "first-act closer."
- *The question-and-answer period that follows the formal presentation is often as important as the presentation.* As with the actual presentation, some rehearsal can be helpful, especially for the questions that are predictable, such as, "Why should we consider a new firm?" Having a ready answer can be convincing; fumbling an answer can be fatal.

Closing

At the presentation—or in a subsequent meeting—there comes a time where the client must be encouraged to make a commitment. This often requires experience in identifying the issues (fee, commitment of principal's time, etc.) that will convince the client to take this critical step. Being a good listener is part of the process. The box below, "Selling and Closing," illustrates this crucial step.

Selling and Closing

This example of interactive selling and closing actually occurred.

A "supersalesman" was booked as a guest on a late-night talk show. The host had not met the guest before he was introduced by the announcer as the person who had just won a salesman-of-the-year award. For some reason, the host was suspicious and aggressive. He began the interview on a hostile note:

"Oh, yeah," he said. "Try to sell me something."

The salesman responded quietly, "What would you like me to sell you?"

Pointing to the top of his desk, the host said, "That ashtray. Try to sell me that ashtray."

"Why would you want an ashtray like that?" the salesman asked.

The host responded, "I'm a pipe smoker and it would help me keep things in order and keep the ashes off my papers."

The salesman said, "Those are good reasons to have an ashtray like that. It will certainly help you keep your desk clean and orderly." He went on, "What about that ashtray interests you?"

The host said, "It's crystal, and has a nice shape, and is heavy, and will hold down my papers, and refracts the light in an interesting way."

The salesman reflected back, "Yes, this ashtray is really attractive and weighty and will refract the light colorfully. How much would you pay for an ashtray like that?"

The host responded, "Oh, $15 or $20."

The salesman said, "I can let you have it for $15."

Case closed.

Debriefing

No matter how this long process turns out (that is, whether you win or lose the project), it is important to request a debriefing from the client. Most are willing to give an insight as to how their choice was made. In our experience, there are almost always surprises, and it can be very helpful to see how you and your presentation were perceived.

In the first year of practice, Brad's firm won an invited competition for a mixed-use project. They naively assumed that they were chosen for the superiority of the design solution. The client said the design solution was important, but what convinced him was the fact that it was a young firm, and he believed he would be its most important client. He also liked the no-frills, low-overhead office, which indicated to him that he would get more effort for the same fee. At the time, this deflated the firm's egos, but later they realized that he had given them important advice on what—as a young firm—they could emphasize in their next presentations.

Conclusion

Young firms tend to focus on marketing and sales only when business is slow, so the first point we want to reiterate here is that your marketing and sales efforts must be continuous, focused, and broadly based. To engage in these efforts only on a sporadic basis while you already have work is a sure way to impair the financial health of a young firm (the subject of the next chapter).

The second point we want to stress is that an essential aspect of a continuous marketing program is staying in touch with former clients. Not only might they have, or know of, other projects, they can also serve as your best sales staff, because a strong reference or a friendly introduction from a satisfied former client can often turn a lead into a project.

Third, marketing and sales require an investment. New firms often have to spend 3 to 6 percent of their net fee revenues on preparing proposals, presentations, and brochures; on photography, entertainment, travel, and other related costs; and an equal amount of their billable time. As a firm becomes established, a range of 5 to 10 percent of gross revenues is more normal. (Chapter 4 defines these finance-related terms.)

Finally, a young firm should regard every potential project as part of the foundation for the firm's long-term practice. Some unglamorous initial assignments—such as a small study or a minor renovation—might help to build a client list, lead to an introduction to an important client for future work, or establish a solid reference. For example, Brad's firm's growing school practice began with a series of two room additions, renovations for a local synagogue and a church, as well as a pro bono project for a school for emotionally disturbed children. The foundation for two other practice areas were small feasibility studies. The point is, assess all opportunities strategically, and remember: "Everything leads somewhere."

4

Financial Management

It is a myth that one cannot make a reasonable living as a design professional. Though few of us get rich, and even fewer have achieved the "instant riches" possible in other fields, making a reasonable income is definitely possible. Many of us have been able to earn enough to buy a home, travel, educate our children, and save enough for a comfortable retirement. And having your own firm is one of the best ways to achieve this goal.

Although financial gain may not be the primary reason for a design professional to start a new firm, there is no escaping the fact that sustaining the firm will depend to a very great degree upon effective management of the firm's finances—with all its ramifications. This chapter describes the basics of financial management necessary to build and guide the financial health of a new firm: the principles, tools, and techniques that founders have to understand to manage their firms successfully.

Basic Concepts

The practice of architecture and other design professions is necessarily a business as well as an artistic pursuit, meaning that the fundamentals of finance apply to those practices regardless of size. Although the level of detail will vary with the volume of business, the number of staff, the size and complexity of projects, and other factors, maintaining a financially healthy firm is a prevalent concern for any business enterprise.

The objective of a firm's general management will be to ensure that the firm's efforts are integrated, balanced, and directed toward achieving goals. Marketing, project services, and general business cannot operate independently. Financial management is the core of business management and can be viewed as the integration of several components:

- *Funding:* Sources and applications of money.
- *General accounting:* Record of monetary transactions.
- *Project cost accounting:* Record-keeping of revenues, reimbursable expenses, direct expenses, and direct personnel time.
- *Profit planning:* Goals for profit and uses of capital and operating budgets.
- *Cash flow:* Change in the firm's cash position during a given period. Positive cash flow (more cash received than disbursed) increases the cash account; negative cash flow decreases the cash account.
- *Cash management:* Billing, collecting, and disbursing cash.
- *Remuneration:* Salaries and benefits.
- *Firm valuation:* Pricing for ownership transition.

Good management practice involves *understanding* what has to be managed, *planning* (establishing appropriate, realistic, and achievable goals), and *controlling* (achieving those goals through the effective employment of resources: people, time, money, facilities, and technology).

Essential Vocabulary

One of the most important of the basic financial concepts to master is the vocabulary. The world of financial management has its own language, and although much of it can be understood from context, we list here a few words and phrases that either have special meaning or whose particular understanding is essential to this chapter.

Accounts payable: Current liabilities in accrual accounting, representing the amount owed by the firm to vendors, consultants, or others for merchandise or services that have been provided to the firm.

Accounts receivable: Money owed by clients to the firm for services rendered or for reimbursement of expenses.

Accrual accounting: Accounting method that recognizes revenues as having been earned when services are performed, and that recognizes expenses when they are incurred, without regard to when cash is received or disbursed.

Asset: Resource owned by the firm on which a monetary value can be placed.

Backlog: Value of services contracted for but not yet earned.

Balance sheet: Statement of the firm's financial condition as of a specific date. It is a statement of the balance between the asset accounts (cash, accounts receivable, equipment, etc.) and the liability (consultants payable, loans payable, etc.) and owners' equity accounts.

Book value: The owners' equity accounts representing the net worth of the firm; the firm's assets less its liabilities.

Cash accounting: Accounting method that recognizes revenue when payment is received in cash, and that recognizes expense when cash is disbursed.

Cash flow: The change in the firm's cash account during a given period. *Positive cash flow* (more cash received than disbursed) results in an increase in the cash account. *Negative cash flow* decreases the cash account.

Direct expenses: Costs that can be charged to specific projects. Included are the costs of staff working on the project, outside consultants, and other costs associated with the project such as printing, travel, and long-distance communication.

Equity: Value of the firm's assets in excess of its liabilities; the total claims the owners would have to the value of the business if all assets were liquidated and all liabilities paid, as reflected on the firm's balance sheet.

Expenses: In cash accounting, actual cash disbursements made for goods or services (which do not result in acquisition of an asset, distribution of profit, or reduction of a liability). In accrual accounting, expenses are recognized when they are incurred without regard to when payment is received.

Founder: The person or persons initiating the firm.

Gross revenues: Total value earned by the firm as a result of providing services or from aspects of the business not central to the primary purpose, such as rents or royalties, including value provided by the firm's consultants and owed to them.

Income: Profits remaining after expenses have been subtracted from revenues.

Income statement: The basic operating financial statement showing the activity of the firm for the accounting period specified; synonymous with *profit and loss statement*.

Indirect expenses: Expense items paid in operating the business that are not chargeable to specific projects; collectively often called *overhead*.

Liabilities: Debts or obligations of the firm owed to others.

Loss: Expenses exceeding revenue in an accounting period.

Net income: Profit after corporate income taxes.

Net revenues: Value generated by the firm's employees, excluding value attributable to consultants or to nonlabor project expenses for reproductions, travel, and so on.

Net worth: The value of the owners' equity in the firm; basically, assets less liabilities: in a proprietorship, the proprietor's capital account; in a partnership, the total of the partners' capital accounts; in a corporation, the total of capital stock, plus paid-in capital, plus retained earnings.

Operating costs: The cost to operate the firm, including salaries, rent, supplies, and so on, usually expressed as a monthly total.

Operating income (or operating profit): Revenue remaining after direct and indirect expenses.

Owner: Anyone with a financial interest in a firm, whether as a sole proprietor, partner, or corporate shareholder.

Owners' equity: See Equity.

Partnership: Form of organization in which two or more persons share in the ownership, risks, and rewards of the business.

Principal: In this book, any individual with an equity position in a firm; sometimes expanded elsewhere to include anyone with a significant leadership role.

Profit: Excess of revenue over expenses.

Proprietorship: Form of business organization owned entirely by one person.

Reimbursable expenses: Project-related expenses that, by agreement with the client, are to be directly reimbursed.

Revenue: Primarily, value received from clients as a result of the firm providing services.

Shareholders' equity: See Equity.

Basic Finance Principles

This book constantly emphasizes the need to plan. This is especially true for a new firm's finances. And there are 10 principles to keep in mind when formulating that plan:

1. It is possible to make a reasonable living in your own practice, but it cannot be done without careful financial arrangement.
2. The core of financial management is knowing your costs, knowing your revenues, and keeping both in the proper balance.

3. You live on the cash basis of accounting, but you can die by ignoring accrual; you must know and monitor both.
4. Profit margins are narrow and limited; it is easy to lose more in a month than you make in six months. The easiest way to increase profit margins is to reduce overhead, and for new firms low overhead is a major competitive advantage.
5. Professional help is essential. This may include a bookkeeper, an attorney, and a tax adviser.
6. Design professionals and their limited profit margins are very vulnerable. Good contracts and careful negotiation are important to reducing this vulnerability.
7. Doing something for nothing usually reduces the likelihood of it happening. Some things, however, are worth doing, even at low rates, if they fill in a hole or help build toward a long-term goal.
8. Old accounts receivable are like dead fish. They do not improve with age. Firm, friendly pressure on collections is necessary with most clients.
9. Having adequate working capital is critical. Cash flow problems can become all-consuming.
10. Remember Pharaoh's dream: If you have seven fat years, save for the seven lean years. They will happen.

Fees Projection

This book constantly emphasizes the need to plan. This is especially true for a new firm's finances. One of the most important financial tools is a fee projection—that is, you project the fees you think you can earn each month. This gives you a clear view of your financial future. The goal is to earn each month more than you think it will cost you to cover your monthly expenses (advice we will repeat throughout

TIP

After the contract negotiation, the most effective thing you can do to enhance project success is to plan the project at project initiation.

this chapter), including fair compensation for your own time.

The Cash Flow Worksheet on page 57 begins with an earnings projection for seven months. Shown each month are the amounts expected to be billed at the end of each month.

The Cash Cycle

For a new firm, another important basic concept to understand immediately is *cash flow*. In the final analysis, and at virtually every step along the way, cash is required to operate any business. Goods and services, labor and materials, must be paid for with cash, sometimes at the very moment those goods and services are purchased, sometimes when the credit card or vendor's bill arrives, or soon thereafter. The process by which cash is produced can be understood as a never-ending cycle, as shown in Figure 4.1. This cycle is depicted as a circle whose arcs represent actions that generate assets, and the segment divisions the assets that are created. Since circles have no beginning and no end, imagine that the cycle begins with the action of providing services.

The professional provides services to a client or clients. The professional pays for his or her own labor and that of others as the firm grows. In addition to those labor expenses, the professional also incurs other expenses, both direct and indirect, in order to provide services. He or she may pay for travel, reproductions, postage, and other expenses in connection with executing the project. He or she will also pay for all those indirect, or overhead, items necessary to "keep the door open," including rent, utilities, insurance, taxes, and so on. The asset produced by performing services is called *work in process*.

The next action in the cycle is *billing*, or *invoicing*. The professional prepares an invoice requesting payment for the services provided—the fee—in whatever form he or she and his or her client have agreed. The asset produced by that action is called *accounts receivable* and represents the value of the services performed.

The next action is called *collecting*, and the asset produced is cash. Sometimes, collecting monies owed to the firm for services provided requires little or no specific action; simply sending the bill is enough. However, if payment is not made in a reasonable time, follow-up may become necessary to ensure that the payment will be forthcoming.

Once collected, cash is used to pay for obligations that have been incurred in the course of business and

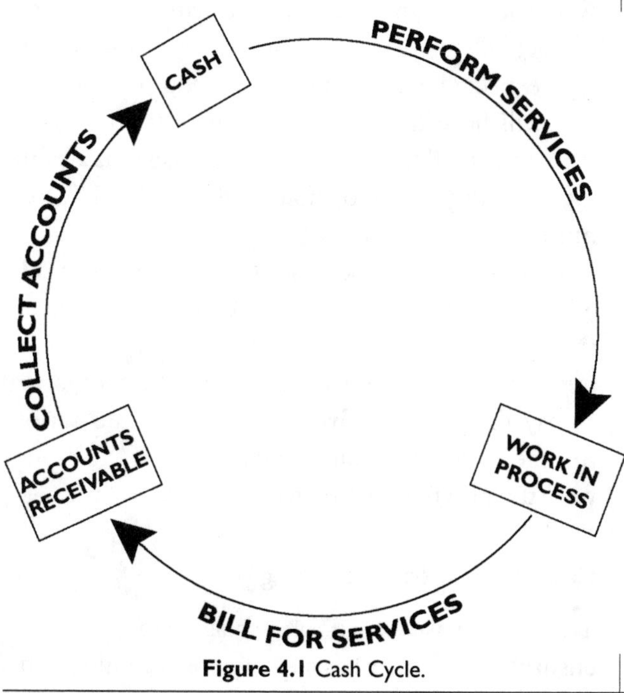

Figure 4.1 Cash Cycle.

that will be incurred in the immediate future as the firm continues to provide services—capital expenditures necessary to grow the firm, and operating expenses for salaries, consultants, other direct (project) expenses, and indirect (overhead) expenses. The cycle continues as long as the firm stays in business.

Cash Flow Projection

The projection of earned revenues described earlier can be combined with the concepts of the cash cycle to create a simple tool that allows you to project your cash position in the future (that is, determine whether you still have some or will run out). This tool is a *cash flow projection*.

You create this information by taking the *revenues* (fees earned) as the first step in the Cash Flow Worksheet, Figure 4.2, and estimating when they will actually be received. This will give you the total cash expected each month. Then you project when you will have to pay your expenses (rent, salaries, etc.). Eventually, you will have a good estimate of the total monthly cost to operate (and most of these costs must be paid monthly).

The only major expenses that can sometimes be deferred until you have received client payment are the consultant fees. If you have been paid or reimbursed for a consultant's fees, however, it is important to pay them. Many firms have gotten into serious trouble by treating consultants' fees as if the money were their own, rather than the consultant's money.

Cash and Accrual Accounting

The most basic financial management task is to ensure, on a regular basis (preferably monthly), that

	Month 1	Month 2	Month 3	Month 4	Month 5	Month 6	Month 7
Billings	$36,000	$34,000	$33,000	$38,000	$40,000	$35,000	$32,000
Collections							
First Month (25%)	9,000	8,500	8,250	9,500	10,000	9,000	8,000
Second Month (60%)		21,600	20,400	19,800	22,800	24,000	21,600
Third Month (15%)			5,400	5,100	4,950	1,425	6,000
Other (nonoperating) Receipts			1,000	1,000	1,000	1,000	1,000
Total Cash Receipts (Cash In)			**34,050**	**35,400**	**38,750**	**35,425**	**36,600**
Cash Disbursements							
Direct Expenses			14,900	15,500	17,000	15,940	16,000
Indirect Expenses			16,000	17,500	15,200	17,500	20,750
Other (nonoperating) Disbursements			200	0	600	0	0
Total Cash Disbursements (Cash Out)			**31,100**	**33,000**	**38,200**	**33,440**	**36,750**
Net Cash Gain (Loss) during month			2,950	2,400	550	1,985	(150)
Cash Balance at beginning of month			1,500	4,450	6,850	7,400	9,385
Cash Balance at end of month			4,450	6,850	7,400	9,385	9,235

Figure 4.2 Cash Flow Worksheet.

Adapted from *Financial Management for Architects* by Robert F. Mattox, The American Institute of Architects, 1980.

the firm's revenues are consistently greater than the firm's expenses. We emphasize the need to do this every month because design professionals have narrow profit margins. It is easy—if workload declines sharply—to lose more in one month than can be earned as profit in three to six months. If a firm can accomplish this positive relationship

TIP

You can make or lose more in the contract negotiation than in any aspect of project execution.

between income and expense, it should be financially successful. So what are the tools you need to use to help you be successful?

If the firm recorded its finances the way many ordinary household finances are recorded—that is, on the cash basis—revenue would be recorded when it was received, and expenses would be recorded when they were disbursed. If positive, the difference between revenue and expense would indicate profit (or surplus); if negative, loss (or deficit).

Now imagine that a firm starts in business on January 1, and chooses to record its finances on the cash basis, as described. In January, then, the firm would pay its staff, rent, insurance, taxes, and other expenses, direct and indirect, that were due. By the end of January, it probably would not have invoiced for the services it provided that month, nor collected any money for those services. Using the cash basis of accounting the firm would record no revenue and all expense, and therefore would report a loss for the month's operations.

In February, the firm would likely prepare and send an invoice for the work it had done in January. It also would pay its staff, rent, insurance, taxes, and so on, but still might not have received payment for services that it performed in January and invoiced at the beginning of February. Again, on the cash basis of accounting, the firm would record all expenses and zero revenue, and report a loss for that month also.

In March, the firm would invoice for services performed in February. It would pay its incurred direct and indirect expenses for the month, and might have received payment for the services performed in January. Now the firm would record the value of the revenue received in March for services performed in January, and would record the expenses paid in March. On the cash basis, the firm would record a profit if the revenue it received exceeded the expenses it disbursed that month, but would record a loss if expenses disbursed exceeded revenues received.

Clearly, this method of recording revenue and expense does not accurately or fairly describe what happened in the firm with respect to profit or loss. The firm may actually have practiced profitably in January and February, but since it did not receive the cash that would have represented the value the firm was entitled to for having performed the services, using cash basis accounting, it had no way to record that value. Conversely, in March, the firm may or may not have been profitable; there is simply no way to know by counting only cash received and disbursed.

Despite this anomaly, the importance of emphasizing cash at the beginning cannot be exaggerated. Cash will always be important, but particularly at the beginning of a firm's existence. Typically, the founders of the new enterprise will have invested their own money; in fact, they may have exhausted their personal resources. It will take cash receipts to keep the practice solvent, and sooner rather than later. Later, as the firm develops a body of work and the expectation (but never the certainty) of a consistent flow of new work, management on the accrual basis becomes more important as the only way to truly understand whether the firm and its projects are profitable. Counting the cash on hand is not, and never will be, an accurate way to do so.

Recognizing that cash accounting can be misleading (if not balanced by additional tools described in this chapter), it is, nevertheless, still a critical measure of a young firm's financial health. All young firms are cash-starved; and cash accounting will help guide a new firm to a healthy beginning.

Accrual Accounting

The *accrual* basis of accounting is a method established to reflect the true financial performance of a firm during a specific period of time by matching revenue earned with expenses incurred. In the accrual basis of accounting, revenue is recognized (recorded) when it is *earned,* and expenses are recognized (recorded) when they are *incurred*. Profit (or loss) again represents the difference between the two, regardless of whether cash has been received or disbursed. In an architecture or other similar design firm, the most important objective of accrual-basis accounting is to match revenue with expenses during the period in which the revenue was generated, to determine profitability on a current basis. Using accrual-basis accounting, the firm can accurately record whether it is making or losing money on both a project- and firmwide basis for any month and the year.

Though more accurate, accrual accounting is just one tool. You will almost certainly calculate and pay your taxes on a cash basis, and most new firms are so cash-poor that cash accounting is an extremely important short-term indication of financial health. In the long term, you may live on a cash basis, but your firm can die if you ignore accrual. The staff at the first firm Brad worked for as a consultant thought they were doing fine because each month their cash receipts totaled more than their monthly expenses. What they failed to recognize was that the cash receipts were for work done earlier in the year. On a current basis, they were actually earning less than their expenses. This soon became a crisis.

It need not be said that to succeed, firms must remain both profitable and solvent. The firm's principal(s) should regularly monitor both the firm's cash position and its profitability. Failure to practice profitably over time will, in the short term, inhibit the firm's ability to provide appropriate rewards to the people who contribute to success. In the longer term, lack of profitability will cause the firm to deplete its cash and/or its access to cash, creating insolvency—the inability to pay debts when they become due—leading to bankruptcy.

TIP

Most firms calculate and pay taxes on a cash basis, so it is very important to have tax advice before year-end. Sometimes you may want to delay receipt of a client payment to beyond year-end, or prepay some expenses to minimize tax exposure.

Projecting Workload

As noted in Chapter 3, securing a steady flow of work is an essential step in building a successful firm. The next is to match a projection of the fees that will be earned against the expenses that will be incurred in providing the commissioned services.

Envision two partners, Able and Baker, who are setting out on their own after several years doing moonlight projects while working full-time in a larger firm. To start, they have four projects: three house additions from friends and family, plus a small office renovation that their former employer has given them.

The first step is to estimate the fees they will earn over the next 12 months from these four projects (the *contracted backlog*), as well as what additional work they might get as the year goes on. This projection is always an estimate, of course, but it serves to

Fictitious Firm

Throughout Part 1, we use a fictitious firm, Able & Baker Architects, to exemplify the concepts, principles, and procedures presented. Able & Baker Architects is described in the case study on the next page.

CASE STUDY

Introducing Able & Baker Architects

John Able and Jean Baker, 32 and 28 years old, respectively, decided to start a practice together. Though they attended different schools before their internship, they were both hired as staff architects in a 40-person firm owned by three architects, all more than 10 years older than they were. Although the three principals had acknowledged the gradual growth in Able's and Baker's professional capabilities by assigning them more complex and important project responsibilities, the two were not comfortable with the firm's overall direction, nor with what they thought would later be significant limitations on their future professional growth and compensation.

In spite of their different personalities, interests, and skills, Able and Baker had developed a comfortable and productive working relationship in the firm, so much so that they began doing small-scale "moonlight" projects together.

Baker's outgoing personality enabled her to connect easily with people and inspire their confidence. She became active in her community's civic organizations, and expanded her undergraduate interest in the arts to become involved in arts-related organizations, as well. In collaboration with Able, whose technical skills complemented her own design and people skills, the duo created a team capable of acquiring and executing small projects successfully while they were still employed. Determined to depart on good terms and not burn bridges, they planned to set up their own practice only after they had completed the large projects on which they were working. Ultimately, they left with the blessing of their employers, along with a referral and recommendation for a project that was too small for the larger firm to want to execute, plus two small projects of their own that were nearing completion, and another about to start.

provide some key information. Figure 4.3 indicates the fee projection that Able & Baker prepared three months after they started their firm. The projection records the net fees (excluding consultants and other nonsalary direct expenses) for projects for which

Project	Gross Fee	Net Fee	Net Fee Earned to Date	Net Fee Remaining	Schedule
A	$ 20,000	$ 20,000	$20,000	$ 0	3 months
B	30,000	25,000	15,000	10,000	3 months
C	60,000	45,000	15,000	30,000	6 months
D	140,000	120,000	30,000	90,000	9 months
Proposals @ one-third of proposed fees	150,000	120,000	0	120,000	12 months
Total	$400,000	$330,000	$80,000	$250,000	

Figure 4.3 Able & Baker Fee Projection at Three Months.

they had secured contracts, the value of their services to date (again, excluding consultants), and the amount remaining—the backlog. Their projection also includes the amount they expect to receive from the prospective commissions on which they expressed interest and were asked for proposals. Since they know they will not likely get all of them, they projected the value at one-third. As they gain more experience and develop a track record, these projections will become more accurate.

Invoices and Accounts Receivable

We strongly recommend that firms bill for services monthly (or on an even shorter cycle if clients permit) and that they follow up if the invoice is not paid within 30 days. Many clients will hold up payment if they have questions. Some invoices do get lost (but not as many as some clients claim), and some clients pay only when asked. Friendly follow-up is essential. Remember that accounts receivable are like dead fish; they do not improve with age.

Expense Projection

At the same time that fee projections are being estimated for the first year, it is important to project the expenses that the firm expects to incur during the same period. These are typically divided into start-up expenses (setting up the office, rent deposits, stationery printing, etc.) and ongoing operating expenses (e.g., rent, supplies, and the modest salaries the partners expect to be able to pay themselves, at least until they can assure themselves of profitable operations and adequate cash flow). (A checklist of start-up expenses is shown in Chapter 12.)

By matching the timing of expenses and the likely timing of fee payments, it is possible to form a reasonably good picture of the capital needed to start the firm and keep it afloat during the first year. The document traditionally used to match receipts and disbursements is called a cash flow projection. Figure 4.4 details Able & Baker's cash flow projection for their first year in business together.

The Income Statement

The income statement, sometimes called *a profit/loss* or *income and expense statement*, records the *operations* of the firm over a specific period of time, usually a month, quarter, or year. It categorizes and summarizes the operations of the firm into three major areas: *revenues*, *expenses*, and *profit* (or loss). We strongly recommend that all design firms divide, allocate, and record expenses into three subdivisions: reimbursable, direct, and indirect expenses. These categories of expenses are explained in the following subsections, and Figure 4.5 portrays the accrual-basis income statement of Able & Baker Architects at the end of its first year of practice.

Category Total	1st Quarter	2nd Quarter	3rd Quarter	4th Quarter	First Year
Billings	$50,000	$60,000	$80,000	$60,000	$250,000
Collections	40,000	40,000	60,000	60,000	200,000
Total Receipts	**40,000**	**40,000**	**60,000**	**60,000**	**200,000**
Disbursements					
Salaries	30,000	30,000	30,000	30,000	120,000
Consultants	5,000	5,000	10,000	10,000	30,000
Other Direct Expenses	2,000	2,000	2,000	2,000	8,000
Nonsalary Indirect Expenses	13,000	13,000	13,000	13,000	52,000
Total Disbursements	**50,000**	**50,000**	**55,000**	**55,000**	**210,000**
Net Gain/(Loss)	**(10,000)**	**(10,000)**	**5,000**	**5,000**	**(10,000)**
Beginning Balance	10,000 loan	0	(10,000)	(5,000)	10,000
Ending Balance	0	(10,000)	(5,000)	0	0

Figure 4.4 Able & Baker First-Year Cash Flow Projection.

Income Statement on December 31, 2002		
Revenues		
Gross revenues	$250,000	
Reimbursable revenue: consultants	(40,000)	
Reimbursable revenue: reprographics, travel	(10,000)	
Net revenue: architectural fees	$200,000	100.0%
Direct and Reimbursable Expenses		
Direct salary expense	$ 72,000	36.0
Consultants' expense	40,000	20.0
Reprographics, travel, etc.	10,000	5.0
Total direct expenses	$122,000	61.0%
Indirect Expenses		
Indirect salary expense	$ 48,000	24.0
Payroll and benefits expenses	22,000	11.0
Occupancy expenses	10,000	5.0
General administrative expenses	20,000	10.0
Total indirect expense	$100,000	50.0%
Profit (Loss)	$ 28,000	14.0% of net revenues
		11.2% of gross revenues

Figure 4.5 Able & Baker Architects Income Statement.

Regarding direct salary expense, note that even if a principal is a proprietor, or the principals are partners, for management purposes it is useful to treat their profit draws as if they were salaries. It is the only way to track the true cost of performing services (on the reasonable assumption that the principals work on projects), and it is the only way to compare the firm's performance against the norms established by all other firms.

Self-Payment

The statement in Figure 4.5 indicates that for the 12 months ending December 31, 2002, Able & Baker Architects generated revenues (but not necessarily cash) of $250,000: $200,000 was generated by its own forces; $40,000 was generated by consultants, whose expenses were reimbursed; and $10,000 was generated as reimbursement of project expenses incurred in the interest of the project.

Direct expenses included direct salary expense of $72,000, representing the portion of the principals' salaries expended on projects (there being no other employees in the first year of practice). The $40,000 and $10,000, respectively, represent expenses for consultants and other nonsalary direct expenses, both reimbursed by the owner in this example.

Indirect expenses included indirect salary expense, representing the portion of the principals' and employees' salaries expended on overhead activities such as vacation, holiday, sick, and personal time; marketing, management, secretarial, and bookkeeping services. In addition, indirect expenses include all other expenses incurred to "keep the doors open" (payroll taxes and other mandatory and customary benefits, occupancy expenses, and general and administrative expenses).

Segregating direct and indirect expenses allows the principals to examine the firm's performance on projects, as well as their control of overhead. Also, when broken down in finer detail, these delineations can be used to develop a budget for future projects and for the next accounting period, generally one year.

Although some firms prefer to allocate benefits to direct salaries and record the resulting direct personnel expense, the great majority record benefits as indirect expenses.

Balance Sheet

Unlike the *income statement*, which is a statement of operations that reports financial activities that occurred over the span of time identified in the statement, the balance sheet is a report of *status*, that indicates the firm's financial condition at a specific point in time—specifically, at the date of the report.

Balance sheets are divided into two sections of equal value (hence the balance):

- Assets
- Combination of liabilities and net worth

Assets can be understood as those tangible and intangible resources with monetary value owned by, or owed to, the firm. Liabilities are debts or obligations the firm owes to others; *net worth* is the value owned by, or owed to, the firm's owners. The sum of the assets minus the sum of the liabilities equals net worth. In theory, if the firm were able to collect or redeem all its assets, and pay all its liabilities, the owners would realize their net worth in the firm. Standard double-entry bookkeeping procedures are designed to maintain this essential balance whenever a financial transaction is recorded.

Figure 4.6 shows the accrual-basis balance sheet of Able & Baker Architects that reveals the financial condition of the firm at the end of its first year of practice: December 31, 2002.

Current assets include all those expected to come due within one year. The firm's current assets on December 31, 2002, indicate that Able & Baker Architects owned $5,000 in cash and deposits, and was owed $45,000 by clients who had not yet paid their invoices for services rendered. Work in process records the value of services performed but not billed by the date of the report. Once billed, that amount, $10,000, will be added to accounts receivable and subtracted from work in process; because

Balance Sheet at December 31, 2002	
Assets	
Current Assets	
Cash	$ 5,000
Accounts Receivable	45,000
Work in Process	10,000
Deposits	2,000
Total Current Assets	$62,000
Long-Term Assets	
Furniture and Fixtures	$11,000
Computer Equipment	10,000
Less Depreciation and Amortization	(3,000)
Total Long-Term Assets	$18,000
Total Assets	$80,000
Liabilities	
Current Liabilities	
Credit Line Payable	$20,000
Note Payable: Equipment, Current Portion	2,000
Accounts Payable: Consultants	10,000
Accounts Payable: Trade	2,000
Other Accrued Expenses	3,000
Total Current Liabilities	$37,000
Note Payable: Long-Term Portion	$8,000
Total Liabilities	$45,000
Net Worth	$35,000

Figure 4.6 Sample Balance Sheet for Able & Baker Architects.

the firm recorded the asset when it was earned, the conversion from work in process does not change the value of total assets, nor will it change the value of assets when the client pays the bill and Able & Baker Architects receives the cash. Once earned, the receipt of cash represents the exchange of one asset for another asset that was reported when the revenue was earned.

On December 31, the firm owned $21,000 worth of furniture, fixtures, and equipment, of which $3,000 had been depreciated or amortized by the end of one year. The firm owned no other assets.

The firm's liabilities included $20,000, which had been drawn down on a bank credit line that was arranged by the founders, and a $10,000 equipment loan, of which $2,000 was due within one year and $8,000 over the balance of the loan. Liabilities also included $10,000 payable to consultants (within the $45,000 accounts receivable), $2,000 in trade accounts payable (such as credit cards, reprographics, etc.), and $3,000 in miscellaneous accrued expenses (e.g., vacation, salaries).

In sum, then, as of December 31, 2002, the owners of Able & Baker Architects had a firm whose net worth, or *book value*, was $35,000. That means that if the owners chose to go out of business at the end of the accounting period, and they were able to realize (collect) cash for everything that they owned or were owed, and then used that cash to pay their debts to consultants, vendors, and the bank, they would have $35,000 (on which they would be taxed for any amount over the cash value of their initial investment).

Office Earnings Report

Although it is possible to produce any number of reports that will explain or clarify a particular financial transaction or condition, the Office Earnings Report, shown in Figure 4.7, best serves the design professional.

The Office Earnings Report displays critical financial information for each project in the firm, line by line. It indicates for each project, from its inception to date:

- The amount earned (again, regardless of how much was billed or collected)
- Of the amount earned, how much was billed
- The amount unbilled at the time of the report
- Of the amount billed, the amount received
- The amount unpaid and receivable
- The amount spent to earn the amount billed
- The profit (or loss) to the firm

This report also indicates how much was earned and spent and how much profit (or loss) was achieved in the year to date by each project.

The Office Earnings Report for Able & Baker Architects on December 31, 2002, the end of their first year of practice, indicates that the firm worked on four projects. On Project A, the firm expended $20,000 to earn $20,000, all of which was billed and received by the end of the year. On Project B, the firm expended $26,000 to earn $30,000, of which $30,000 was billed and received. On Project C, the firm expended $50,000 to earn $60,000 ($60,000 was billed and $45,000 was collected, leaving $15,000 in

Office Earnings Report on December 31, 2002
(In thousands of dollars)

	Project to Date							Year to Date		
Project	Earned	Billed	Unbilled	Rec'd	A/R	Spent	Profit (Loss)	Earned	Spent	Profit (Loss)
A	$ 20	$ 20	$ 0	$ 20	$ 0	$ 20	$ 0	$ 20	$ 20	$ 0
B	30	30	0	30	0	26	4	30	26	4
C	60	60	0	45	15	50	10	60	50	10
D	140	130	10	100	30	126	14	140	126	14
Total	$250	$240	$10	$195	$45	$222	$28	$250	$222	$28

accounts receivable). On Project D, the firm expended $126,000 to earn $140,000, of which $130,000 had been billed and $100,000 had been collected, leaving $30,000 in accounts receivable and $10,000 remaining to be billed. In total, the firm earned $250,000, of which $240,000 was billed and $195,000 collected, leaving $10,000 remaining to be billed and ultimately collected, along with the $45,000 in accounts receivable. The overall profit for the firm in its first year was $28,000.

The year-to-date values for each project are identical to those for project-to-date because the firm started in business that year, hence no project went beyond one year. Since projects can start in one year and not be completed until the next, year-to-date values on projects will typically be less than those for project-to-date.

During the year, the firm incurred both direct (project-related) and indirect (overhead) expenses in the course of doing business. The direct expenses (direct salary expense, consultant fees, reproductions, travel, accommodations, etc.) incurred for specific projects were directly attributed and assigned to those projects for which they were incurred. Since indirect expenses are expended in the interest of the firm as a whole, not for a given project, they must be allocated in some way so that each project shares its portion of the total. Although there are several ways to allocate indirect expense (overhead) to projects, the most conventional is to allocate indirect expense to each project in proportion to that project's direct salary expense relative to total direct salary expense.

On Able & Baker Architects' Office Earnings Report, the "spent" amount for each project includes direct salary expense and consultant fees, plus other direct expenses such as reproductions, travel, and so on; and that project's pro rata portion of the firm's total indirect expense in the period reported.

In addition to ensuring that each project bears its portion of the firm's overhead, the allocation of indirect expense to projects in this way makes it possible to integrate the management reports, so that the bottom line of the income statement—profit or loss—equals the profit (or loss) at the bottom of the Office Earnings Report.

Economic Structure

In the 1960s, the American Institute of Architects (AIA) commissioned the management consulting firm of Case & Company to study the economic structure of architectural practice (see Figure 4.8). Case found that for each \$1.00 in salary expense that firms spent on a project, they incurred an additional dollar to cover that project's portion of the firm's overhead cost. Therefore, the breakeven for such operations was \$2.00 (\$1.00 + \$1.00 = \$2.00). Firms were accustomed to adding \$.50 for profit, to create a billing multiple of 2.5 times direct salary (2.5 × \$1.00 = \$2.50). This provided a 25 percent markup on cost (.50 ÷ 2.00), and a 20 percent profit relative to revenue (.50 ÷ 2.50).

By the mid-1970s, the economic structure had changed. Whereas overhead relative to direct salary expense had been 1:1 in the two preceding decades, average overhead in established firms had risen disproportionately to other expenses to 1.5:1. That is, by the 1970s, most established firms were incurring overhead costs of \$1.50 for each \$1.00 of direct salary, creating a breakeven of \$2.50, where it had been \$2.00.

USING DIRECT SALARY EXPENSE AS THE BASE

Expense Calculation	Revenue Calculation
$1.00 Direct Salary Unit Cost	$1.00 Direct Salary Unit Cost
+ 1.50 Indirect Expense	× 2.50 Billing Multiple
2.50 Breakeven Cost	2.50 Invoice Amount (Revenue)

Profit Calculation

$2.50 Revenue
− 2.50 Breakeven Cost
0

USING DIRECT PERSONNEL EXPENSE AS THE BASE

Expense Calculation	Revenue Calculation
$1.00 Direct Salary Unit Cost	1.30 Direct Personnel Expense
+ .30 Benefits (Included in Indirect Expenses)	× 2.50 Billing Multiple
$1.30 Direct Personnel Expense	3.25 Invoice Amount (Revenue)

Profit Calculation

$3.25 Revenue
–2.50 Breakeven Cost (benefits are included in Indirect Expenses)
.75 Profit

Figure 4.8 Basic Economic Structure of Architectural Practice.

Firms that were accustomed to proposing and getting fees based on a multiple of 2.5 times direct salaries found that they were barely covering the cost (including overhead) of doing the work. Since overhead costs could not be cut, two options were possible: *increase the billing multiple* or *increase the billing base*. Believing that the 2.5 multiple had become ingrained in the minds of those purchasing architectural services, the leaders of the profession suggested increasing the base. They achieved this by creating a new base, called *Direct Personnel Expense* (DPE), which was defined as the cost of the architect's employees engaged on the project and the cost of their mandatory and customary benefits.

Mandatory benefits are few and universal: Social Security (FICA) tax and workers' compensation insurance. Unless required by state or local law, virtually all other benefits are customary, but not mandatory. These include vacation, holiday, and personal time, and health insurance. Not universal, but widely recognized, are life insurance, profit-sharing plans, continuing education reimbursement, and professional dues. These mandatory and customary benefits fall in a range of .25 to .40 times salary, depending primarily on the size, age, and profitability of the firm.

Using a mean of .30 for benefits, the economic structure changes substantially. The base for fee determination changes from direct salary to direct personnel expense, or \$1.00 + .30 = \$1.30. Using the same 2.5 billing multiple, one hour of billable time could be billed at \$3.25 (2.5 × \$1.30 = \$3.25). Now the profit relative to revenue is 23 percent (\$.75 ÷ 3.25).

At the end of its first year of practice, the basic economic structure for Able & Baker Architects was:

Expense Calculation

1.00	Direct Salary Unit Cost
+ 1.39	Indirect Expense Factor (Indirect Expense ÷ Direct Salary Expense)
2.39	Breakeven cost

If Able & Baker had been able to bill each dollar of direct salary at its intended billing multiple of 3.0, its revenue calculation would have been:

Revenue Calculation

1.00	Direct Salary Unit Cost
× 3.00	Billing Multiple
3.00	Net Revenue

However, the firm incurred $72,000 in direct salary expense to generate $200,000 in net revenues (regardless of the billing method it used to bill for services). Therefore, the firm had an earned multiple of 2.78, not the 3.0 it intended.

Able & Baker Profit Calculation

2.78	Revenue
− 2.39	Cost
.39	Profit

The $.39 profit the firm earned was 14 percent of net revenues. However, if the firm had used DPE as the billing base, or had been able to negotiate higher fixed fees or a higher billing rate regardless of the base, then profits could have been higher. For example, if the firm had a benefits rate of .25, then the firm's basic economic structure would have looked like this:

Revenue Base Calculation

1.00	Direct Salary Unit Cost
+ .25	Benefits Factor
1.25	Direct Personnel Expense

Revenue Calculation (using a 2.5 billing multiple)

1.25	Direct Personnel Expense
× 2.50	Billing Multiple
3.125	Billed Amount (Revenue)

Profit Calculation

3.125	Revenue
– 2.39	Cost
.735	Profit

Young firms frequently have lower benefits and total overhead ratios in the first years of practice. Moreover, they often work more than a standard 40-hour work week for their clients. In the early years at Brad's firm, they kept overhead ratio below 1.0, which enabled them to survive on the low-profit-margin projects that they often took to build the practice.

Capital Needs

Start-up capital is crucial for any new firm. Two important questions must be answered at this juncture:

- How much will I need?
- Where will I get it?

How Much?

The answer to "how much?" is a function of two different needs. First is the amount of money needed to pay for start-up organizational expenses. These might include:

- Legal and accounting assistance
- Acquisition of office space and leasehold improvements
- Furniture, fixtures, and equipment
- Printed office materials such as stationery, business cards, and transmittal forms
- Marketing materials such as announcements and brochures

To these must be added the money required to fund operations until enough cash is generated as payment for services in the normal business cycle, as indicated previously in Figure 4.1.

As stated repeatedly, it is common for architects to start a practice after developing a relationship and a commission (or the promise of a commission) that enables them to leave their current firms. The cash cycle begins when services are performed but, as explained earlier, cash payment for services usually comes in 60 to 90 days later. If the firm starts without a commission in hand, it will need to market its services, secure commissions, perform services, send invoices, and, finally, receive the first payment that establishes positive cash flow. In this case, the amount of capital required is the amount necessary to cover all disbursements that must be made until the firm begins to collect for its services.

Considering that even a firm with a project already in hand will not likely receive payment for services immediately, all start-up firms should capitalize sufficiently to cover three to six months of operating expenses, *plus* the amount needed for start-up organizational expenses.

Of course, even with work in hand, the start-up cash may not be all the investment that is required. Most new firms have very uneven cash flow in their early years. Most founders of firms can regale you with stories of their "near-death" experiences with cash flow in their early years. Brad's father, for example, recalled the weeks they were down to their last $100 (in the 1930s). They debated whether to shut down immediately and save the $100 or continue for another week. The point is, persevering is part of the history of even the most successful firms. The lesson is that having a cash reserve in the beginning and building it up over time are important to the survival of a new firm.

Where to Get the Money?

Sources for initial capital include:

- Personal savings
- Equity in personal real estate (mortgages and equity loans)
- Loans from relatives and friends
- Personal credit cards
- Small Business Administration (SBA) loans
- Commercial (bank) loans

Regarding bank loans, it is important to understand that lenders do not want to be *investors* in your firm. Their business is based on the certainty of a return on capital in the form of interest on loaned funds, rather than the uncertainty of a return in the form of profit from successful operations, which would be the right of an investor, but not a lender.

Banks will want the start-up design professionals to have some of their own capital invested in the firm, usually more than half the invested equity. Otherwise, the bank would be the primary stakeholder *and* risk-taker. Consequently, architects and other design professionals are usually required to provide a substantial portion of the necessary start-up capital from sources other than bank loans.

There are times when no commercial lenders are interested in a young design firm. Brad's firm ran into this in its sixth year, which coincided with the deep recession at the end of the 1980s. A number of the firm's developer clients went bankrupt, resulting in a cash flow crisis for the firm. Their regular bank refused to discuss a loan, and a second bank offered to loan them 70 percent of the value of cash and securities they put up as collateral.

There are two "takeaway" points from this story:

- First, it is important to establish a banking relationship and good credit early. If you do take a loan, pay it back on time. Make your banker your friend. The bank the firm finally found to help through the crisis has since proved invaluable in providing references, letters of credit required by leases, equipment leases, and many other services beyond the firm's line of credit.
- Second, it is critically important to build up reserves during the good years. Design professions are very vulnerable to business cycles. Having a supportive banker and adequate reserves of cash and credit can help get you through a downturn without it becoming a firm-threatening crisis.

To reiterate from the beginning of the chapter, seven years of plenty may be followed by seven (hopefully far fewer) years of famine.

One of the best ways to help build a strong financial base is to negotiate appropriate compensation for the services you provide. This is the subject of the next chapter.

5 Negotiating Fees and Contracts

Sales and finance come together when it is time to negotiate the fee for the services being offered. Obviously, it is essential to a firm's financial health that the design professionals learn to do this task well. All design professionals find setting fees a challenging task, especially because most clients want to know in advance what the fee will be for their project, even when the scope is unclear and the services will be provided over several years.

One approach is to do what Brad's brother-in-law did with his first client. He sent a letter of proposal for an energy audit of the client's building and left a blank for the client to fill in the fee. The client filled in $300. Most experienced professionals do not recommend this approach.

In the past this task was far simpler because most of the professions published recommended fee curves to help guide their members' efforts in setting fees. These curves have been declared anticompetitive and illegal, and the only people who still use established fee schedules are some of the large public and institutional clients. Needless to say, these client-generated fee curves are lower than those created by the professions.

The demise of the standard fee curves was a positive step not only from a legal standpoint, but in other ways as well. These curves were built on the fallacious concept that any two projects that were of the same construction budget, building type, and mix of new and renovation would require the same effort and cost to carry out. In fact, the research done on the costs to complete various types of projects, which formed the underlying basis for the fee curves, showed widely varying results for projects that were supposed to be similar. In national surveys, for example, almost 25 percent of the projects lost money.

Projects, clients, schedules, required services, and many other factors have continued to grow in complexity since the cessation of fee schedules. This has forced the design professionals to face the fact that calculating and negotiating appropriate fees is a major task requiring considerable skill and effort.

Analyzing the Cost of Providing a Service

There are five basic steps to setting a fee:

1. Calculate costs.
2. Do a competitive analysis.
3. Do a risk analysis.
4. Choose a fee method.
5. Negotiate the fee.

Calculate Costs

One method, often referred to as *top-down* budgeting, starts with the assumed or desired fee and calculates how much can be allocated to the various direct

Top-Down Budgeting

When the fee is established, either as a lump sum amount or a percentage that can be converted to a lump sum, the process used to budget the project is:

1. Start with fee dollars.
2. Subtract desired profit.
3. Yield cost of professional services.
4. Subtract cost of consultants and nonlabor direct expenses.
5. Yield cost of architectural services.
6. Divide by overhead rate.
7. Yield direct salary expense.
8. Divide by average hourly rate.
9. Yield hours available.
10. Allocate hours to phases and tasks.

costs of doing the work, as shown above. Alternatively, you can calculate what it might cost to provide the service. This was documented by the AIA as "cost-based compensation" and is often referred to as "bottom-up" budgeting, as shown below.

Cost-Based Compensation (Bottom-Up) Budgeting

The bottom-up budgeting process follows this sequence:

1. Identify or estimate tasks required to execute the project.
2. Multiply by average or specific hourly rates.
3. Yield direct salary expense.
4. Multiply by overhead ratio.
5. Yield cost of architectural services.
6. Add cost of consultants and nonlabor direct expenses.
7. Yield cost of professional services.
8. Add contingency and profit.
9. Yield fee required.

Probably, the first pass at the bottom-up method will yield a higher number than the expected fee, and further analysis will be necessary to reconcile it with the top-down calculation. If and when both methods yield the same results, this can be a good starting point. Nevertheless, it is not necessarily the right fee to quote if you are still competing for the project.

Do a Competitive Analysis

The next step in establishing a fee is to research the "going rate" for the service and the fees your competitors are likely to quote. A common range for comparable jobs exists in most cases and can often be checked with other experienced firms that are not competing for the same project. This "comparing of rates" is done all the time, and a principal in either a new or established firm should not be shy about asking for advice.

Determining what your competition will charge is much more difficult. Sometimes, other firms can help you, but in most cases you have to guess at this. Established firms are likely to quote within a certain range if it is consistent with their own bottom-up and top-down analyses. Smaller, younger firms are far harder to evaluate.

Do a Risk Analysis

The next step in determining a fee is to analyze the risks. This subject, too, requires judgment, which will improve with experience. Among the most common areas of potential risk encountered on many projects are:

- *An indecisive client.* These can be hard to spot in advance, but benchmarks include: reputation from previous jobs, a vaguely worded description of their proposed project, and the impression they give during preproposal contacts. A client with poor decision-making capabilities always adds to the cost of providing services.

- *An unreasonable client.* Good clients expect their design team to make a profit, and will work to help ensure that happens. An unreasonable client does not care, and argues against even reasonable requests for additional compensation when the scope changes. Other clients—such as the large committees set up for some projects—are inherently indecisive even if they are well meaning. These clients often cannot be avoided, but some contingency should be built into the fee or contract to account for the extra time it takes to deal with them.
- *An extremely tight budget.* A tight budget can significantly increase the effort necessary to reach a final design. If the budget is so tight that it is unreasonable, it may be indicative of an unreasonable client. Moreover, it may make it difficult to make the proposed fee seem reasonable in proportion to the total project cost.
- *A very tight or an unpredictable schedule.* Many clients talk about unreasonably short schedules. As with budgets, if it is too tight, it may be indicative of a naïve or unreasonable client. Conversely, tight, reasonable schedules are advantageous to the design firm since many of the design team's costs increase over time. Thus, of equal concern is an indefinite schedule that stops and starts or extends beyond the time required, because many of the design team's costs are a direct function of time.
- *An interrupted work process.* Some projects are done in phases with indefinite breaks between

stages to secure financing, obtain land-use approvals, and the like. Each interruption can add to cost as a firm shuts down or remobilizes its efforts.

- *A difficult approval process.* Clients often like to shift risk. For example, if they foresee risk in obtaining financing or land-use approvals, they often will try to shift fee payments until after these hurdles have been overcome. Moreover, if these steps are risky, they are likely to require added effort by the design team.
- *Slow payment.* Some clients are notoriously slow payers. This can place a real burden on a young design firm, hence should be a factor in both the fee and the contract negotiation. To reward prompt payment, therefore, it is often worth giving something extra to a client that does so. One of Brad's first clients paid within 24 hours of receiving the invoice. This sensitivity to the firm's cash flow needs resulted in the client being given first priority throughout the life of the project.
- *A difficult construction phase.* With a good contractor or construction manager, one site visit a week is more than required; with a bad one, five days a week is not enough. As for an indecisive client, a difficult construction phase is almost impossible to predict at the beginning of a project. Therefore, it is important to clearly tie the basic fees to an assumed level of service (number of site visits, length of construction, etc.), with any overages compensated as extra services.
- *An insecure client or a client in trouble.* Many in the profession believe that the most dangerous client is one that is insecure or already in trouble. If a client gets into financial or other difficulty,

expect it to impact the design team. The only protection is to be sensitive to early signs of trouble.

Choose a Fee Method

The next step is to select the most appropriate fee method. There are many, each with its advantages and disadvantages, and no one works for all situations. The final choice often depends upon client preference. The most common are defined in the following subsections.

Percentage of Construction Cost

For decades, this was the most common method for setting fees. Its great advantage is that the fee increases automatically as the scope (as reflected in the budget) increases. Its major disadvantages are: it is arbitrary (if not based upon a project cost analysis); it penalizes the effort to contain or reduce budget, and clients view this conflict with suspicion; and the fee goes down if the cost goes down. Because of these disadvantages, this method should be used with caution, though it can be the right choice if the client has set an unrealistically low budget.

Percentage of Approved Budget

This method resolves any perceived conflict of interest. It is best used when the scope is unclear at the start of the design process.

Lump Sum

This is becoming the most commonly used method for some firms and experienced clients. If based on a careful cost and risk analysis, it can be the appropriate choice. Its major disadvantage is its underlying assumption that the scope is fixed. Lump sums are inflexible and clients usually resist requests for extra services.

Hourly

Hourly billing is the ideal method when the scope is unclear. Most clients will, however, accept this method only for small projects or for the phases for which the scope clearly cannot be defined.

Hourly with a Cap (or Limit or Maximum)

The cap is the most common way to respond to clients' concerns about the open-ended nature of hourly billing. Some agreements permit hourly billing without an *upset amount* or fixed cap until the scope is defined and a maximum upset can be set. If a maximum, or cap, is set, it should be higher than the lump sum that could have been negotiated. In a lump sum, the design team keeps any amount under the maximum. In hourly up to a cap, the client keeps the difference. Of course, any amount over the cap is a loss to the design professionals under either arrangement.

Dollars per Square Foot or per Unit

Some fees are quoted on a unit basis (square foot, residential unit, etc.). This is common for corporate interiors, multifamily housing, and a few other building types. This is the equivalent of a lump sum if the unit total is known in advance.

Prototypes and Reuse Fees

In certain circumstances, a builder may ask the architect to design several prototypes (such as houses or chain stores) that will then be used repeatedly. In this case, part or all of the basic cost of designing the prototype is recovered in the original prototype fee, with a smaller additional amount paid for each reuse to cover site adaptation and the rest of the prototype fee. In some cases this does not have to cover continuing services and is thus a royalty for reuse of the original design.

Performance Bonus or Success Fees

Some clients will offer bonus or success fees if certain targets (budget, schedule, etc.) are met. Since so many of these targets are under the client's control, the agreement must be clear.

Composite

Among the many other approaches to setting fees, one of the most common is to combine two or more of the preceding methods. For example, when there is a variable scope, a variable form such as hourly charges can be used for design, public approvals, and construction administration, and a fixed fee is used for the scope (usually design development and contract documents) under the design team's control.

Negotiate the Fee

Fee negotiation is more an art form than a skill, but to some extent it can be learned. The most effective teacher is experience. Absent experience, keep these basics in mind when negotiating fees:

- *Avoid setting fees while still selling.* When your priority is to be selected by the client, you may lose your focus on maintaining the fee you need. If a client asks you to set a fee during the marketing/ sales process, try to build in the flexibility to negotiate a more accurate fee later. Also, quote fee ranges rather than a single number; provide separate fee estimates for any consultants so that their fees do not distort your own proposal; and try to get the client to accept a fee *quote* for a limited initial phase of work where the scope and risks can be clearly defined. If all else fails, be as vague as possible, in the hope that it will gain you some negotiating room later.

- *Avoid setting fees before the scope has been clarified.* If a client asks for a fixed fee before the scope has been clarified, be very clear about the assumptions that form the basis of the fee. Make it plain that any material changes in the assumptions are likely to require an adjustment to the fee quotation. Refer to the risk areas discussed earlier in the chapter for the issues (such as schedule, number of meetings, scope of construction phase services, etc.) to be covered by assumptions.
- *Avoid the volitional fallacy.* The "volitional fallacy" is the assumption that because you want something to be true it will be true. Analyze your probable costs, keep and refer to records of actual costs on past jobs, and don't talk yourself into believing an unrealistically low fee will somehow work out because "this job is different."
- *Ask the client to commit to a limited first phase.* This is called "setting the hook." Once most clients have agreed to retain you for an initial scope of service, such as a site selection study or a master plan, you can usually avoid negotiating the overall fee while still competing with others. It is worth offering a very competitive fee for a limited first phase to avoid setting fees while still selling or while the scope is largely unknown.

- *Play on the client's sense of fairness.* If you think the client is fair, it's a good idea to try to make fairness a part of the negotiation. Consider sharing the underlying cost analysis that you prepared for your fee estimate. If the client asks you to cut your fee, counter by asking which part of the labor estimate they think you should cut. Most reasonable clients will not push back too hard when confronted with this choice. Some clients, even large, corporate clients, will respond favorably when faced with the fact that their unfairness is inconsistent with the company's corporate ethic.
- *Get it up front.* When setting the overall fee, try to negotiate a fee that covers the full list of known services. Some firms like to leave open the potential to negotiate extra services later, but experience proves that most clients resent this. No two clients are the same, but it is often easier to get a fair fee at the beginning rather than by detailing a long list of extra services.
- *Be prepared to walk away.* One of the easiest ways to get a fair fee is to not need the job. If you can walk away, it strengthens your negotiating stance. Unfortunately, it is rare for a new firm to be in this position. There are, however, times when even a new firm should walk away.
- *Remember, some low-fee jobs are worth taking.* As discussed in Chapters 3 and 4, there are times when it is worth taking a project for which the fee is too low; for example, if the project is relatively small, if it will lead to future work, and/or if it uses time that is uncommitted. Remember, some income is better than none, especially for a struggling young firm.

These important points are reiterated in the box below, titled "Guidelines for Setting Fees."

Contracts and Contract Negotiation

The core of any contract is a *description of the services to be provided* and the *compensation to be paid for those services*. Most of the other clauses in a typical agreement deal with the eventualities of problems or changes in scope and compensation. At least in theory, the contract can be as simple as a handshake or a one-page

Guidelines for Setting Fees

- Don't set fixed fees while still selling or when the scope is unknown.
- Know the competition and understand the norms.
- Always estimate the cost to provide the service and define the net direct labor that will be available for the likely fee.
- Understand the areas of risk.
- Keep records and know your costs.
- Pick the most appropriate fee method:
  - Percent of construction cost (actual final cost or approved budget)
  - Lump sum
  - Hourly (open-ended or an agreed-to limit)
  - Square footage
  - Prototype and reuse fee
  - Bonuses, success fees, shared savings, and so on
  - Mixed methods
- Present the fee in the most attractive manner possible.
- Negotiate with consultants the following:
  - Consistent terms
  - Fees that work within the overall budget
  - No open-ended terms within a fixed fee contract
- Build in clear limits on open-ended scope items.
- Negotiate a fair deal up front rather than through extra services.

letter agreement. Such a limited contract is appropriate, if at all, only for very small projects or services of very limited scope. In virtually all other cases, a full agreement should be discussed and agreed upon before a project proceeds.

Whenever possible we strongly recommend that you use one of the standard AIA contract forms as the starting point for an agreement. These standard forms are usually modified to reflect the specific understandings between the owner and the design team. That said, you will also find that some clients have their own standard forms, and that some overenthusiastic client attorneys insist on rewriting the standard forms. Beware of these other standard forms and major rewrites because they are usually one-sided and contain clauses that can create unacceptable risks for the design team.

Some of the more common issues encountered in negotiating the standard clauses of an owner-architect agreement (such as AIA B141—see the box on the next page) are as follows:

It is beyond the scope of this book to cover all aspects of the typical contract negotiation, and none of the information in this section should be considered legal advice. When in doubt about the legal implications of any contractual issue, consult an attorney with relevant experience, your liability insurance carrier, or another design professional with substantial experience in contract negotiation.

Contracting Parties

The contract usually begins by naming the parties to the agreement. Note here that you want the client to be an *entity with assets*. If the client signs the agreement in the name of a shell corporation, the design team may have no recourse in the case of a dispute over money.

The Project

The description of the project (the program, the concept, the schedule, etc.) is important because it sets a baseline against which to judge whether the client is making material changes after the fee has

AIA Agreement B141–1997

Table of Contents

1.1 Initial Information

1.2 Responsibilities of the Parties

1.3 Terms and Conditions

1.4 Scope of Services and Other Special Terms and Conditions

1.5 Compensation

2.1 Project Administration Services

2.2 Supporting Services

2.3 Evaluation and Planning Services

2.4 Design Services

2.5 Construction Procurement Services

2.6 Contract Administration Services

2.7 Facility Operation Services

2.8 Schedule of Services

2.9 Modifications

been set. If there is a written program, a schedule, concept drawings, or other descriptive material, attach them as exhibits to the contract.

Scope/Services

This section of the contract should be modified to:

- Reflect the services to be provided
- Clarify for an inexperienced client the design team's role
- Establish limits or assumptions for some of the major variables

For example:

- If the design team is to develop the space program, develop studies of possible future phases, negotiate special land-use approvals, or provide a full-time on-site representative during construction; these services should be included in Article 12 or in a modified Article 1 in the B141 form. The description of the scope of services in the standard form is too generic to be good for either the client or the design team.

- If the owner does not understand what your responsibilities are (versus those of the builder, the interior designer, or the owner), it is worth clarifying these up front. Too many client relationships deteriorate when the owner learns—after the fact—that the design team does not have control over the construction subcontractors or that essential services were not included in the agreement.
- If consultants will be included as subcontractors to you, make sure they agree to the same terms that bind you. It is particularly important that they agree to be paid only after you are paid, that they have insurance, and that they do not take exception to any of the contract terms.

Additional, Optional, or Contingent Services

The standard form provides a checklist of some of the more common reasons for additional services. Be clear how such services will be authorized. If a client wants to approve additional services in writing and in advance, be careful not to proceed without this written authorization. In addition, make sure this list includes any changes in the assumptions (number of site visits, etc.) that form the foundation of your fee quote. In some areas you may want to agree with the client that you will include a stated amount of time (say, 100 hours) in your base fee for analysis of change orders and contractor substitutions, and charge only excessive time as an additional service.

Construction Costs

Do not guarantee the construction costs. At the same time, make sure that if cost is the basis for the fee, the estimate is realistic and contains everything, including the CM fee and any contingencies.

Ownership of Documents

Owners often insist on removing this clause, though usually it is possible to get clients to agree to accept copies for their use. If the clause is removed, you should be aware that you may be losing rights otherwise provided to you under federal copyright law. In addition, you should insist on a clause that holds you harmless from any reuse of the documents. When liability problems arise in a future addition, the plaintiff's attorney will sue everyone on the title block.

Arbitration

Most owners strike this clause, which you may find acceptable. It is, however, worthwhile to insist that disputes be subjected to at least nonbinding mediation prior to any litigation.

Termination

Owners like to strike termination clauses. While there are some valid arguments for protection from arbitrary termination and for reimbursement of costs, most owners refuse to pay even if the clause remains. Therefore, these clauses are often sacrificed in exchange for keeping other clauses.

Payment

Insist on monthly billing and timely payment or the right to stop work if payments are not made.

Payments Withheld

To the extent possible, make sure that the client understands that achieving perfection in the drawings and services is an unrealistic standard, and that some change orders, omissions, and problems are inevitable. Discuss a reasonable change-order contingency during the initial budgeting phase of the project, as well as during the contract negotiations.

Too many clients believe in a different golden rule: that is, they have the gold so they make the rules. Make it a mutual understanding that if they arbitrarily withhold payment, you can stop work.

Basic Compensation

The best advice for this key section of the contract is to get advice on how to fill it in. But, basically, the following points are essential elements of the contract and should be clearly documented:

- Most owners object to markups on consultants and reimbursables, but such markups merely reflect the real liability and administrative costs of including these expenses in your contract. One device that usually helps bring this point home is to give the client the opportunity to retain consultants directly (so that they incur the extra administrative and liability burden and no longer have your liability insurance covering the consultants). They will almost always refuse.
- Owners will rightly ask for prior approval in writing for additional services. Agree to this, but always insist on getting approval in writing before you *provide* the services.
- The rate of interest is often listed as the legal rate since some states limit the permissible rate.

Other Provisions

This is the section where all other understandings should be documented.

With work in hand, it is now time to focus on how the firm should be organized. This is the subject of the next chapter.

6 Organization and Personnel

All firms grow to be a reflection of their founders, in part based on interests and abilities, and in part due to how the founders choose to organize their practice. A principal committed to a *strong idea* practice will make different organizational choices from one committed to a *strong service* model. (This is discussed more fully in Chapter 10 and in Appendix B, Charting Your Course.)

Legal Forms of Organization

Even if the new firm will be staffed by only the person starting the firm, that person should decide on the nature of the organization he or she is launching, following the guiding principles given in the box titled "Basic Organizational Principles." The most common options are:

- Proprietorship
- Partnership
- General (business) corporation (C-corporation)
- Professional corporation (PC)

- S-corporation (strictly speaking, the S-election in a business corporation)
- Limited Liability Company (LLC) or Limited Liability Partnership (LLP)

Unless there is a specific reason to do otherwise, it is advisable to begin practice in the simplest, most economical, and most flexible organization, keeping in mind that eventual change may be desirable and

Basic Organizational Principles

- Design professions are team sports. Few people are good at everything, and most successful firms are led by principals who possess a balance of the essential design, technical, management, and marketing skills.
- The roles and personal goals of a firm's leaders must mesh.
- Agree on the strategic goals, but expect diversity in tactics and short-term objectives.
- Look for strength in your colleagues; you don't want weak subordinates.
- Most new firms with more than one leader operate as if they were partnerships even if they use another form of organization.
- Partnership is an inherently difficult form. Mutual respect, a commitment to make it work, and trust are essential.
- When selecting and documenting the firm's organization, seek professional advice on the legal options, decision making, initial contributions of capital or other assets by the principals, distribution of profits and losses, changes in ownership, departure (forced or voluntary) of the owner, retirement, death or disability, dissolution of the firm.
- People are not fungible or expendable; they are a firm's most important assets and should be treated that way.
- Growth demands organizational change.
    - 1 → 2 Adding an employee or a partner is the most fundamental change.
    - 8 → 12 An informal start-up must become a "firm."
    - 20 → 30 The founder can be involved in everything but cannot run everything.
    - 25 → 60 The founder cannot even be involved in everything.
- Plan for eventual transition or change of ownership—begin to look for your successor right from the beginning.

will be possible. Regardless of the form, think of the practice as a separate entity with its own requirements, organization, procedures, and accounts. Each of the organizational forms is described in the following subsections.

Proprietorship

A *proprietorship* is an entity in which the firm and the individual who owns it are synonymous. All revenues and expenses of the business are treated as if they are the personal revenue and expenses of the proprietor, who is the 100 percent owner.

It is generally possible and permissible, but it is not advisable, for proprietors to run their businesses through their personal checkbooks. In theory, a proprietor of a design firm, even one with employees, could deposit clients' payments into his or her personal checking account, and from that account disburse payments for salaries, taxes, and other company expenses, thereby effectively merging personal and company accounts. This practice should be avoided because it is likely to obscure the operations of the firm and increase the risk of incurring serious tax problems. Even though, in the final analysis, the firm's income is the proprietor's personal income, and even if the start-up firm is small, a proprietor should open a separate checking account to record just the firm's transactions.

For a design professional starting very small, it is reasonable and perhaps even advisable, to start as a proprietorship. The advantages outweigh the disadvantages. A proprietorship:

- Is simple to begin and operate.
- Requires no special legal creation and may not require business registration.

- Requires no special personal tax filings, since the firm's taxes are the proprietor's.

The singular disadvantage is that the proprietor's personal professional liability is limitless, as it would be in any other form of organization in which the individual was the sole owner.

Partnership

Some new firms, as is our case study firm, Able & Baker, are organized by two or more professionals who elect to form a firm together as equal (or unequal) co-owners. In this circumstance, the most common organization chosen is a partnership. Unlike a proprietorship, a partnership is a legal entity unto itself. Although it is strongly advisable, it is not required that professionals entering into partnership execute a partnership agreement that defines the particular conditions they want to apply to their new firm. If they choose not to, their partnership will be *understood* to be operating, and disputes will be resolved in accordance with the conditions of their state's uniform partnership code.

Following are the most important issues to consider in establishing a partnership agreement:

- *Initial investment:* Who will be contributors and in what proportions?
- *Additional investment, if needed:* Who will provide it, and in what proportions?
- *Distribution of profits and losses:* These are generally in proportion to ownership interests, but should be spelled out.
- *Decision making:* By dictate, vote, or consensus? If by vote, vote of individuals or shares?

- *Valuation* (and decision making where appropriate) for death or permanent disability, normal retirement, voluntary early withdrawal, and involuntary separation.
- *New owners:* Who decides whether and whom to bring in as additional owners?
- *Noncompete provisions:* If owners leave the practice, what limits are placed on their ability to compete with the remaining owners?
- *Expectations of owners:* What particular commitments are required? Is it full-time? Does all professional income go to the firm?
- *Sale to others:* What conditions apply to a prospective sale? Who decides?
- *Liquidation of the practice:* How is it decided, and by whom, to terminate or liquidate the practice?

Because a partnership is a legal entity disconnected from the personal circumstances of the partners, financial records must be kept that identify the partnership's revenues, expenses, and profit or loss. The tax effect, however, is that profits (*net income*, in accounting terms) or losses "pass through" the partnership and are allocated to the individual partners in proportion to their ownership interests. The partners, therefore, assume personal responsibility for federal, state, and local income taxes on their allocated portion of partnership income.

In a *general partnership*, liability extends to the partners, "individually and severally," meaning that each partner is responsible for 100 percent of the liabilities of the partnership. That condition precipitated the enactment of laws permitting professional practice in limited liability partnerships (LLPs) or companies (LLCs), described later.

General or Professional Corporation

A *corporation* is a legal entity owned by its stockholders or shareholders pursuant to a certificate, or articles, of incorporation and bylaws, which it must file in the state in which it is organized. In a typical corporation, a design firm's professional, technical, and clerical staff, including the shareholders, are all considered employees of the corporation. Shareholder employees receive salaries, from which taxes are withheld and filed by the corporation.

Corporations must keep separate financial accounts and records. And because corporate income (profit) after all expenses, including salaries and bonuses, is taxed at corporate income tax rates, and because dividends distributed to stockholders are also taxed, corporate owners generally choose to distribute profits in the form of bonuses in the year in which they are earned.

Liability of shareholders in general corporations is limited to their proportionate ownership share in the company. For that reason, many states prohibit the practice of architecture and other design professions in corporate form, because they want *professional* liability to extend to the responsible professionals, regardless of their level of ownership. Consequently, several states have enacted a new corporate form—the *professional corporation*—to allow design professionals to enjoy the business benefits of corporate practice while maintaining their professional responsibilities in the public interest. Professional corporations (PCs) generally differ from general corporations in that professional liability in PCs extends to those professionals in the corporation found to have been responsible for a professional error or omission; in most other ways, PCs are like general corporations.

S-Corporation

The *S-corporation* (more strictly, the S-election available within general corporations) is a corporate form closely following the requirements of more traditional corporate forms, but treating the shareholders as if they were partners in a partnership for tax purposes. In that way, income or loss flows through the corporation, which has no liability for taxes, and is allocated to the shareholders in proportion to their share ownership.

Limited Liability Company or Partnership

Responding to a situation some years ago in which the acts of partners in a satellite office of a national accounting firm (organized as a partnership) were found to be fraudulent, resulting in the eventual collapse of the company, several states enacted laws that permitted professional practice as a limited liability partnership (LLP) or limited liability company (LLC). An *LLC* is a legal entity distinct from its owners, who are called "members" and who own membership interests in the LLC.

These entities typically combine the management flexibility and tax advantages of general partnerships, with the liability protection of a corporation. More specifically, the members in an LLC have business liability only to the extent of their membership interest in the company, likewise professional liability only for their own professional acts and those for which they had supervisory responsibility.

Professionals forming an LLC typically file a Certificate of Formation with the state, and operate the company pursuant to an Operating Agreement that is similar to a General Partnership Agreement. Like a partnership, an LLC permits pass-through

TIP

Remember, unless there is a specific reason to do otherwise, organize your practice in the simplest, most economical, and most flexible way possible.

taxation to its member owners with no entity-level tax.

Project and Firm Organizational Structures

Most firms start small with one architect serving one client—although there certainly are exceptions, including some notable ones. When you start small, the project and firmwide organizational structure looks as shown in Figure 6.1.

On projects, the sole proprietor—the architect—forms the client relationship; negotiates the owner architect agreement; establishes the program; designs, documents, checks shop drawings; visits the job site—in fact does everything that needs doing on the project. It's the same for the firm: that same person

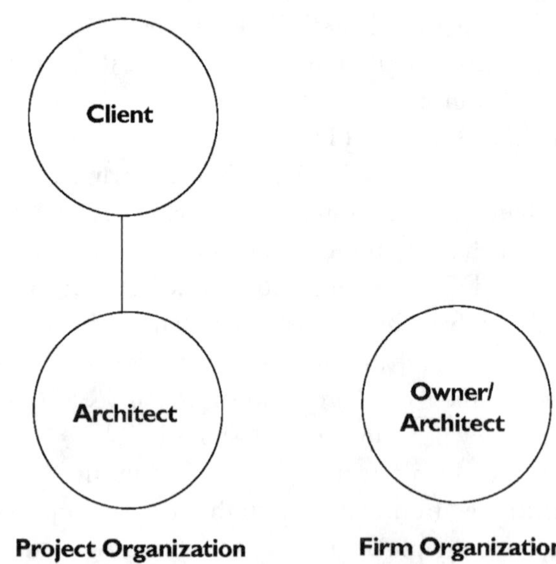

Figure 6.1 Project and Organizational Structure for Small Start-Up Firms.

plans, markets, manages, and administers, in short does everything that needs doing for the firm, as a whole.

As the demands on the owner-architect's time increase, eventually becoming greater than he or she can reasonably handle, the owner-architect will hire an assistant to help with projects, administrative matters, or both. At that point, the project and firmwide structures will change, as shown in Figure 6.2.

As client and project loads increase gradually, the owner-architect is likely to replicate the project structure, maintaining his or her direct relationship to the client, initiating the project and assigning to

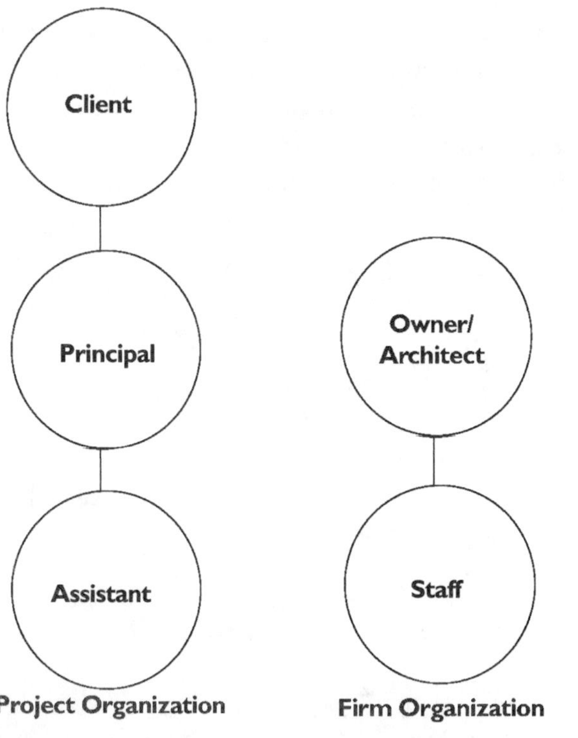

Figure 6.2 Project and Firmwide Structure after Modest Growth.

his or her professional/technical assistant the tasks that he or she chooses to delegate because he or she has less interest or insufficient time to accomplish them.

If, however, the client/project load increases dramatically, that solution may become impractical. Clients require the attention of the firm's principal; but if the client's need for attention exceeds that which the principal can provide, something has to give. Either the principal must delegate more responsibility for client contact to his or her professional assistant, or the principal must add another staff member capable of doing what he or she does; that is, the owner-architect must take on a partner.

If the principal opts to delegate some of his or her responsibility to an assistant, the project structure will again change, to resemble the one shown in Figure 6.3. This diagram displays a structure in which the usual role of the principal is to get the job,

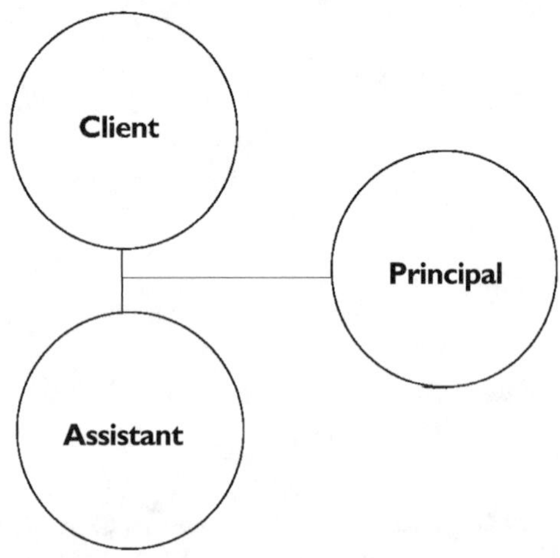

Figure 6.3 Project Structure after the Addition of an Assistant.

negotiate the contract, assemble the internal and external project team (i.e., staff and consultants), and initiate the project. Thereafter, the principal assumes as much responsibility and control as he or she can, given his or her other tasks, and delegates the rest to the staff. The assistant (who may fill the role of architect, staff architect, or project architect, and on larger projects with larger project teams, project manager) meets those responsibilities delegated to him or her, normally in design and documentation, though sometimes in project management and construction administration, as well.

In addition, since the organization is now composed of two professionals, but no administrative/clerical support, either the principal, the professional assistant, or both must also take on the administrative/clerical tasks necessary to keep the firm functioning. These include a wide range of activities, including receiving visitors, answering the telephone, preparing correspondence and invoices, keeping personnel and financial records, paying bills, remitting taxes, maintaining the physical plant and equipment, providing marketing assistance, and many others.

TIP

The farther down the line of command that a task can be delegated and performed effectively, the better managed the firm will be.

However, the architect may choose to resolve the workload problem by adding a partner, in which case it is likely that each principal will become the principal-in-charge for his or her own projects. The project and firmwide structures change (see Figure 6.4) to reflect the addition of a second owner with responsibilities as described, in which case, the partners run the firm together, either dividing firmwide responsibilities between them or conferring on all matters, probably making decisions by consensus.

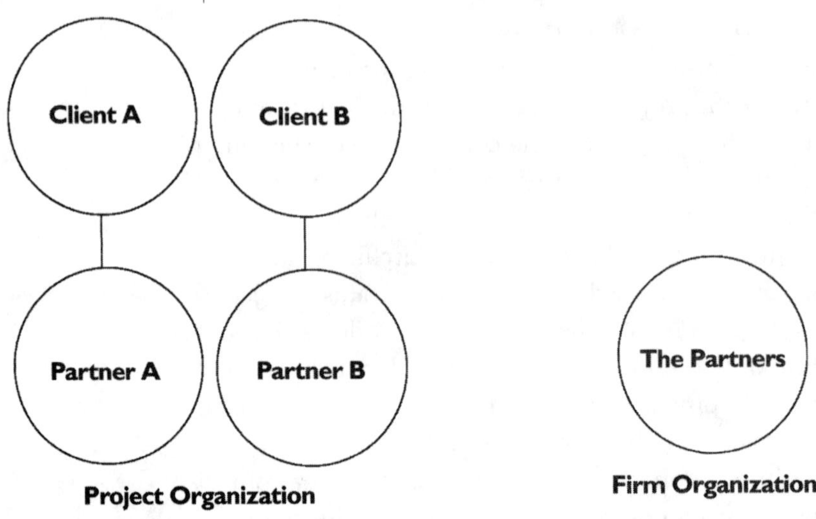

Figure 6.4 Structure Showing Addition of a Partner.

As the firm continues to grow, the same issues arise, albeit on a larger scale. The likely result will be that the partners will add staff to assist them in meeting both project and firm needs. But until the firm becomes substantially larger, the project staff will probably be organized as a series of ad hoc teams that form and re-form as necessary to meet changing client/project needs. The structure of those teams will likely resemble those shown in Figure 6.3 or Figure 6.4, depending on whether or not the principals have added staff to assist them to execute projects. In contrast, the firmwide organization may become more specific to meet certain functional needs, particularly those related to marketing, finance, and administration, specifically, bookkeeping, invoicing, and control of accounts receivable, accounts payable, and cash flow. The firmwide organization will then look like that shown in Figure 6.5.

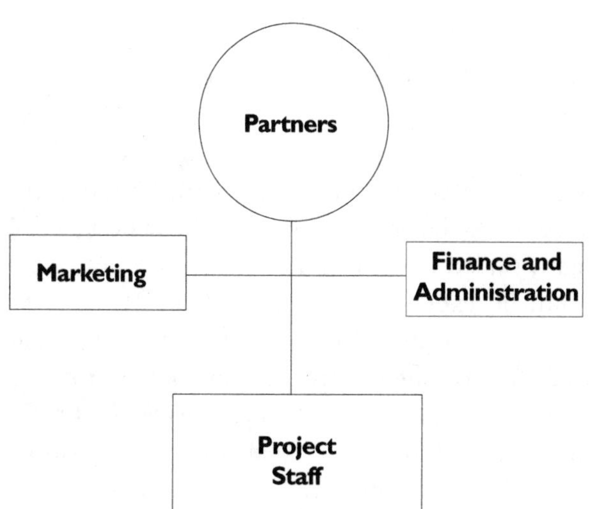

Figure 6.5 More Specific Firm Organization.

Growth Plateaus

When the firm's project workload and revenues first begin to grow sufficiently to require assistance, but not enough to add more than one person, the principal must make a choice between adding a professional/technical or clerical/administrative person as the firm's first employee. Hiring the first employee marks a plateau reached by the firm. Previously, the owner was likely functioning as a proprietor, responsible only to and for him- or herself, and accustomed to paying for the firm's operating expenses and keeping and paying personal income taxes on the monies remaining as the difference between project revenues and direct and indirect expenses. The addition of the first employee changes all that.

First Hires

As explained earlier, the first growth plateau for a new firm occurs when the founder hires his or her first employee, the need for which arises when the project load becomes too great for the founder to execute without assistance. Hence, the founder begins to seek a person whose primary role will be to assist in executing projects. But what level of assistance? Does the principal need a brilliant designer? A highly skilled CAD technician? A well-educated but minimally experienced recent graduate? The answer must be made after considering both the immediate need and the longer-term direction of the firm.

If the founder is developing a *strong idea* firm—one organized to deliver singular expertise or innovation on unique projects, or to solve one-of-a kind problems for "patrons"—then the founder's first hire will have to come from among "the best and the brightest," a talented, young professional who will join the firm to work with the "guru" who is creating those innovative solutions on which the firm is building its reputation.

If, instead, the firm is being developed as a *strong service* firm—one that delivers experience and reliability, especially on complex assignments with high management components and difficult approval procedures—then the founder will want a well-balanced, career-oriented professional with a strong commitment to client satisfaction.

Or, if the founder's objective for the firm is to provide highly efficient service on routine or even repetitive assignments for clients who seek more of a standard product than a service, then the best first hire will be someone who is committed to getting the job done efficiently and who is comfortable using standardized procedures to do so.

All that said, the best first employee may not be a project assistant at all. The best choice might be a clerical/administrative assistant who can free the founder from administrative duties that take him or her away from his or her primary responsibility: obtaining and satisfying clients.

An important management principle, well proven in practice, is that the best way to manage a firm is to delegate every task to the lowest member of the hierarchy who can execute it effectively. Thus, if the founder can delegate bookkeeping, record-keeping, invoicing, or even routine marketing and collections tasks to a competent clerical/administrative assistant, then he or she will have more time to seek new clients and satisfy current ones. Such an assistant could come from the clerical ranks, a secretary or bookkeeper, for example, with experience in the profession and the necessary interest and ability to take on more responsibility. Or that person could be a recent graduate, perhaps with a degree in marketing or business administration, with little experience but with enough intelligence and drive to learn quickly. Either way, the founder will free up time to devote to clients and projects.

If a firm's workload is growing fast enough to require assistance, but not fast enough to afford someone full-time, the founder can often hire, on a temporary basis, quality personnel that would otherwise be unaffordable to them on a full-time basis. Many cities have agencies that provide such temporary professional staff. Their ranks are composed variously of highly qualified professionals or technicians between permanent jobs, those who prefer the flexibility afforded by semipermanent jobs, or those who prefer the challenge and novelty of a changing work environment.

Another option is to establish a *cooperative venture*. In this arrangement, professionals without immediate interest in, or prospects for, growth in the near term, pool their talents, energies, financial resources, and office space to provide project assistance to each other on an as-needed basis.

The addition of the first employee, whether professional/technical or clerical/administrative, automatically gives the owner-proprietor a new role, that of employer, with responsibility for meeting a limited but important list of requirements: income tax withholdings and remittances on the employee's compensation, FICA (Social Security) tax payments, worker compensation taxes or insurance (depending on the state in which the firm practices), and OSHA-monitored health and safety conditions.

If the principal has carefully considered the workload and financial conditions (both profitability and cash flow) leading to the decision to add an employee, and if the principal keeps a finger on those pulses, formally or informally, then the added responsibilities attendant to becoming an employer will not be overwhelming and the rewards will mount.

As stated previously, an important management theory, one proven in practice, is that the farther down the line of command a task can be delegated, and performed effectively, the better managed the firm will be. By adding an assistant, the principal can now delegate tasks, freeing him- or herself to use those skills that he or she uniquely provides. In effect, a structure has been created that enables the principal to function at his or her highest level, hence be most effective for the firm.

The growth of a firm can be seen as a series of numerical plateaus, as delineated here:

1 + 1
1 + 1 partner
10 people
25–35
50–60
100

The first plateau, 1 + 1, refers to the founder plus the first employee.

The second plateau, 1 + 1 partner, means the firm was not founded by two partners (two relatively equal owners regardless of the legal entity in which they choose to operate). This plateau occurs when the firm's work has grown to the point which the single founder cannot comfortably, or chooses not to, handle alone. At that point the founder brings in a partner or elevates an employee to partner.

The third plateau occurs if the founder has not already brought in a partner and the firm grows to about 10 or 11 staff members. This is also the point at which a new office will start to have the appearance of an established firm, with regular hours, multi-person teams, marketing materials, and professional accounting support. The economics of the field of architecture and similar professional design firms generally preclude the addition of staff without projects for them to work on, so firms add staff in response to project requirements, usually when the firm wins more projects, or larger projects, and/or more complex projects. When this occurs, the sole principal usually finds him- or herself with more than he or she can conscientiously address—more clients and more team members requiring his or her attention on projects, and more firm management issues to resolve, particularly those resulting from increases in clients, projects, and staff.

That size is reached when the number of staff the principal must manage exceeds his or her reasonable realm of control. In architecture and similar professional service firms, the normal control ratio—of principals to staff—runs from 1:7 at the low end to 1:11 at the high end. In most circumstances, when the ratio of staff to principals (defined here as those in the firm who do what principals normally do to ensure the success of the firm, including capitalizing the firm, securing new work, managing at the top, establishing acceptable quality levels, and providing necessary leadership) exceeds 11:1, the lone principal will likely feel the attendant stress from having too much to do, and will begin thinking about adding a partner.

The fourth plateau is typically reached when the firm grows to 25 to 35 people. At that size, the staff will likely have become more diverse, and a layer of intermediate staff will have been identified. Initially recruited or elevated to assume higher-level project responsibilities, such as project manager, these people are also the most likely to have their elevated status recognized in a title such as "associate." Although they may not be designated as managers per se or have substantial management responsibility, they constitute a "middle management" level that the firm must have to operate successfully. They fill the gap in experience and capability between the principals at the top and the junior staff below. Thus, the senior staff develops and manages projects, thereby freeing the principals to perform where they're most effective, at leading, directing, and mentoring.

In addition, senior staff may seek and/or be given other firmwide responsibilities, because the firm will have grown to the point at which certain centralized functions are necessary to improve its effectiveness. For example, the principals may need assistance in marketing, creation of administrative policies, development of firmwide project standards, and the like. Who better to call on and involve than the most experienced people?

The fifth plateau is reached when the firm grows to about 50 or 60 people and requires full-time management, again largely as a direct result of its project load. Until that point, the firm will likely have been managed by the principals, who assume collective responsibility for the firm and individual responsibility for various firmwide functions, such as marketing, finance, recruiting, professional development, physical plant, administrative staff, and so on, with each principal spending a small portion of his or her time "running" the area assigned. When the firm reaches the fifth plateau, it will likely require full-time management, generally in the form of a single person who may be called managing partner, president, CEO, general manager, director of operations/operations manager, COO, or the like. Depending on the values of the principals and their need for, and comfort level with, focused responsibility, the singular manager may be directive or facilitative in nature, but will be likely to spend the great majority of his or her time running the firm, as opposed to running projects.

The sixth plateau is reached when the firm grows to approximately 100. Up to that point, the firm's project operational structure may have been composed of a series of project teams that come together to execute a project, then disband and reform in other project teams to execute other projects. By the time the firm has reached 100, if it has not already done so for market or project delivery reasons, it will probably implement a substructure of some kind between the entity of the firm and the project team so that the staff have a "home" in the firm; that is, they know where they belong. Based on the values of the owners, the leaders will decide on the substructure that will best address the issues at hand: studios, departments, studio-department combinations, or matrix organizations.

Care and Feeding of Partners

Unless the firm stays very small, either by choice or circumstance, the founder will typically choose to have one or more partners, and one of the most complex aspects of running a practice is the care and feeding of partners. Regardless of the organizational form of the firm, the interrelationships among principals can be either a foundational strength or a fatal weakness.

Both of us have had many partners and have helped mediate partner relations in many other firms and have come to the conclusion that mutually supportive teams of principals create far more successful firms than any one of the principals could have achieved alone. Conversely, problems between principals have caused significant damage to a firm's future.

Partnerships between unrelated individuals have been compared to marriages without the "glue" of children or sex. As with marriages, it is hard to specify the secrets to successful partnerships, but some general guidelines can be established:

- You do not have to be close friends (although it helps), but you should like and respect each other. It usually takes more than a partnership or shareholders' agreement to hold a group together.
- Do not expect every principal to put in equal effort or achieve equal results. That is the ideal, but it is unrealistic. Instead, ascertain whether each individual is filling a principal's role and making a principal-level contribution to the firm's success.
- Be wary of inherently unstable situations. Among the most common is a husband and wife with a third partner. Several third partners in famous firms have not survived the dynamics of this combination.
- Respect diversity. Most really successful partnerships have principals with complementary personalities and skills who respect the different capabilities of their partners.
- Even weak partnerships can appear successful in good times. The real test of a partnership is how it holds up under adversity.
- Strive for fairness in the allocation of financial distribution, professional credit, and the other rewards of ownership. Seemingly minor differences or omissions of credit can be very disruptive.
- Put in writing the basic understandings of the shareholders' or partnership agreement.
- If it is not working, end it. If a partnership dissolves, make every effort to avoid litigation or the other typical nastiness of a divorce. In the long run, it is far better to get it over with, as quickly and cheaply as possible.

Project Delivery Process

The project delivery process is an important aspect of a firm's design operations. The process the firm puts in place to execute projects and how it delivers projects to its clients affect every area of its practice.

The project process includes these aspects:

- Team organization
- Project schedule and deliverables
- Roles and responsibilities
- Accountability for decisions

There is no one right way to organize and schedule projects, nor is there one right way to assign responsibility or accountability. Rather, there are many variables to consider, including project location and scope, project schedule and compensation, and staff ability and availability. The best advice is to consider each project situation as unique within the context of a process that is flexible enough to be applied differently for each unique situation. The objective is to determine individual solutions for each specific situation, within a project process that is consistent for the firm as a whole, and consistent with its goals.

The prototypical process has four steps:

1. Identify the project delivery unit.
2. Prepare a project process chart.
3. Define each person's functions and duties.
4. Assign ultimate decision-making responsibility.

We'll go through each of these steps in detail.

Step 1: Identify Project Delivery Unit

The project delivery unit refers to the individual, project team, department, studio, or some combination of those used to execute projects. Each firm will establish its preferred method of organizing personnel to deliver projects to clients. If, for example, the firm starts as a single proprietor with no staff, the project delivery unit will be the proprietor, who will perform all project tasks. If the proprietor adds staff to assist, then certain responsibilities will be delegated.

Regardless of the delivery unit, each must accomplish the design, technical, and managerial aspects of completing projects in accord with the owner's (or owners') preferences. The involvement of the owner(s) can vary within a unit type, depending on the client, the project, and the size and capability of the firm at that point in time.

It is important to think about your delivery unit choice early because it will influence many important aspects of your practice, including, at the very least, the way the principal will spend his or her time, the choice of staff, and the economics of the practice. Also, as a firm moves through the growth plateaus, and evolves, the organization and processes will likely change and require new thinking.

In a principal-led team, the principal typically maintains overall authority for project implementation. Little essential responsibility or authority is delegated to key staff members below the principal level. Rather, the principal retains responsibility for actively running the project on a day-to-day basis. That said, to increase his or her span of control, the principal may delegate significant project responsibility to key people below the principal level, while retaining overall project supervisory responsibility. This, of course, is the typical structure of a new firm, but the principal of a firm of any size that is planning to grow or to take on larger, more complex projects should understand that this project leadership structure will likely change over time.

The options of principal-led teams include:

- A *project architect–led team* structure places prime responsibility and authority in the hands of one person who has overall project responsibility and is expected to make both design and management decisions on a day-to-day basis, communicating with the principal in accordance with a protocol he or she has established.
- A *designer-led team* structure places prime responsibility in the hands of a designer, who may have a subordinate manager, or subsumes those management functions.
- In a *project manager–led team*, prime project responsibility and authority are placed in the hands of a manager, who may have a subordinate designer as part of the project team.
- A *co-equal designer and manager team* has managerial and design responsibilities assigned to two persons (e.g., a project manager and project designer) who have equal authority but different responsibilities. In such structures, it is common, and usually required, that the two key people agree on decisions affecting both project design and management.
- *Manager-led departments* that concentrate on specific aspects of the work, such as design and production, are often established by firms seeking to maximize design and technical efficiency. In such structure, a partner-in-charge or project manager represents both the client's and the firm's overall interests and shepherds the project through the firm's departmental

system. Often responsibilities are shared, with the manager responsible for the program and schedule and department heads responsible for design and technical quality.

- *Studios* are often organized to focus on specific markets or project types (e.g., a commercial or healthcare studio), especially where the market, client, and/or projects require specialized knowledge and technical skills. The studio staff may have developed special interest and knowledge of the kind of work on which the studio is focusing, or may be generalists who are assigned to the studio for a specified period of time.

Combination structures (such as those structured as studios at the top and departments at the bottom) are organized to take advantage of the need for specialization and efficiency.

There are pitfalls inherent to each of the prototypical structures:

- Principals who elect to retain day-to-day responsibility automatically limit their availability to assume other important responsibilities in the firm. They also limit the number, and perhaps size and complexity, of projects that the firm is capable of executing. And, finally, the potential growth of junior professionals of the firm is limited because there are no supervisory project positions into which they can grow.
- Firms that choose to organize projects in architect-led teams often do so to increase the principal's span of control, while keeping a generalist at the project helm. However, as workload increases, these architects (sometimes called project directors or architects-in-charge) may

find themselves deluged with managerial and administrative tasks, thus less and less involved in the actual design and technical development of projects, which may have been the reason they and the firm elected such a structure in the first place.

- Firms interested in the primacy of design often will want a designer to lead the team, but a dilemma arises if the designer finds him- or herself unwilling, and sometimes unable, to deal with expanding managerial and technical project needs. Or, if the designer is able to undertake those responsibilities, he or she may become less available to address the design issues that are important to both the designer and the firm.
- Manager-led teams are usually formed because there is an emphasis on both the client's and the firm's management needs (such as budgets and schedules). The danger with this structure is that managers may fail to realize the level of design achievement desired by the firm. In this situation, it helps if the manager has not only basic architectural experience and basic managerial skills—planning, scheduling, budgeting—but also the interpersonal skills important to effective management—communication, negotiation, delegation, and team-building.
- The co-equal designer and manager team would appear to solve the problem of the manager-led team, but this organizational structure requires not only firms that are large enough, and with enough projects, to necessitate and support double leadership, but also clearly defined limits of responsibility and solid working relationships.

- A departmental structure achieves efficiency by focusing knowledge, effort, and energy on narrower tasks, but often at the expense of broader project understanding and continuity of decision making. And for this structure to work, the apparent conflict between the project manager's responsibility for the "what" (program) and the "when" (schedule), and the department head's "who" (staff) and "how" (design and technical procedures and quality), must be resolved, which requires a clear delineation of responsibilities at all levels.

Each firm must choose an organizational structure that meets its needs. Start-up *strong idea* firms will be most effective beginning with single-point leadership—an architect or designer with responsibility for all aspects of the project. Start-up *strong service* firms will be most effective beginning with project teams led by capable management—a principal, project manager, or architect who is clearly focused on the management needs of the client and project.

Step 2: Prepare a Project Process Chart

A project process chart shows the percentage of time expended by role and phase. It identifies the deliverables to be provided and indicates the level of project profitability (see Figure 6.6).

When the firm starts in practice, the projects are likely to be small in size, simple in scope, and executed by the principal. When only one person's time is involved, it should be relatively easy to plan a new project by identifying the tasks to be performed in each phase. Even if the project is of a type unfamiliar to the architect, making it difficult to estimate the

Phases						
	Predesign	*Schematic Design*	*Design Development*	*Construction Documents*	*Bidding/ Negotiation*	*Construction Administration*
Percent of Total	%	%	%	%	%	%
Deliverables						
Roles						
Principal-in-Charge	%	%	%	%	%	%
Project Manager	%	%	%	%	%	%
Project Designer	%	%	%	%	%	%
Project Architect	%	%	%	%	%	%
Drafter/ Technician	%	%	%	%	%	%
Other	%	%	%	%	%	%
	100%	100%	100%	100%	100%	100%

Figure 6.6 Project Process Chart.

time per task, he or she can estimate the overall time in each phase of the work, understanding that all necessary tasks must be accomplished within that time frame.

As the firm develops experience over time, the principal will be better able to identify the amount and percentage of time necessary to accomplish particular tasks, on "typical" projects and on all projects. Going further, the firm will be able to identify how that time was expended on a task-by-task basis in each phase. From this information, it will be possible to prepare a pro forma project process diagram that can then be adjusted on a project-by-project basis to reflect the conditions of a particular project.

For example, experience might show that the firm typically expends 10 to 12 percent of total project time in schematic design, of which 40 percent is allocated to a project manager, or project management activities; 40 percent to a project designer, or project design activities; and 20 percent to an assistant designer, drafter, or CAD technician (for documentation activities in that phase). The result is usually a schematic design package of a site plan, ground floor plan, floor plan for each level, sketch elevations, and a three-dimensional representation of some kind.

Based on its experience, it might become clear to the firm that the review and approval requirements of the new project will require an unusually high level of management effort to successfully shepherd the project through to completion and acceptance by the owner, the local planning board, and other review groups. At the same time, the project might be deemed to require at least twice as much design effort as the firm's norm. In this case, early identification of these issues would enable the firm to schedule and prepare interim presentations to serve multiple purposes and to isolate certain aspects of the agency review process as additional services.

Step 3: Define Individual Functions and Duties

In this step, you clearly delineate the functions and duties of each person involved with the project, and estimate the percentage of time it will take each person to fulfill his or her role.

Again, in a start-up firm, all the functions and duties probably will be performed by a single person, the principal. This will change as the firm grows. People, especially those at higher levels, will do more than one kind of task. A principal might have responsibilities in management and administration, project management or design, marketing or public relations, personnel management, and a host of other areas. A project manager might be responsible for particular projects, monitor project quality assurance/quality control, and coordinate certain staff assignments.

Using the project roles and duties form, shown in Figure 6.7, the principal can list the various responsibilities of each person and the percentage of time needed to complete each task. This will result in an array of each person's productive time, leading to identification of total staffing availability and utilization.

For example, a partner in the firm might spend 30 percent of his or her time marketing, 50 percent with clients and leading the project team as principal-in-charge, 10 percent in firmwide management, and 10 percent in paid time off (holidays, vacations, personal time, etc.). A staff-level project manager might spend 75 percent of his or her time on active project management tasks, 5 percent on marketing assistance, 7 percent on firmwide quality assurance, 3 percent on professional activities, and 10 percent on paid time off (vacation, holiday, sick, and personal time). Then if, for example, it was determined that a new project would require all of the project manager's time, and that project manager already had other projects to monitor, the firm would have to consider alternative solutions, perhaps extending the project schedule, requiring overtime effort, or temporarily extending the principal's responsibilities.

	Time Allocation
Title:	
Function:	%
Duties:	%
	%
	%
	%
	100%

	Time Allocation
Title:	
Function:	%
Duties:	%
	%
	%
	%
	100%

	Time Allocation
Title:	
Function:	%
Duties:	%
	%
	%
	%
	%
	100%

Figure 6.7 Project Roles and Duties.

Step 4: Assign Decision-Making Responsibility

In start-up firms with no employees, it is clear who will make all decisions: the principal. But as soon as more than one person is involved on a project, unless it is absolutely clear who will make the decisions, and how, chances are they will be made ad hoc, or according to status rather than responsibility, or by default, or perhaps not at all. Also, depending on who is assigned to the project, the system and structure established by the firm will necessarily be tested, because no two people will act precisely the same way in the same situation; each will perform pursuant to particular individual experiences and personalities. Therefore, a rigid, unalterable system that is uniformly applied is doomed to failure, as no two people will meet the requirements of the system in the same way. It is far better to be flexible and allow for modification and manipulation of the system, to reflect the individual capabilities of the people responsible for implementing it.

One way to achieve this flexibility is to allow key project people to negotiate essential responsibilities among themselves. The benefits of doing so are twofold: all responsibilities will be accounted for, and individual responsibilities will be more clearly defined, more readily accepted, and more likely to be performed well. For example, assume the project manager is unusually adept at keeping on top of collections, even though it is the firm's usual policy to assign that responsibility to the principal-in-charge. If the project manager and principal-in-charge can negotiate the responsibility for collections on the project at hand, the firm may benefit by more timely collections and by having the task performed at a lower level, thereby freeing the principal-in-charge for more level-appropriate work.

A relatively simple way to negotiate responsibilities in this way is to use a responsibility form like the one shown in Figure 6.8. You can use this form to identify, for example:

- Primary responsibility
- Secondary responsibility
- Contribution or participation

A more sophisticated and precise way would be to identify four different levels of responsibility:

Level 1: Deciding or acting ("primary responsibility")

Level 2: Consulting (before the decision is made)

Level 3: Approving (after the decision is made, but before it is implemented)

Level 4: Being informed

The effective result is a project-specific decision-making process based on the firm's own goals, history, procedures, and personnel; project delivery unit organization and structure; project schedule and deliverables; personnel roles, responsibilities, and time allocations; and individual and collective accountability for decisions.

The process (and its forms) described here encourages individual project planning based on individual project needs. There is no need to replicate specifics from project to project. Rather, once the firm has established its overall goals and project objectives, and has selected a project structure based on these goals, projects can be planned and then monitored according to their unique characteristics and those of the firm.

1. Decide/act *2. Consult* *3. Approve* *4. Inform*	**Responsibility**				
	PIC	**PM**	**PD**	**PA**	**Other**
Determine fee					
Negotiate contract					
Select consultants					
Identify project staff					
Determine client needs					
Prepare program					
Conceptual design					
Schematic design					
Design documentation					
Make technical decisions					
Document format					
Complete specifications					
Track construction changes					
Monitor team progress					
Prepare invoices					
Collect receivables					
Other					

Figure 6.8 Project Responsibility Chart.

Legal and Ethical Issues

7

An architect must be legally qualified to practice. All states and the District of Columbia require individuals to be licensed (registered) before they may call themselves architects or contract to perform architectural services. In short, you are not legally considered an architect unless and until you have been licensed by the state(s) in which you seek to practice. And in some states, architects are required to apply for licenses (but not necessarily to have been licensed) even before they attempt to solicit work.

The purpose of this chapter is to introduce you to the legal and ethical issues involved with becoming a practicing architect.

Registration and Certification

Licensure requirements in all states include the following:

- A professional degree in architecture
- A period of practical training or internship
- Passage of all sections of the Architectural Registration Examination (ARE)

And as to the first requirement, note that in many states, the professional degree in architecture must be from a school of architecture whose program is accredited by the National Architectural Accrediting Board (NAAB). That said, be aware that state architectural registration boards set their own standards, so graduation from a non-NAAB-accredited program may meet the education requirement for licensure in some states.

Each state and each U.S. territory has a governmental authority that registers and regulates architects. Typically, the authority is vested in a State Board of Architecture composed of architects and laypersons appointed to the board by the governor of the state. Without registration issued by the state, no one may engage in the practice of architecture nor use the title "architect" within that state. In addition to issuing registrations, the state boards watch over the practice of architecture within their state boundaries and discipline architects whose practice does not meet minimum standards of professional conduct established by the board.

In 1920, the state boards created a national system for identifying qualified architects, called the National Council of Architectural Registration Boards (NCARB). NCARB is not a governmental agency; it is a federation of all the state boards that register and govern the practice of architecture. Its only members are those state registration boards.

The state boards formulate the rules and policies of NCARB and elect NCARB's officers and directors. Working with the state boards, NCARB establishes national standards for certifying qualified architects. Those standards have been recognized by every state board as adequately rigorous to allow the state board to register the NCARB certificate holder, generally without further examination or other demonstration of qualifications. Once identified and certified as qualified by NCARB, architects are readily granted registration in almost all United States jurisdictions.

Every state board uses the NCARB ARE as its written examination to test the skills, knowledge, and abilities of applicants for registration, and all state boards require a training (internship) period before candidates may sit for the ARE and become licensed. A few states, such as California, have additional requirements. Many states have adopted the training standards from the Intern Development Program (IDP), which is administered by NCARB. NCARB, of course, similarly requires its candidates for certification to have passed the ARE after completion of an internship program. Like most state boards, NCARB requires a degree accredited by the National Architectural Accrediting Board in the study of architecture.

In addition to setting standards for national certification, NCARB recommends to the state boards rules of conduct, which a majority of state boards have adopted as their own and which serve as a basis for disciplining architects. In addition, several state boards have made continuing professional development a requirement for registration renewal, and it is likely that most other states will follow suit in the future.

Therefore, because you must be licensed (registered) by the state board to practice in any one state, the easiest way to obtain licensure in more than one state is to become certified by NCARB. Furthermore, before starting in practice, it's a good idea to heed the advice given in the "Guiding Principles" box on the next page.

Guiding Principles

- Seek professional advice. Then take it seriously. Your advisers should include: accountants, attorneys, business advisers, public relations advisers, bankers, insurance providers, and other experienced individuals.
- Put everything in writing: contracts, meeting records, confirming notes.
- Keep complete records and set up a good filing system.
- Make use of the published standard forms and contracts, then adapt them to fit the specific scope of the work, business arrangement, and other key parameters. No two projects are identical.
- Protect your image as an ethical professional. Remember you will meet, and need help from, many people during the course of your career.

Starting Up

The legal requirements of starting up depend on the organizational structure you choose:

- *Proprietorship:* Typically, there is no specific legal obligation for starting in a practice as a proprietorship; you just start.
- *Partnership, corporation, or limited liability company or partnership*: You must file the appropriate organizational documents with the state (and sometimes local) authorities. For a partnership, you typically file a partnership agreement; for a corporation, a certificate of incorporation and/or articles of incorporation and bylaws; for a limited liability company, a certificate of formation.

Going forward, owners are responsible for filing their own personal tax returns and paying the appropriate personal income taxes, FICA tax, and workers' compensation tax or insurance. If the company has employees, the employer is required to withhold employees' income and FICA taxes and file quarterly tax returns with payment of the employer's portion and amounts withheld from employees.

Owners are also legally obligated to notify the appropriate authorities of any change in the ownership or location of the business.

Professional Liability

Because of the special education and knowledge deemed essential for the proper practice of the profession, the laws that established registration for architecture (and other "learned professions," including engineering, landscape architecture, medicine, dentistry, law, and accounting) effectively gave duly licensed practitioners of these professions a monopoly to practice, denying that right to all those who are not similarly qualified and licensed.

It is understood that, in the practice of their profession, architects do not offer standardized solutions or products; rather, they are expected to exercise discretion and judgment as to their clients' interests, based on their education and experience, in a wide variety of nonstandard situations and conditions for which there is never a single "correct" solution. And because under such circumstances, perfection is impossible to achieve, design professionals are not required to be perfect. They are, however, required to perform in a manner consistent with that of other competent professionals practicing in the same jurisdiction under similar circumstances. Anything less may constitute *negligence,* for which the professional can be held personally liable and be penalized.

The test by which design professionals are judged in the event of an error or omission is a comparison against the standard of care that would have been provided by other competent professionals practicing in the same jurisdiction. Negligence is a legal determination that, unless the professional agrees that he or she has been negligent, must be determined in a legal process—a court of competent jurisdiction or previously agreed arbitration. In most cases, the determination of negligence is addressed as a civil matter; penalties, if any, are financial. In a few rare but significant cases, however, malpractice was found to have been so severe as to call into question the professional's ability to continue to practice. In one such case, involving the collapse of suspended walkways in the lobby of the Hyatt Hotel in Kansas City, which resulted in property damage, injury, and loss of life, the structural engineer was found to be negligent and lost his license to practice, first in the state where the incident occurred and then, by extension, in other states in which he had been licensed.

Liability Insurance

Because design professionals can be held personally liable for their own negligence (errors and omissions), they should purchase liability insurance. Several major insurance carriers offer professional liability insurance to design professionals. Such policies include exclusions for certain conditions, deductibles, and per-claim and aggregate limits.

These policies are almost always written on a "claims made" basis, requiring that the insurance be kept "in force," that is, the premiums must continue to be paid to be applicable in the future.

The face value of the policy (e.g., $500,000) is applied as claims are made against the insured in any given year (as long as the policy is maintained in force), until the full amount has been exposed. For example, if three successive claims for damages of $300,000, $200,000, and $100,000 were tendered in a given year against a firm with $500,000 coverage limit, there would be no coverage for the third claim (if damages were awarded in those amounts).

Premiums for such policies are generally written on the basis of annual billings, and depend upon several variables, including the discipline(s) being insured; the types of clients, projects, and services being offered; and the amount of the deductible. Services that historically have not resulted in liability problems, such as planning, are insurable at relatively low rates. Professional liability insurance for professional services on building types that have poor liability histories are generally subject to higher premiums. In recent years, professional liability insurance premiums for architects have ranged from 2 to 3 percent of gross revenues.

In some cases, clients or the design team will buy insurance for a single project. Such "project insurance" is the exception, but can be appropriate for unusual projects or projects needing higher-than-normal coverage.

Certain activities and relationships can substantially reduce the potential for liability claims and/or the likelihood that such claims will result in the award of damages. These include:

- Preparing sound written agreements
- Developing good personal relationships with clients and contractors (people are far less likely to sue people they like and respect)

- Maintaining clear and regular written communication with clients, consultants, and contractors
- Addressing problems proactively when they arise
- Managing risk in client selection, fee negotiation, and project design and execution

The last, risk management, comprises five steps:

1. Identify the potential risks.
2. Weigh the possible value of these risks.
3. Avoid the risks that are not worth taking.
4. Reduce the impact of risks that are.
5. Transfer risk to others, when possible, such as your insurance provider.

Legal and Ethical Obligations

As stated throughout this book, most design professionals start their own firms only after they have worked for others. In fact, there is no other way to gain the appropriate experience or meet the normal prerequisites to sit for the Architectural Registration Examination unless one has worked for others. Therefore, design professionals starting a new firm begin with preestablished relationships with their former employers and with the clients for whom they provided services when employed by another firm.

There are at least two kinds of obligations to the firm: legal and ethical. Legal obligations include prohibitions against tortuous interference, against abrogating the general fiduciary responsibilities that owners and certain other high-level employees have to the firm, and contractual responsibilities such as those embedded in partnership or shareholder agreements or in separate confidentiality and/or noncompete agreements.

No one has a right to interfere with another's contractual relationships, including a firm's contract to perform and be paid for client services; anyone interfering with such a contractual relationship, such as by encouraging the client to break a contract, is exposing him- or herself to a potential claim for tortuous interference. If a professional shares ownership with others, then he or she has a fiduciary responsibility to his or her co-owners and the firm not to take any action that would harm the firm in any material sense. Also, if in becoming an owner, or being elevated to a higher status level in the firm, a professional signs an agreement restricting his or her future acts in any legally binding way, then that professional is constrained from doing what he or she had promised not to do. For example, if on becoming an associate in the firm (a title generally signifying increased status, and sometimes signifying additional privileges and responsibilities, as well), a professional signs a noncompete or confidentiality letter, then any act that abrogates the terms and conditions of that agreement exposes him or her to the possibility of legal action. The courts will generally support confidentiality and noncompete agreements that are not unduly restrictive, that is, do not totally restrict the professional from being able to practice his or her profession in the locale where he or she lives and works.

Ethical Responsibilities

The American Institute of Architects (AIA), the oldest and largest professional organization for architects in the United States, with a current membership exceeding 80,000, offers many programs, services, and benefits. AIA has developed and promulgated a

Code of Ethics & Professional Conduct. The code is arranged in three tiers: Canons, Ethical Standards, and Rules of Conduct. *Canons* are broad principles of conduct that cover general obligations, and obligations to the public, the client, the profession, and to colleagues. *Ethical standards* set more specific goals, to which (AIA) members should aspire in professional performance and behavior. *Rules of professional conduct* are mandatory, meaning that violation of a rule is grounds for disciplinary action by the Institute.

The Code of Ethics includes 24 rules, some of which incorporate language that generally reflects legal obligations. For example, Rule 1.101 under General Obligations states: "In practicing architecture, Members [of AIA] shall demonstrate a consistent pattern of reasonable care and competence, and shall apply the technical knowledge and skill which is ordinarily applied by architects of good standing practicing in the same locality." Similarly, Rule 2.102, under Obligations to the Public, states, "Members shall neither offer nor make any payment or gift to a public official with the intent of influencing the official's judgment in connection with an existing or prospective project in which the Members are interested." Rule 3.103, under Obligations to the Client, states, "Members shall not materially alter the scope or objectives of a project without the client's consent."

The ethical rules that may affect professionals starting in practice are those that address obligations to colleagues. There are three such rules, and they describe situations that frequently occur, usually without incident or contention.

- Rule 5.201 states, "Members shall recognize and respect the professional contributions of their employees, employers, professional colleagues, and business associates."

- Rule 5.202 states, "Members leaving a firm shall not, without the permission of their employer or partner, take designs, drawings, data, reports, notes, or other materials relating to the firm's work, whether or not performed by the Member."
- And, correspondingly, Rule 5.203, states, "A Member shall not unreasonably withhold permission from a departing employee or partner to take copies of designs, drawings, data, reports, notes, or other materials relating to work performed by the employee or partner that are not confidential."

It is reasonable and understandable that professionals starting new firms will want to use examples of work they performed while employees of others, to demonstrate their capabilities as professionals. To that end, Rule 5.203 informs employers of their obligation to permit this. Rule 5.202 informs former employees of their obligation to seek their employers' permission; and Rule 5.201 informs them of their obligation to take and give appropriate credit.

In sum, a professional is obliged to act ethically. For most professionals, this behavior will be easy and natural. For those who need guidance, the AIA's Code of Ethics & Professional Conduct describes what such ethical behavior "looks like."

As already explained, a professional's ethical responsibility may go beyond the legal. If, for example, the owner of a start-up firm acts legally, scrupulously respects his or her employer's relationship with the client, and does not seek to damage his or her employer's relationship with the client in any way, he or she might still discover ethical obligations he or she must meet.

NOTE

The AIA's Code of Ethics & Professional Conduct is not concerned with, and does not address, reasonable and normal business activities. In fact, the antitrust laws of the United States and most states require that architects maintain a free and competitive business environment. As a result, matters of marketing and pricing are deemed to be business, not ethical, matters, and therefore are not directly addressed in the code.

Assume, for example, that a client's project has come, or is about to come, to the end of a designated phase, and that the client learns that a key employee on the project will be leaving at that point to start a new firm. In such a circumstance, the client is typically free to sever his or her relationship with the architect who started the project and commission the new firm on mutually agreed terms, as long as the client has not been induced to do so. Regardless of who initiated the possible shift of the project, if the departing architect accepts the project, he or she would be well advised to ensure that he or she will not suffer any damaging contractual or financial consequences.

And when information is published about a project, each party is ethically obligated to give appropriate credit to others who have contributed materially to the project, and to not take inappropriate credit for any work for which he or she has not been directly responsible.

The box titled "Typical Ethical Questions" raises a number of dilemmas you should be prepared to face during your career. The box lists just some of the many situations that can arise. Where the law or the terms of a contractual relationship are clear, the right decision should be obvious; moreover, most architects have an innate sense of what is appropriate ethical behavior and what is not. Many situations, however, are not clearcut. In these situations, it is usually very important to avoid burning bridges or making enemies. Most young professionals are unaware of how often professional paths cross. Consultants, former employees, and others you deal with

Typical Ethical Questions

- One or more clients you are handling on behalf of your current employer offer to follow you with their current projects if you go on your own. Do you act on this opportunity?
- A potential project comes to you while you are working for someone else. Do you keep it to yourself and develop it or tell your employer?
- You have decided to leave your employer while in the middle of several important projects. How much notice do you give?
- You are pursuing a potential project with another firm that gave you the lead. The client tells you that you can have the project without the other firm. Do you accept?
- A client offers to pay you in cash and not report it. Do you accept? (*Hint:* Your failure to report income is tax evasion.)
- An employee asks to be paid as a consultant rather than an employee with the standard payroll deductions. Your accountant advises that the person does not qualify, but that this issue is unlikely to be caught. Do you agree to the request?
- You are preparing a proposal and you include projects that you did while employed by another firm. Do you credit your former employer in the proposal?
- Some of your projects are being included in a book or exhibit, including projects you did while employed by another firm. How do you credit that firm?
- A client asks you to take over a project currently being done by another firm. The other firm has not been told yet that they are to be replaced. What are your obligations to the other firm?
- An employee of a potential client offers to help you get a project in return for a finder's fee. Should you agree to pay it?
- Your workload drops off and you cannot afford to keep some or all of your employees. How much notice should you give them? Should you pay severance? Help them find other work?
- A client pays you only 75 percent of your fee and refuses to pay the rest, citing dissatisfaction with you and your consultants' work. What do you owe your consultants?
- To be considered for certain public projects, you are expected to contribute to the fund-raising efforts of some elected officials. Do you make these contributions? (*Hint:* Refer to Rule 2.102 of the Code of Ethics & Professional Conduct described earlier.)
- An employee brings his or her own computer loaded with unlicensed software. Do you ignore this?
- You are offered the opportunity to participate in a profitable real estate investment by one of your firm's clients. What do you owe your partners, if anything?

may be in a position later to return the favor, so it's best to treat everyone fairly and equitably.

Here are a few situations that require special attention:

- *Moonlighting.* As stated throughout this book, architects start by working for others, because the only way to become qualified to take the registration examination is to fulfill an internship requirement. Those who choose to start their own practices usually continue working full-time for someone else while building skills, forming relationships, and making contacts that will enable them to go out on their own. When opportunities to practice in their own name come along, they find a way to serve their private clients while remaining employed. In short, they moonlight. If you decide to do this, here are a few pointers: use your own identity, time, and resources, not the firm's; don't imply that you represent your employer for your own work; continue to work conscientiously for your employer, to the full extent of your capabilities.
- *Removing documents.* Always ask permission; your employer is ethically obliged to provide copies of documents on which you worked. Volunteer to pay for them; it is your obligation, though your employer may be generous.
- *Taking and giving credit.* Take credit only for what you have done. Be sure to cite your employer on every project on which you participated as an employee.
- *Taking clients.* If you signed a noncompete agreement with your employer, simply put, you probably can't take a client with you when you

leave. If you don't have such an agreement, you are still proscribed from interfering with your employer's contract, but you are free to inform clients for whom you have worked that you are beginning your own practice. The clients may give you work in the future and may even opt to engage you on the project on which you have been employed. Again, don't burn bridges, ever.

- *Soliciting employees, from your firm or another.* As with clients, only a noncompete agreement to which you are a party effectively prevents you from soliciting employees; but keep in mind, reputation is everything, so it is best to inform others of your intention regarding starting in practice. Then let them decide to join you.
- *Cutting fees.* There was a time that fee-cutting was deemed unethical, but since the mid-1970s, it has been viewed as a business matter, not an ethical one. And as a starting practitioner, you will likely have lower operating expenses than established firms and will, therefore, be able to offer lower fees and still be profitable. However, though offering lower fees is legitimate, it is a dangerous tactic because the client, and possibly others, may continue to expect you to charge low fees.
- *Stretching payables.* Stretching payables means failing to pay others, typically consultants, when you have been paid. This is a matter of business, but one that borders on the unethical. You may have a contractual obligation with either the client or the consultant to pay when you have been paid. Can you get away with not paying for short periods of time? Probably. Should you? Probably not. In addition to expecting

your consultants to be responsive to you—which failing to pay them in a timely manner will preclude—you don't want to dig a financial hole that will be difficult to get out of. Also, never, ever fail to pay the Internal Revenue Service for taxes due, not withheld employee taxes or your own.

- *Seeking free goods or services.* This is not only unethical, but is illegal in some cases. Although you are unlikely to go to jail for accepting a sample, even a large sample, from a contractor, vendor, or supplier, you do not want to feel, or be, obligated or beholden to that supplier; and by accepting a "freebie," you will be. Keep in mind how difficult it may be in others' eyes to draw the line between gift, payoff, bribe, and extortion.
- *Asking employees to work for free.* Pure and simple, this is unethical, not to mention illegal.

Contracts

The architect starting in practice will likely encounter three kinds of contracts:

- *Project-related contracts*, especially including the owner-architect agreement, the architect-consultant agreement, and the owner-contractor construction contract.
- *Internal contracts*, especially including ownership agreements for partnerships, corporations, or limited liability companies.
- *Ordinary business agreements*, especially including lease or lease/purchase agreements for facilities or equipment, and loan documents.

By law, a contract is defined as an agreement between two parties to provide goods or services for a consideration, generally money. In essence, an owner-architect agreement records that the architect will provide certain design, documentation, and construction administration services for the owner for an agreed-upon fee. A lease records a lessor's agreement to provide space or equipment to a lessee into exchange for a monthly lease payment. Although oral contracts are permissible and binding (although in a dispute, it's often difficult to prove that such a contract existed), a written contract is always recommended because you have a piece of paper to prove a contract exists, in the case of a dispute.

In general, an architect starting a firm would be well advised to consult the standard contracts and agreements published by his or her professional organization before assuming any contractual responsibilities, and in particular before accepting contracts offered by others that might include language favoring the presenter.

The American Institute of Architects, the American Consulting Engineers Council, the American Society of Landscape Architects, the American Institute of Graphic Artists, and other professional organizations have developed model agreements for virtually all project situations, which are available at modest cost. These model agreements are updated regularly and are generally considered to be fair to all parties.

As with every other aspect of practice, it is hard for any individual to deal with all the legal and ethical issues that arise without some outside advice. Some of these outside sources and resources are discussed in the next chapter.

Resources and Support

8

Though it is possible to go out on your own without any professional assistance at all—essentially, winging it—a wiser move is to launch your firm only *after* you have gathered and coordinated a core group of professional advisers and other resources—organizations and associations—on which you can rely for necessary information, advice, and support. Winging it certainly may seem more gratifying—but only if you're successful—and in the long run, it is far better to have backup support in the wings, to answer a question, suggest a direction, or offer advice that will help you avoid potentially dangerous mistakes and move forward in the best way.

Legal Advice

If you decide to organize your firm as a proprietorship or partnership, it may be possible, as explained in Chapter 6, to do so without filing legal documents of any kind, although putting it in writing in an agreement is advisable. After you launch, however, inevitably situations will arise that will make it necessary to have a relationship with an attorney on whom you can rely and with whom you are comfortable speaking. Typical situations for which you would need to seek legal advice include contractual matters, such as those that arise during client agreement negotiations; liability matters arising out of potential or alleged professional negligence; space and equipment lease issues; employment and labor law issues; and insurance and tax matters. Frequently, a five-minute telephone conversation with a knowledgeable attorney can give you exactly the right information that will save you hours of misdirected effort or needless concern.

In Chapter 7, we briefly mentioned that a number of professional organizations for architects, engineers, landscape architects, planners, and graphic designers have developed standard documents for use by their members (and nonmembers, as well). Although relatively straightforward, time-tested, and widely accepted, these agreements do include conditions and language that may be difficult to understand by the uninitiated or uninformed user.

For example, an architect intending to invoke standard contract forms may not know that AIA Document B141, Standard Form of Agreement between Owner and Architect, is meant to be used in conjunction with AIA Document A201, General Conditions of the Contract for Construction, which it incorporates by reference, and can be used with architect-consultant agreements, as well. Attorneys familiar with professional practice, however, will be well-versed not only in general contractual matters, but in these and other standard documents, as well.

Although it is not likely that professionals starting new firms will be confronted by liability problems immediately, accidents do happen, relationships go sour, and we live in a litigious society. Attorneys who are experienced in dealing with construction-related problems can be of immense value when such matters arise. Explaining to you how to proceed in a manner that will protect your interests can be a most valuable piece of information.

And if you decide to set up your practice outside the home, then purchasing—or more likely leasing—an office will be one of the first, and most significant, financial decisions you will have to make. Real estate leases are special forms of contract that are frequently developed by real estate agents and brokers for simple or small transactions. However, for larger and more complicated transactions, you would be well advised to seek the counsel of a qualified attorney experienced in real estate transactions. He or she can review and suggest appropriate revisions to pro forma lease documents, as well as negotiate on your behalf.

Finally, because many start-up firms are launched by the initiating proprietor or partners, without other employees, initially, employee and tax issues are likely to be minimal or nonexistent. But as firms grow and add employees, a whole new set of conditions enters the picture, generally involving labor and tax laws. Problems in these areas are generally infrequent and are not likely to exist at all when firms are small, but with growth, problems are more likely to arise.

For example, the notion of how to pay employees—whether on an hourly or salaried basis—is a matter prescribed by the Fair Labor Standards Act and administered by the United States Department of Labor. The act states that employees subject to the terms of the act must be paid time and a half for hours in excess of 40 hours per week, excluding those employees who are "exempt." Exempt are those employees with professional, managerial, and supervisory responsibilities. Sounds simple enough, but note that the definition of "professional" used in the act is different from the common understanding, leading to unknowing breaches in the law that can result in severe penalties for a new firm. Similarly, dismissed employees who feel that they have been wrongfully terminated or denied appropriate compensation may cause legal problems for a new firm. Again, such a situation is unlikely to affect the start-up practitioner; nevertheless, it is useful to have someone at the other end of the telephone to talk to, just in case.

Accounting Assistance

It is not uncommon for design professionals to begin practice without accounting help. And, if the firm stays very small and operates as a proprietorship, it may never need accounting assistance, since the net income of the firm becomes the proprietor's personal income for which he or she files a personal income tax return. If, however, the firm is initiated as a partnership, subchapter S-corporation, or other more complicated form of organization, then more record-keeping will be required and more complicated tax returns will have to be prepared, both of which typically require the services of an accountant.

It's also a good idea to hire an accountant for an important piece of front-end advice: how to organize the firm's chart of accounts. In even the simplest accounting configurations, income and expense items are charged to different categories (accounts) with different names, and usually numbers, as well. A firm with the very simplest chart might have as few as three income statement accounts—revenue, expenses, and profit/loss—in which all revenue items would get charged to revenue, all expenses to expenses, and the arithmetic difference would be recorded as profit or loss. This firm might similarly maintain only three balance sheet accounts—assets, liabilities, and net worth.

More useful, even in the early days, is to set up a somewhat more sophisticated chart of accounts, so that income and expense items can be recorded in categories that provide the owner with valuable information regarding his or her business. For example, a start-up firm would be well advised to set up a chart of accounts with several revenue accounts (fees, reimbursables, consultants, and miscellaneous revenue) and several direct and indirect expense accounts (labor, consultants, reproductions, travel, occupancy, insurance, benefits, taxes, and other general and administrative expenses, at a minimum). Then, as the firm grows, the chart can be expanded, from which reports can be generated that produce the financial information that allows the owner(s) to better understand and manage the operations of the firm.

Banking

Bankers are important members of the community, especially in small communities. In addition to developing broad understanding of money and real estate markets, they serve a wide variety of individuals, companies, institutions, even governmental agencies, and consequently can develop a keen knowledge of the arenas in which they operate. A helpful banker willing to share this knowledge and the related contacts can be very useful for design professionals.

It hardly need be said that there is no practical way to operate a firm without a bank account. From the very first day it is open for business, the firm will deposit receipts and make disbursements through a checking account. As the firm grows, the bank may become the depository for withheld and employer taxes, as well. At the same time, it's wise to establish a personal relationship with a banker. If in the future, the owner chooses to expand the firm's facilities, add staff, purchase equipment, or otherwise grow the firm without contributing personal funds, it will be necessary to secure a loan, and this will be easier to do if you have made yourself and your firm known to a banker. And help securing a loan is only one of the many services a bank can provide a growing design firm. Banks can, for example, also help obtain a letter of credit, required by an office lease, or make cost-effective lease terms for computer hardware and software. In sum, get to know your banker and keep him or her informed of the firm's progress and success.

Management Consultants

Within the last generation, management consulting for design professionals has become identified as a discipline unto itself. Comprising primarily individuals who leave architecture or engineering firms to set up individual consulting practices based on their personal knowledge, experience, and skills, a few management consulting firms are in their second or third generation of ownership. Some management consultants develop singular capabilities, such as marketing or financial management, that they then offer to the marketplace. A few firms, like The Coxe

Group, Inc., have developed larger, multidiscipline practices that offer a wide range of services including marketing and financial management, key personnel search, ownership transition, project partnering, strategic planning, and assistance with mergers and acquisitions.

Consultants of many kinds can provide information, expertise, perspective, and impartiality to design professionals. Because they are hired to help address management issues for a wide variety of client types, they have the opportunity to experience situations of all kinds. The best consultants assimilate what they learn from these situations, understand the underlying issues and principles, and apply their knowledge to address each new problem they face. In addition, as consultants, they can be more impartial, which is a big advantage for their clients as they struggle to reach solutions that are in their best interest.

But a few words of advice are in order before you hire a consultant of any stripe. Find one who:

- Listens well and understands your problem
- Has the requisite experience and knowledge to minimize the learning curve
- Suggests an approach that appears to be effective and proportionate to the issue
- You will feel comfortable working with and can trust
- Proposes costs that are appropriate to your situation

Professional Organizations

Each of the design professions has an organization that represents its members' interests in the profession, with related professions and industry, in the marketplace, and in government. These groups provide a vehicle for professional exchange; develop standard instruments, documents, and practice aids; recognize contributions of significance (e.g., give awards for excellence in design and practice); and generally set the standards for the profession they represent. These organizations include:

- American Institute of Architects (AIA) (www.aia.org)
- American Council of Engineering Companies (ACEC) (www.acec.org)
- American Society of Civil Engineers (ASCE) (www.asce.org)
- American Planning Association (APA) (www.planning.org)
- American Society of Landscape Architects (ASLA) (www.asla.org)
- American Society of Interior Designers (ASID) (www.asid.org)
- American Institute for Graphic Arts (AIGA) (www.aiga.org)
- Society for Environmental Graphic Design (SEGD) (www.segd.org)

The aforementioned professional organizations do not regulate design practice, so membership in them is voluntary (recall from Chapter 7 that the state registration boards take care of licensing design professionals). Nevertheless, start-up professionals are advised to become members in the appropriate organization, then use them as a valuable resource. Most have staff to answer professional questions and provide guidance or to refer you to others who may be better able to help.

As noted repeatedly, these organizations generally produce agreements, contracts, forms, instruments, guides, checklists, and other practice aids; but they may also publish books, tapes, CDs, and electronic newsletters, all of which make it easier for members to stay abreast of new developments in the field and to improve their own practices.

For example, the AIA's publication, *Architect's Handbook of Professional Practice,* now in its fourteenth edition, provides an excellent overview of virtually every element of practice that one might want. And the organization's Standard Form of Agreement between Owner and Architect and the accompanying document, Standard Conditions of the Contract for Construction, were developed in concert with the Associated General Contractors of America (AGC) and have become the standard in the industry—widely used and widely respected by most participants in the building process.

Another organization, the American Council of Engineering Companies (ACEC), has instituted a peer review process, which professionals can use to have their firms reviewed by a committee of their professional peers.

Technical organizations, too, are excellent resources for information in their specialties. These include:

- American Society for Testing and Materials (ASTM) (www.astm.org)
- Building Owners and Managers Association (BOMA) (www.boma.org)
- American Institute of Steel Construction (AISC) (www.aisc.org)
- National Concrete Masonry Association (NCMA) (www.ncma.org)

- Precast/Prestressed Concrete Institute (PCI) (www.pci.org)
- Brick Industry Association (BIA) (www.bia.org)
- Associated General Contractors of America (ABC) (www.age.org)

And for information about the market sectors in which design professionals work, or want to work, client organizations are good resources. They include:

- American Hospital Association (AHA) (www.aha.org)
- American Association of School Administrators (AASA) (www.aasa.org)
- Society for College and University Planning (SCUP) (www.scup.org)
- American Association of Homes and Services for the Aging (AAHSA) (www2.aahsa.org)
- International Council of Shopping Centers (ICSC) (www.icsc.org)

Similarly, business, civic, political, and charitable organizations can be excellent resources to learn about the community in which you live and work. Some of the most well known are the Better Business Bureau, Chamber of Commerce, Republican and Democratic clubs, Rotary, Lions, Elks, and others.

Former Employers and Colleagues

We've said it many times in this book, but it bears repeating: Don't burn bridges. Former employers and professional c olleagues are great sources of information, assistance, inspiration, and sometimes even clients. Design professionals are generally willing to help one another. Not only do they understand that, as a matter of principle, they have an obligation to train their successors—hence, future competitors—but they are generally disposed to want to help on a personal level. They are usually willing to provide all manner of detailed, often confidential information (salaries, multiples, fees, costs, etc.), as long as it is not being requested in a competitive situation.

Former employers are also excellent sources of advice, and they will sometimes refer prospective clients they cannot or don't want to serve. This is a win-win-win situation: it helps the prospective client by providing a reference to a professional better equipped to serve him or her at that time; it helps the referring professional by providing an effective and face-saving way to turn down an unwanted client; and certainly it helps the professional to whom the prospective client is referred.

Former employers may also agree to, even enjoy, participating in a mentoring relationship with a former subordinate employee, especially when the relationship is the continuation of a mentor-protégé relationship that began in the employer's firm. Imagine having a senior professional available to ask questions of any kind, and who can offer the fruits of his or her long experience in the profession. Although it might be difficult to hire such a person, some professionals will give of themselves, if asked. One recent retiree we know was so pleased to be asked for advice that he joined the new firm on a consulting basis.

Software Programs and Web Site Sources

Like so many others in the last decades, the design profession has been revolutionized by computerization, to the extent that virtually all design professionals who are starting practices nowadays are well versed in the use of computers for word processing, calculations, design and construction documentation, three-dimensional representation, e-mail, and Web site research.

You may find the following software programs, which are widely used in the profession, to be very helpful as your firm grows:

- *For word processing*:
  Microsoft Word (www.microsoft.com)
- *For marketing*:
  ACT! (www.act!.com)
  FileMaker Pro (www.filemaker.com)
- *For e-mail*:
  MS Outlook (www.microsoft.com)
- *For project management*:
  MS Project (www.microsoft.com)
- *For financial management*:
  Deltek Advantage (www.deltek.com)
  Sema4 (www.deltek.com)
- *For spreadsheet applications*:
  Excel (www.microsoft.com)
- *For graphics*:
  Adobe Photoshop for image editing, Adobe InDesign for page layout, and Adobe Illustrator for illustration and 2-D graphic design (www.adobe.com)
- *For image viewing and sorting*:
  ACDSee (www.acdsystems.com)
  Paint Shop Pro (www.jasc.com)
- *For database administration*:
  Microsoft Access (www.microsoft.com)
  FileMakerPro (www.filemaker.com)

And check out the following Web sites to access professional organization news, general information, programs, and documents quickly and easily:

- American Institute of Architects: www.aia.org
- National Council of Architectural Registration Boards: www.ncarb.org
- American Council of Engineering Companies: www.acec.org
- American Society of Landscape Architects: www.asla.org
- Society for Environmental Graphic Design: www.segd.org
- American Planning Association: www.planning.org
- American Society of Interior Designers: www.asid.org

And these Web sites will be useful in accessing books and software, technical, marketing, and other building-related information:

- *For information about AutoCad:* www.autodesk.com
- *For books and software:* www.buildnet.com
- *For books, software, and estimating tools:* www.buildersbookloft.com
- *For books and software:* www.constructionlounge.com
- *For MicroStation CAD product literature and technical assistance:* www.bentleysystems.com
- *For general resource information:* www.deathbyarch.com
- *For professional issue chat rooms:* www.aol.com
- *For GO ARCH, a professional issue chat room:* www.compuserve.com
- *For building material and product specs, tables, illustrations and drawings:* www.sweets.com
- *For technical standards:* www.ansi.org

- *For market analysis and lead tracking:* www.fwdodge.com
- *For regional construction industry information:* www.thebluebook.com
- *For organization and business directories useful in marketing:* www.galegroup.com

Although no one starts fully formed, there is a wealth of fellow professionals, consultants, professional organizations, and vendors who are ready, willing, able, and usually eager, to help.

9 Strategic and Business Plans

A central theme of this book is the recommendation to build your firm within the framework of a plan. Though this plan may be as simple as making a list of goals, itemizing a budget, and conducting research on potential clients, almost always it is worth the extra effort to take a more comprehensive planning approach, one that establishes an integrated plan for all aspects of the practice.

There is no standard format to follow for devising a comprehensive plan, but many experienced firms find it advantageous to develop both strategic and business plans. Most also institute a process for updating their plans (usually annually), and then commit the plan to writing. Both the process and the written plan are important.

The process is important because it provides a way to think about, refine, and document the various elements of the future practice. The plan derived from the process documents the results of the planning and serves as a checklist for measuring the progress toward achieving the stated goals. In this chapter, we'll delve into the benefits of both strategic and business planning. First, however, familiarize yourself with the 10 guiding principles given in "The Practice Plan" on the facing page.

Strategic Planning

A strategic plan in this context is defined as a clear and coherent *vision* for the future as seen by the firm's stakeholder(s), and an *action plan* for implementing the vision, with clearly identified tasks, responsibilities, priorities, and milestones.

When you begin to consider your vision for the future—a vital step in the planning process—recognize that some front-end "blue-sky" thinking is acceptable, and may even be energizing; but it is important to keep in mind that your vision should identify a future that is reasonable, achievable, and, to the greatest degree possible, measurable, so that the stakeholders can ensure that they are making progress toward realizing their goals.

Strategic Planning Process

Here we look at two strategic planning models—one longer and more complex than the other—both of which provide a useful framework for incorporating frequently used planning terms and issues. First we'll look at the long-form model, which is a nine-step process.

1. *Values*. Establish the underlying, philosophical concepts on which you intend to build your future, that lead to a . . .
2. *Mission*. Make this an inspiring, but general, description of what you want to be, leading to definition of a . . .
3. *Vision*. Articulate your overall goals, the description of which should include major

The Practice Plan

1. *Follow the leaders.* Most successful firms plan their future. At a minimum, your plan should include: a vision statement and summary of goals, a marketing plan, a financial plan, an operations (including technology) plan, and a human resources plan.
2. *Set realistic goals.* Have an intermediate and a long-term vision of where you want to go.
3. *Know yourself.* This means know your strengths and weaknesses. Perform a strengths, weaknesses, opportunities, and threats (SWOT) analysis (defined later in the chapter).
4. *Build a firm with the required skills.* Plan to build or acquire the capabilities to accomplish your goals.
5. *Focus on ways to get work, build momentum, and establish the desired image.* A realistic marketing plan is a central feature of any plan.
6. *Create a financial foundation.* This will enable you to support the practice and build reserves.
7. *Accept change.* Change occurs whether we like it or not, so be prepared for inevitable changes that will take place in personnel, organizational structure, the marketing and financial climates, and others.
8. *Plan for excellence.* Excellence is not achieved by talent alone. Plan for it.
9. *Never be satisfied.* No successful firm rests on its laurels.
10. *Be flexible.* This means be ready and willing to take advantage when opportunity knocks. As Yogi Berra once said, "When you reach a fork in the road, take it."

areas of emphasis to move you toward your mission, leading to identification of . . .

4. *Obstacles.* Identify anything or anyone that stands in the way of you fulfilling your mission, leading to identification of . . .
5. *Areas of focus.* Know where you have to focus to overcome the obstacles, leading to definition of . . .
6. *Goals.* Do this for each focal area listed in Step 5, leading to the shaping of . . .

7. *Strategies*. Decide on the approaches you will take to achieve your goals, leading to the development of . . .
8. *Action plans*. Specify how you intend to implement the strategies, leading to the . . .
9. *Business plan*. Annualize, budget, follow up, and keep implementation on track.

For a start-up firm, however, this long process is probably more layered than is really necessary to develop a strategic plan. When the founders have an intuitive understanding of their own values, which they undoubtedly do, then they can use the relatively simple three-step process:

1. Perform a SWOT analysis.
2. Formulate a vision.
3. Do action planning.

We'll explore each of these steps more fully, using case studies of our fictional firm, Able & Baker Architects.

SWOT Analysis

SWOT is an acronym for strengths, weaknesses, opportunities, and threats. In a SWOT analysis, founders start by identifying what they understand to be their strengths, weaknesses, opportunities (in the marketplace), and threats against potential success. This will provide information, in a general way, to help complete the more specific visioning process in Step 2.

Visioning

In this step, founders reflect on, and then document, their vision of what they intend the firm to be at a fixed future time, usually between three and five

CASE STUDY

Able & Baker Architects SWOT Analysis

As the partners in Able & Baker Architects approached the end of their third year of practice, they decided to develop a strategic plan for the next three years. At an evening meeting, they performed an informal SWOT analysis and identified the following:

- *Strengths*: design ability, client service, growing reputation as experts in healthcare facilities
- *Weaknesses*: staff quality and quantity, inefficient principal-to-staff ratio, inconsistent quality assurance procedure (although no serious liability problems)
- *Opportunities*: large and diverse healthcare marketplace, large and diverse employee pool
- *Threats*: other capable healthcare firms in the market

years out. (Less than three years rarely provides sufficient time for substantive change and achievement, and more than five is usually too far out, considering the substantive change, either internally or externally, that could occur in that time frame.) For the point in time chosen, at a minimum, the firm's founders should consider the firm's:

- Location
- Capabilities
- Services offered to the marketplace
- Design philosophy
- Size, in numbers of people
- Volume of fees (to be) sold, in net revenues
- Profit to be earned
- Markets, expressed geographically and by client type
- Human resources (the nature and quality of staff)

- Technology (nature and quality)
- Reputation in the marketplace, in the eyes of both clients and prospective employees
- Culture (what it "looks and feels like" inside the firm)
- Ownership (who will own the firm)

In addition, the founder(s) should document how they define:

- Their roles
- Their base salaries
- The time they expect to expend in the interest of the firm

By thinking about and documenting these key elements, founders will have identified virtually every important aspect of the firm they're planning.

CASE STUDY

Able & Baker Architects Visioning Process

During the week following their SWOT analysis, the partners thought about and documented their personal visions for the firm at the end of the next three-year period. The following Saturday they met to discuss their respective visions. At that meeting, both partners presented their personal vision, which revealed both a great deal of congruence, but also incongruence regarding the firm's size and markets. Able expressed a desire to grow at an aggressive rate of 20 percent per year, compounded, while Baker wanted to grow at a more modest rate.

Moreover, Able also articulated a desire to expand the firm's markets into medical office buildings and nursing homes, which he saw as connected to the firm's essential expertise while creating some diversity; Baker wanted to continue to focus on the firm's core strengths. After discussing the issues, Able agreed to modify his vision to reflect a more modest growth rate of 15 percent, and to treat medical office buildings and nursing homes as "targets of opportunity," rather than seek that work proactively.

CASE STUDY

Able & Baker Architects Three-Year Vision (2005)

- *Location:* New space in the same city
- *Size:* Staff of six
- *Volume:* Net revenue, $500,000
- *Profit:* Fifteen percent of net revenue
- *Capabilities:* Comprehensive architectural services
- *Markets:* Healthcare institutions within a one-and-a-half-hour radius
- *Human resources:* Well-educated, well-trained, client-centered staff
- *Technology:* Fully integrated at an appropriate level for the practice
- *Reputation:* Expert in our field; firm of choice in our market; professional and caring place to work
- *Culture:* Professional, ethical, hard-working, focused on project success
- *Ownership:* Same as current

They will have, in a manner of speaking, painted a picture of their firm in a way that enables them to begin to identify specific steps to take to realize that vision.

Action Planning

With a vision for the future clearly drawn, the founders are ready to begin action planning. Appropriately, the visioning process is the responsibility of the stakeholders, as only those who are, or will be, at risk have the right to determine the firm's future. Metaphorically, they decide where their train is going. In contrast, the action planning process is more successful when a broader group of people participate. Employees, advisers, colleagues, and others who "are on the train" but who do not set its direction, can, nevertheless, make a significant contribution to the quality of the action planning.

A proven successful technique for participants to use in the action planning process is to time travel; that is, to imagine themselves in the future, celebrating the successful achievement of their vision at the end of the defined planning period. After visualizing a successful outcome, it is easier to identify the things they *would have done*, individually and collectively, to be successful. This visualization process frees the action planning participants from the constraints and limitations of the present, and allows them to think more freely and expansively about the future.

To that end, each of the participants in the action planning process (guided by a facilitator, if possible) makes a list of actions that they imagine would have been done to realize the vision established by the stakeholders. They then share their lists with each other and discuss them. The participants then set relative priorities on each of the items on their list—to identify which items they see as more or less important to achieving the overall vision.

Next, the participants identify the individual or group of individuals they believe to be best equipped to ensure that each identified action is accomplished, along with a reasonable milestone for each.

In the end, the strategic plan should include every important element necessary to success, as determined by the stakeholders, plus an action plan for accomplishing them.

Strategic Planning Summary

When firms are very small, most of the work involved in carrying out the action plan will fall on the

CASE STUDY

Able & Baker Architects Action Planning

Once they had articulated a clear and coherent vision for the next three years, the partners and the new staff member they had hired met to develop an action plan to implement the vision. Working individually, they identified the specific actions that they believed would have to be taken to realize the vision; they then shared their thoughts, documenting suggested actions as they were mentioned. The actions they suggested included:

1. Recruit and hire an experienced healthcare architect.
2. Initiate a firmwide 401(k) plan.
3. Prepare project sheets to use as promotional pieces.
4. Develop a manual of drawing standards and guidelines.
5. Upgrade the CAD software.
6. Write articles on new developments in healthcare design.
7. Start every new project with a formal kickoff meeting.
8. Become active in the Academy of Healthcare Architects.
9. Schedule "client satisfaction" meetings with all clients.
10. Institute regular staff reviews.
11. Delegate budget and schedule monitoring responsibilities to key project staff members.
12. Develop a specific marketing plan.
13. Write program for new office for the firm when it grows.
14. Create a specific description for every position.
15. Plan firmwide social events.

During the discussion, the participants also determined that for the firm to realize its vision, the most important actions they had to focus on were numbers 1, 7, 11, and 12:

1. Recruit and hire an experienced healthcare architect.
7. Start every new project with a formal kickoff meeting.
11. Delegate budget and schedule monitoring responsibilities to key project staff members.
12. Develop a specific marketing plan.

Therefore, they immediately assigned responsibilities and initial milestones for each of those items and agreed to meet quarterly to review progress.

principals. As the firm grows, however, it will be possible for many of the actions to be accomplished by others.

Like all planning activities, strategic planning is dynamic, not static. Regardless of the thoroughness and specificity with which you prepare a strategic plan, a number of factors may cause the plan to change over time—perhaps the people and their goals, the clients and their needs, technology, the macro-economy, or something else. Therefore, you should review your strategic plans periodically, ideally annually or semiannually.

And because strategic plans typically are made to cover several years, keep in mind that the goals explicit in the vision are not intended to be accomplished in a few weeks. Rather, the goals are meant to express longer-range aspirations that require time, energy, and money over the long term. In the meantime, business must continue as usual, meaning that the time, energy, and money required to meet future goals must be expended *in addition* to the resources being used currently. By conducting a semiannual or annual review, you'll be able to easily identify which short-term objectives have been realized, or have failed to be realized. The review will also help guide you as you change the plan to reflect or respond appropriately to any external changes that have occurred during the established time frame.

Business Planning

In contrast to the strategic plan, which identifies goals that can be achieved over relatively long periods of time, generally three to five years, the purpose of a business plan is to integrate the firm's marketing, finance, operations, and human resources in a shorter time frame, usually on an annual basis. The business plan is the instrument that helps principals to plan, in both a general and detailed way, exactly how they expect to use the firm's resources in the coming year.

Each element in the plan relates to the others. Revenue targets generate marketing goals and the need for appropriate professional/technical staff and overhead support. Staff growth (in numbers of people or expense) creates the need to produce revenues to pay for them, and technical and other indirect expenses, to support them. The desire to step up the marketing effort or to increase any other component of indirect expense adds to the total overhead expense, thereby increasing the overhead rate, thus creating the need for additional revenue.

Clearly, then, business planning is an iterative process. As noted in Chapter 4, there are only three parts to the financial equation: revenue, expense, and profit or loss, and it is possible to start the planning process with any one of those three factors. That said, the conventional approach for firms that have been in business for several years is to begin the planning process with revenues—the fees and other monies it expects to earn the following year. Firms that have a more sophisticated management structure and that have sufficient knowledge of their marketplace usually can reasonably and accurately project the next year's revenue. Less sophisticated firms will simply extrapolate from what they have earned in fees during the current year. In either case, the business planning process starts by identifying next year's revenues. The initiating assumption might be something like this: "We'll do \$*x* in net revenues this year; next year we can do $x + y$."

With a defined revenue amount as the starting point, planners can next specify the expenses likely to be related to those revenues. To do this they must answer a series of questions:

- What will we have to do to earn those revenues?
- How many people will we need? With what level of experience and ability? At what salaries?
- How much consulting help will we need?
- How much will we have to spend in other direct expenses? How much in nonsalary indirect (overhead) expense?
- What will those revenues and those expenses leave in profit?
- Is that profit sufficient?

If the answer to the last question is no, the planning process is reiterated with different assumptions that will yield the desired profit.

Smaller or newer firms with insufficient historical data on which they can rely may choose to start the planning process from the point of costs, from which they generate income. Their initiating assumption might be: "We have a current payroll of \$*a* to which we expect we will have to add raises of \$*b*, yielding a new payroll cost of \$*c*. Based on current payroll utilization and our traditional salary multiplier, those labor dollars will generate \$*d* in net revenues. We also expect that overhead expense will increase by *e* percent, so our total cost will be \$*f*." Subtracting the total operating cost (f) from revenues (d) yields profit. Again, if profit is sufficient, and an examination of the various line items does not turn up other significant problems, the planning process is over. If, however, profit is insufficient, the planning process is reiterated using different assumptions.

A very few firms begin the planning process by identifying the amount of profit they wish to earn in the coming year. Then, starting with profit, they identify the overall revenues and expenses that will be required to produce that profit; next, they analyze those amounts to ascertain that they are reasonable, achievable, and consistent with the firm's vision for the future. Again, the process becomes iterative if any element is deemed to be unreasonable or unachievable.

Take a look now at two business plans for Able & Baker Architects, first using the revenue generation method and then the cost projection method.

Business Planning Summary

Regardless of the starting point, whether revenue, labor cost, or profit, the result is a business plan that identifies the relationship between productive (utilized) staff salaries and revenue, the revenues that must be produced by those responsible for marketing the firm, the staff required to produce those revenues, and the related overhead expenses (including marketing, of course) that will be required to operate the firm.

The numerical relationship between direct and indirect salary expense is called the *utilization rate*: direct hours or direct salary expense divided by total hours or total salary expense. As explained in Chapter 4, the range within which most profitable firms operate is .60 to .65.

The numerical relationship that describes the amount of indirect (overhead) expense that must be covered by each dollar of direct salary expense is called the *indirect expense* (or *overhead*) ratio: total indirect expense divided by direct salary expense.

CASE STUDY

Able & Baker Architects Business Plan Using the Revenue Generation Method

Using as a template the firm's Income and Expense Statement (refer back to Figure 4.5) at the end of the first year of practice, Able and Baker set about developing a business plan for the following year. Confident they will be successful in securing new commissions, they intend to add a professional/technical staff person to enable them to allocate more time for marketing. They start by creating a revenue target based on their goal to increase the firm's net revenues by 25 percent, or $200,000 × 1.25 = $250,000 for the first year.

Assuming that consultants and other direct expenses will grow proportionally, they project $50,000 for consultants and $15,000 for other direct expenses.

They calculate direct salary expenses as a function of their first year's history of achieving a net multiple of 2.8 times salary (though they had hoped to do better). Although they expect their own utilization to drop, they also anticipate that the new employee will be highly utilized.

They expect payroll and benefits expenses to increase in proportion to salaries, to $30,000, while occupancy and general and administrative expenses are expected to increase to $11,000 and $24,000, respectively, bringing indirect expenses to $125,000, a combined 25 percent increase.

The resulting profit planned for the year is $35,000, 14 percent of planned net revenues and 11.1 percent of planned total revenues. Able & Baker Architects' planned income statement using the revenue generation method for the end of the next year is shown in Figure 9.1.

Although the current norm for established firms approximates 1.50, it will probably be lower for start-up firms and each firm should establish the level at which it can operate comfortably and be profitable. Most new firms will operate at an overhead ratio of 1.0 or less in their early years.

Revenues		
Gross Revenues	$ 315,000	
Reimbursable revenue—Consultants	(50,000)	
Reimbursable revenue—Repro, travel, etc.	(15,000)	
Net revenue—Architectural fees	$ 250,000	100.0%
Direct and Reimbursable Expenses		
Direct salary expense	$ 90,000	36.0%
Consultants' expense	50,000	20.0%
Repro, travel, etc.	15,000	6.0%
Total direct expenses	$ 155,000	62.0%
Indirect Expenses		
Indirect salary expense	$ 60,000	24.0%
Payroll and benefits expense	30,000	12.0%
Occupancy expense	11,000	4.4%
General and administrative expense	24,000	9.6%
Total indirect expenses	$ 125,000	50.0%
Profit (Loss)	$ 35,000	14.0%

Figure 9.1 Able & Baker Architects' Planned Income Statement, Revenue Generation Method.

The numerical relationship between the revenues produced by the firm's staff and the cost of the labor to produce that revenue is called the *net multiple*, or *net earned multiple*: net revenues divided by direct salary expense. Although the current norm is very close to 3.0, each firm should establish the net multiple it is able to charge clients in order to produce good work and make an acceptable profit.

Market and financial planning are, of course, only two of the important parts of the firm's plan for its future. The firm's services should get equal attention. This is the subject of the next chapter.

CASE STUDY

Able & Baker Architects Business Plan Using Cost Projection Method

In thinking about the upcoming year, Able and Baker decide to tackle their planning by projecting their anticipated net costs, that is, before consultants and other nonsalary direct expenses. They expect to keep their salary draws at $60,000 each, $120,000 for both, but they plan to reduce their utilization from 60 to 55 percent in order to devote more time to marketing and training. They plan to hire a professional/technical staff person at an annual salary of $30,000, and expect to have that person working 80 percent on projects, adding $24,000 to direct salary expense and $6,000 to indirect salary expense. The combined principal and staff utilization yields $90,000 in direct salary expense and $60,000 in indirect salary expense.

Although they hope to negotiate better fees, they project net revenues at the same 2.8 multiple that they earned in their first year of practice, which yielded $250,000 in net revenues.

The resulting cost-based projection for Able & Baker's second year is shown in Figure 9.2.

	Total	Utilization	Direct Expense	Indirect Expense
Able salary	$ 60,000	.55	$33,000	$27,000
Baker salary	60,000	55	33,000	27,000
Staff salary	30,000	.80	24,000	6,000
Total salaries	$150,000	.75		
Direct salary expense			$90,000	
Indirect salary expense				$60,000
Net revenue (@ 2.8 × Direct Salary)	$250,000			
Direct salary expense	$ 90,000			
Indirect salary expense	60,000			
Other indirect expense	65,000			
Indirect expenses	$125,000			
Total expenses	$215,000			
Profit	$ 35,000			

Figure 9.2 Able & Baker Architects Cost-Based Projection.

10 Planning for Excellence

The purpose of the firm's strategic and business plans is twofold: to address financial, marketing, and other business issues, and to facilitate the achievement of excellence, the latter which should be the greatest concern of any successful firm.

While it is true that most significant works of architecture are usually developed under the guidance of a single strong design leader, credit for such works must always be given to the role played by the many other participants in the design process. Typically, more than 10 people (architects, engineers, interior designers, specialist-consultants, construction managers, and, of course, clients) are involved in the design decision-making process for most significant projects, and many have 50 or more. Even when Brad's grandfather was starting his practice and sharing office space with Frank Lloyd Wright in the 1890s, this was the case.

NOTE

Though this chapter discusses the goal of excellence using the example of an architectural design firm, the basic guidelines contained here may be applied to any design firm.

As any experienced architect with his or her ego in check will admit, design excellence is, in part, a result of successful management of a complex team, all of whose members contribute to the quality of the final result. Thus, the ability to select, manage, and train this team of individuals is always critical to a design firm's success. David H. Maister, in his book *Practice What You Preach* (New York: The Free Press, 2001), listed nine statements he regards as best predictors of financial performance (see the box below).

Don't misunderstand: We are not saying that design excellence can be achieved by management alone, or even that it is the most important factor. Management skill cannot substitute for high-quality design, but it can make those with design ability more effective. Thus, design quality, and helping to achieve it, must be a central management issue in any firm concerned with design excellence. And, as a central issue, it should be addressed in the firm's plans for its future.

At first, it may seem that saying design quality should be a central management issue blurs the traditional boundary between design and management in architectural practice. Certainly, most design professionals make a careful distinction between

Best Predictors of Financial Performance

- Client satisfaction is a top priority at the firm.
- Firm has no room for those who put their personal agenda ahead of the interests of the clients or the office.
- Those who contribute the most to the overall success of the office are the most highly rewarded.
- Management gets the best work out of everybody in the office.
- You are required, not encouraged, to learn new skills.
- Invest a significant amount of time in things that will pay off in the future.
- People within the office always treat others with respect.
- Quality supervision on client projects is uniformly high.
- Quality of the professionals in the office is as high as can be expected.

management and design; one has to do with finance, administration, and other related matters, while the other is the core of a design practice. We argue that management and design cannot be separated in practices that aspire to achieve consistent quality. Consider these situations that illustrate this point:

- The new firm that is spending so much effort surviving that it cannot focus enough on design. How does it reduce the effort required just to survive?
- The established firm with a solid—but dull—reputation that, more often than not, is losing out on the best jobs and whose staff members are moving to other firms with "hotter" design reputations. How does the firm meet this challenge?
- A firm that is growing rapidly, thanks to the design skills and reputations of the founding principals, who no longer can find the time to design, and so are assigning the work to a constantly changing group of employees, thereby relinquishing consistent quality of design. How do the principals regain control over quality?
- The firm that more frequently is asked to compete on a design basis for jobs, none of which it manages to win. The losses are expensive and demoralizing. Can the firm be restructured to compete more effectively? Should it make the effort to compete at all?
- The firm that has done good work on small projects but that cannot break into larger, more professionally challenging projects. How does the firm obtain the design opportunities it wants and needs to grow?

- The firm that is organized such that design, production, and construction are run by different people, resulting in designs that are often unrecognizable by the time they are built. How can design control be combined with management efficiency?
- The firm that always seems to encounter project problems—whether in budget, schedule, or client dictates—that prevent it from achieving the quality of design it seeks. How can this firm effectively control the process of designing and constructing a building?

As you can see, wherever design is carried out by a team (as is the case in most major projects today), wherever design depends on having and guiding receptive clients (as most good design does), or wherever the process of doing a project has an impact on the result (as most processes do), management is a factor in producing quality design.

If effectively planned and controlled, the interaction between management and design can be a significant help in achieving the highest possible design quality within the inherent constraints of each project.

Achieving Consistent Quality in Design

As stated at the beginning of this chapter, consistent design quality depends primarily on the skill and force of the firm's design leadership (keeping in mind that leadership is a human characteristic and cannot be conferred). But it is also dependent on these other factors as well:

- How the firm defines its goals for design in conjunction with other aspects of its practice

- The types of project the firm secures
- How the firm defines the design process, allocates resources to each phase of this process, and monitors this process as the project is executed
- How the firm is organized
- How the firm relates to its clients
- How, in this media-influenced era, the firm builds its design reputation so that it attracts the clients and staff it requires to perpetuate both its image and the substance of design excellence
- How the firm uses and manages the talent, experience, energy, and will of the entire project team

Each of these factors affects design quality differently in every firm, so we cannot offer a definitive answer to any of the questions raised, but what is clear is that the search for the right framework is an essential step toward achieving consistent design quality.

Setting Goals

The values and objectives of a firm's principals—no matter how loosely expressed—set that framework. To state that the overriding goal is to provide the client top-quality service that results in building solutions that are aesthetically, technically, and functionally advanced, and are of consistently high quality, is not enough. Every goal set by the principals has an impact on how the firm responds to the design quality factors just listed. Firm targets for size, profitability, growth, type of projects, ownership, control, and other areas all have a direct or indirect impact on design quality.

For example, a firm that plans to grow into a 100-person office with a practice targeting the market of hospitals and laboratories will have to pursue design excellence using a different set of constraints than a firm that pursues housing and office projects and that does not want to expand beyond the number of projects that can be personally directed by the firm's founding principals. The former will have to be able to support more than one principal designer, plus a core staff comprised of senior technical specialists who share project leadership; the latter firm, in contrast, will be able to maintain centralized control in the hands of a single design principal.

But what may have the most direct impact on design quality is how the principals define design quality and set goals to achieve it. It is particularly important to avoid the tendency to use only *quantitative values* as the basis for measuring the firm's achievements. When this happens, those primarily involved in design will find the going rough if the firm measures success solely in terms of optimized revenues and minimized expenses. Creativity, taste, and problem-solving skill—factors that defy quantitative measure—must be given significant weight in the final structure of a firm's objectives.

In recent years, ideas about how to measure design quality have proliferated. For example, whether explicitly stated or not, some firms' objectives include one or more of the following:

- *To do something innovative or newsworthy on each project*. This is a common goal of firms focusing on establishing a reputation.
- *To redefine the traditional design response to a particular building type*. This is a goal for many firms with specialized institutional practices (schools, hospitals, etc.).

- *To design buildings that emphasize the functional, maintenance, cost, and other performance objectives of the owner, rather than aesthetic criteria*. This is perhaps the objective of some office, hospital, and housing specialists.
- *To consistently impose on each project a single design theory or vocabulary*. This goal is common among firms dominated by a single strong personality.

No doubt you see the point: Regardless of what your design goals are, once they are defined, they will influence how your firm approaches its work, allocates its resources to a project, guides and judges its own design efforts as the projects develop, selects and develops staff, and deals with many other issues that affect design quality.

Recognizing the Impact of Practice Mix on Design Goals

Design goals, are, as stated, directly affected by a firm's projects. Therefore, the type of projects a firm gets is usually a function of what the firm seeks. If a firm wants to establish a strong design reputation, it must find a way to obtain work from clients with the desire, budget, and program to generate public interest and make design excellence possible.

Obviously, it is far more difficult to build an image from completing, say, small additions to proprietary nursing homes, small industrial buildings, or low-income housing than it is by designing a corporate headquarters building or a college performing arts center. How a firm selects the type of work it wants, and then secures it, was covered in Chapter 3. The point here is that the realism, and even the definition, of the firm's design goals are in large part dependent on the direction and success of the firm's marketing efforts.

Moreover, a firm's design goals must address the needs of the building type and client. Different building types generate very different design constraints. These differences must be reflected in the firm's design philosophy and process. High technology, code-constrained programmatic buildings, such as hospitals and laboratories, often present more difficult aesthetic challenges than those of an office building or a luxury condominium, where a different combination of a client's decision-making process, program, budget, and technical priorities govern.

More than one solid, old-line firm has seen its reputation damaged by breaking away from its roots to embrace design philosophies and processes that are incompatible with its traditional projects' needs. This is usually done in a misguided attempt to rapidly upgrade design quality and image. A typical sequence is:

1. The firm loses several projects in part because of a reputation for dull design.
2. The principals decide they must upgrade their image and skills.
3. The firm hires a designer from a "design firm," and tries to import new process as well.
4. The firm turns its back on the skills that brought in clients.
5. Its image fails to change and clients and old-time staff become alienated.
6. The design "savior" is fired and the firm reverts to its former ways, often in a weakened condition.

An alternative scenario is the following:

1. The firm hires a star designer.
2. The firm fails to alter its project delivery process or budgets to reflect the new, design-driven needs of the new "star."
3. The star designer resigns in frustration.

It is important to remember that design excellence is not imported, but instead requires a long-term effort directed from the top down and integrated with every aspect of the firm's activities. It is a firm's real goals, in conjunction with the projects it works on, that help establish the context for the development of a design process.

Designing the Design Process

The term *design process* is used here to refer to the way a firm allocates and controls its design resources (people, consultants, time, etc.) and manages them to execute a project. To improve design quality and efficiency of the project team, as well as to promote meaningful interaction between the client and the project team, time must be spent on designing the design process.

For each of the participants (owner(s), architect(s), consultant(s)), a clear, well-documented and agreed-upon definition of this process will include:

- Scope of the work
- Schedule
- Work plan

The work plan serves to organize the efforts of the team and is a vehicle for communicating the sequence of these efforts to the client. Note, however, there are major differences even among "design-oriented" firms in this area. Some of the typical ones are:

- *Length of time devoted to each phase.* Some firms spend far more time in program and site analysis; other firms allocate as much time as possible to schematic design and design development; still others are careful to allocate adequate resources to the late design-development, contract-document, shop-drawing, and field phases, in the belief that "God is in the details."

- *Who does what.* In any design-oriented firm, the proper matching of staff with projects is the critical first step in the successful execution of the project. Some individuals are better at small projects; others are best in design development; still others are good at working through complex problems. The natural tendency is to make do with the staff available. This, however, can result in the most important projects being assigned to staff no one knew what to do with, since they are available because the best design talent is busy on other projects.

Asked what his most important job was, legendary ice hockey coach, Scotty Bowman, replied: "To get the right players on the ice."

QUOTED IN *THE GAME*, BY KEN DRYDEN

- *How each phase is carried out.* This refers to decisions about when to involve engineers, which tools (models, renderings, etc.) to use during the design phase, how to study the key design issues, and how to resolve these issues.
- *When to involve consultants.* Most architects will, when asked, say they like to involve engineers at the beginning of design, but in practice, many do not. Moreover, many engineers discourage such early involvement because they want to do the job only once. Still, failure to seek creative engineering input early can significantly affect the development of a building design.

- *How progress is monitored.* At specific times during the development of a project, there is a need to pause for a review. The firm must decide when these reviews are needed, how they should be structured, and who should participate. Sporadic reviews by poorly briefed principals that result in a lot of rework are all too common and often give reviews a bad name. Well-run design firms find some way to provide regular review and participation by the firm's design leadership. In sum, these reviews should evaluate progress based on the management, design, and technical goals established for the project. They should suggest areas for further study and establish guidelines for further development. In an environment where clients want projects "yesterday," it is tempting to cut out the so-called soft parts of the design process, and the design development phase is the most typical victim today. Ironically, it is during this phase that some important details require extra time to work out. What a shame it would be, for example, to see a separate accounting for a chair rail detail that was a central theme in an interiors project because it took several weeks to resolve. These soft periods are often gestation periods, when the design concept matures. Or firms are faced with the need to rethink a design—a decision that cuts into fee budget, project schedule, and client patience. The firms with design ambitions are careful to preserve their flexibility in all aspects of the process in order to bring additional skills, time, and effort to a project when necessary. These factors can all play a role in effectively focusing the resources of a firm so that the design concepts established by the principal designer can result in an excellent completed work of architecture.

- *How the firm deals with other members of the project team.* Over the last several decades, the size of teams has grown and the roles and responsibilities have changed. Now, many specialist consultants, owners' reps, construction managers, and others have direct access to the client. Almost every firm today has lost some important aspect of the project design decision because of the advice of one of these other team members. Conversely, in an era of skeptical clients, a united front of architect and construction manager or other consultant can often serve to resolve an important design issue. Therefore, how a firm controls the entire project team—in particular its relationship with the source of such key owner concerns as cost and time—will have a great impact on the success (or failure) of a given project.

Organizing the Firm

Communication and interaction are central to the effectiveness of every aspect of the design process. In simpler times, when the problems, the project, and the practice were all on a smaller scale, the practice of architecture could be based on individual intuition. Today, with larger projects, complex functional, technical, and environmental problems, and larger groups of client-architect-consultant teams working to solve these problems, organized and effective communication and interaction are imperative to success.

Some firms—even some large national ones—try to centralize design in the hands of a single person. And though management theory says that most individuals can control only the details of four to six complex issues (such as design projects) at one time, this has not deterred some architects from trying to handle more. Centralization of design decision–making is normally most effective only in small firms; it is difficult to achieve in large ones.

Medium and large firms usually take one of three more decentralized options: *departmental*, *project team*, and *studio*. The first breaks the project into specialties—often with different specialists or departments doing the planning, programming, design, production, and construction administration. Under this option, a project manager weaves the common thread throughout each project. The second option has a single team take the project from planning through construction, with specialists and draftspeople added to the core team as required. The studio is an expanded team, with most or all of the skills and personnel to handle several projects organized under a single design/management leadership.

All of these options (and variants) have their advantages and disadvantages. The central organizational issue, with respect to design quality within each option, is the role of the principal designers. More specifically, do designers or managers control decision-making for the project? On this point much blood has been shed. If it is not the designer, how do important design decisions get made? Is the principal designer involved throughout the process?

Firms that confine the principal designer to schematic design and design development have been compared to multistage rockets with each stage controlled by a different guidance system. The satellite may get launched, but not necessarily into the orbit intended by the first-stage rocket. Peter Samton, of the Gruzen Samton Partnership, did a study of how a few of their more respected competitors organized themselves to achieve design quality. While his sample was limited to relatively large firms (with more than 100 staff), his conclusions are relevant for most firms:

- Design excellence is achieved only when there is effective design leadership at the principal level throughout the process.
- All firms studied were very concerned about process, organization, and most of the other issues covered in this section, and were working to find the right approach for their firm.
- No two firms were identical in the way they achieved excellence, but all had found some way to address each issue.

Managing Clients

A key figure in any project organization is the person who manages the client relationship, whether that person is the principal designer or someone else. The design quality of many projects is often won or lost depending on who fills this role. On some projects, it is easier to go along with a client's wishes than to defend a design solution the client does not support. But while it is easier to "ride a horse in the direction it is going," this decision can often lead to a compromised design concept.

Few owners today accept their architect's design decisions unchallenged. Often, owner opinions directly cause key budget and aesthetic trade-offs. If there is no one on the architect's side who understands what is important in the design, and who can sell it to the client, many of the firm's design ideas will fall prey unnecessarily to unsupported arguments based solely on "taste" or budget. This does not need to happen. An understanding client is essential to a good result, and it is part of the architect's job to gain this understanding. To quote Eero Saarinen, "Let's see if we can make this guy into a great client."

One popular architectural argument says that good design does not necessarily cost more. This is often true, but unfortunately it is also true that the heart of many designs has been cut out in last-minute budget reductions because of poor client and construction cost management. Many budget reductions also alienate clients, who end up feeling misled by their architects and lose the essential quality they, too, had counted on. Thus, the careful management of client expectations and project budget is critical to design.

Another essential part of the client management process is the effective communication of the design team's ideas and recommendations. Whoever presents the design must be supplied with adequate visual and technical support to make his or her arguments. It is no coincidence that the best-known design firms typically produce the most compelling design presentations.

Building a Public Image

Obtaining client support for a design proposal is easier, of course, if the firm has a strong reputation for design excellence. When dealing with a recognized design talent, clients generally defer to their acknowledged architectural judgment. Design image also has the more tangible reward of attracting more notable clients and talented staff. This has always been true, but it appears to have become even more important in recent years. The success of developers, such as Gerald Hines, together with a growing public interest in architecture, has made being a design celebrity an important competitive asset.

That said, design celebrity is often created by others, as much as it is earned. Several of the best-known design figures today gained fame before they had completed more than a few houses and small interiors thanks to their promotion by others with power in the market. For example, a former Zeckendorf executive recounted how Zeckendorf promoted his young in-house architect, I. M. Pei, so effectively that Pei was listed among the nation's leading architects before a single one of the projects that later earned him his well-justified reputation was off the drawing boards. Others, far less worthy, are now striving to equal that remarkable public relations achievement. The lesson here is that even a local design reputation requires an active effort at self-promotion.

What is more, self-promotion rarely can be based upon the reputation of an organization; today it must be tied to identifiable personalities. It is irrelevant that many of the buildings and designs that have been attributed to some of the nation's most prominent design figures were, in fact, designed by someone else; the focus of the reputation is almost always on individual talent. This glorification of the individual is one of the reasons that larger firms have trouble building the type of multistar organizations common in other professions. It is also one of the reasons so few large firms have been able to achieve consistent design excellence. Architecture, as art, demands the identification of artists.

One of Brad's father's favorite stories told of Bill Caudill (founder of Caudill Rowlett Scott), who wanted to be pictured with his entire team for an article in *Life* magazine. The editor disagreed, saying, "Bill, everyone knows the MGM lion, but no one thinks he made the movie by himself." The editor was right, of course, about the public's understanding about movies, but not about architecture. The film industry is careful to identify and reward the many different talents that go into the complex task of making a great movie. Such is not yet the case in the equally complex task of designing a building.

Image-building methods employed vary considerably, but those used most often today include:

- Cultivation of the press
- Aggressive publication of the firm's work (In more than one case this has involved subsidizing a publisher to produce a book on the firm.)
- Active participation in the design establishment's activities: teaching, speaking, preservation efforts, art openings, panel discussions, juries, and the like
- Organizing architectural exhibits or writing about architecture, featuring one's own work
- Working to make the firm's office, graphics, and the other visual elements consistent with the desired image

Of course, the time-honored methods of entering—and winning—competitions or design award programs are still among the most effective approaches. Being active and respected in the design community tends to increase success in competitions and awards programs. Merely creating an attractive submission is not always enough.

Promoting Design Talent

This brings us full circle. As stated at the beginning of the chapter, the most important figures in achieving design excellence are the lead designer and the design team that work on each project. No matter how good the goals, the projects, the process, or the salesmanship, great (or even good) design is possible only when you have a good design team led by a superior design talent.

Firms that have strong reputations have little trouble attracting such talent, but building a new organization, or rebuilding an older tarnished one, is a far more difficult task. In the latter case, the firms that have done so have had to aggressively seek out, train, and integrate talent into established organizations that may have had powerful antibodies to resist change. At the very least, this takes several years to accomplish.

It is very rare to see a firm such as C. F. Murphy (now Murphy/Jahn) emerge quickly as a design leader. The large staff layoff at SOM following completion of the Air Force Academy, however, combined with the Richard J. Daley–directed load of public work, gave that firm an opportunity for staff and projects with real design potential. They took this opportunity and ran with it. Some firms have tried the quick fix by importing outside talent to lead the design effort. More often than not this has failed because the effort stopped with the hiring of one or two stars. As many expensive free agents in baseball have proven, a few stars are not enough to make a winning team.

Conclusion

As with any other aspect of successful architectural practice, consistent design excellence cannot be achieved by accident. It is the product of an intense multifaceted effort. At the core of a successful effort is an individual (or individuals) with design talent in a leadership role. But though essential, a strong leader is not enough to achieve consistently high design quality. Consistently high-quality design is also a central management issue, and as such it should be built into the firm's plan for the future.

Potential Causes of Failure

Most books and articles on architectural design focus on how design firms have risen from obscurity to prominence. Few address the equally instructive, if less popular, subject of why some firms fail. There are, of course, many types of failure: failure to achieve the principals' major objectives; failure to achieve a firm's full potential; failure in the form of complete organizational collapse; or just going broke. Fortunately, it is possible to trace the origins of most failures to one or more flaws in the leadership of a firm, and such an investigation can teach founders of new firms a lot about what to avoid and how.

Some flaws are noble, worthy of a Greek tragedy, but most are petty or avoidable. Both the noble and the petty are discussed in the following sections with examples of the common pitfalls presented as brief case studies.

NOTE

All the case studies presented in this chapter are composites of real situations, but sufficiently disguised to be unrecognizable.

We have distilled the most common causes of firm failure to a list of 10, introduced in the following list, then explored one by one in the following sections.

1. *Halley's Comet*: Believing a brief run of luck means you can coast.
2. *The Buggy Whip*: Ignoring the cycles inherent to most specialties.
3. *The Grass Is Always Greener*: Ignoring client/market base to pursue other practice areas.
4. *Cannon Fodder*: Treating key people as expendable.
5. *The Captainless Ship*: Failing to replace a strong leader when he or she retires.
6. *Peter Principle by Primogeniture*: Bringing unqualified relations into the firm's leadership.
7. *Swollen Heads and Feet of Clay*: Relying too much on strengths while ignoring weaknesses.
8. *Financial Management According to the Russian Politburo*: Managing finances incompetently.
9. *Losing Sight of the Big Picture*: Failing to market when busy.
10. *Sometimes the Batteries Run Low*: Running out of energy.

Case 1: Halley's Comet

Probably the most commonly seen form of failure is the firm that has a brief run of luck and then disappears.

Firm A spent 10 years building a reputation for consistent quality on a series of small commissions. The three principals all worked directly on each project and developed a growing list of happy former clients. Then they obtained a "dream" commission, a major project for a client willing to support an innovative design solution. The architects made the most of the job, and following favorable publicity, rapidly became a "hot" firm. As more big projects came their way, the office grew from 10 to 60 people in two years. That's when the problems began.

Too soon, the principals began believing their own publicity and playing the role of "stars." At the same time, they spread themselves too thin—a problem aggravated by their loss of interest in the details of new projects. They spent more and more time enjoying the fruits of their prosperity. Quality became inconsistent and client loyalty weakened. No organized business development program was created. As a result, when a recession hit, their work dried up, they shrank quickly back to a 10-person firm, and eventually faded into obscurity.

Case 2: The Buggy Whip

The design professions are competitive, cyclical businesses. This means a firm can never rest on its laurels, and must be in a position to respond to changes in the market.

Firm B built a strong practice in educational and other public building types in the 1960s and 1970s. The principals were confident their prosperity would continue and so regularly spent the firm's profits. Unfortunately, school populations began to decline, the economy slumped, and local tax revolts applied the coup de grace to their traditional markets by the 1980s. The firm found itself without work and without the financial strength to rebuild in another area of practice.

Case 3: The Grass Is Always Greener

Unlike Firm B, many firms are never satisfied with their current areas of practice. This, too, can lead to problems.

Firm C acquired a strong reputation for planning studies, which occasionally led to architectural commissions. Even though the firm's finished buildings never matched the quality of their predesign studies, the principals wanted to be architects, not planners, so they ignored their study work and put their efforts into getting design commissions. The basis of their reputation soon shifted from excellent planning to mediocre architecture. With this shift came the beginning of their decline.

Case 4: Cannon Fodder

It is good advice to anyone who thinks him- or herself irreplaceable to observe what happens when he or she withdraws his or her finger from a bucket of water. Unfortunately, this lesson has often been translated into the belief that everyone is replaceable, which, in the short term, is not necessarily true.

Firm D prospered for years under the leadership of a man who made it clear that he believed the "everyone is replaceable" axiom. Over time, the firm's reputation became more dependent on the principals who were carrying out the projects (as is generally the case today), but the founder never recognized their growing contributions or shared the fruits of the firm's success. Then a crisis came, and the key principals, who felt no loyalty to the top man, left the firm, taking their clients with them.

Case 5: The Captainless Ship

A variant on the loss of key personnel is the forcing out or failure to replace the person or persons who built the firm.

Firm E's younger partners breathed a sigh of relief when their concerted efforts finally compelled the domineering founding principal to retire. In reaction to his autocratic approach, they decided to manage by committee. All of the committee members were "inside" men who frowned on the founder's egomaniacal and wasteful interest in speeches, parties, travel, and other "nonproductive" efforts. Eventually, though, the committee found that, in the name of prudent management, they had, essentially, "lobotomized" the firm. Devoid of its personality, and constipated in its decision-making, the office muddled its way into mediocrity.

Case 6: Peter Principle by Primogeniture

Like many parents, design professionals often want to pass on what they build to their children. The desire to hand down the leadership of a firm is understandable, but often ends up being a disservice to both the child and the parent-architect's colleagues who helped create the legacy.

Firm F—compelled by the insistence of its founder—promoted the founder's son to fill his father's place upon retirement. The merit of this promotion was not convincing to either clients or key staff, who soon departed.

Case 7: Swollen Heads and Feet of Clay

It is far truer to say that "no one person is a complete design professional" than "no one is irreplaceable."

Firm G, for example, built upon the sales skills of its principals. Unfortunately, its other skills—in design, production, and the many other capabilities necessary to serve a client properly—were not comparable. Ultimately, the principals ran out of new clientele.

Firm H, in contrast, built its reputation on design expertise, but like Firm G, never balanced its forte with other requisite skills. Tough competition and bad references cut short their moment of success.

Achieving balance is a challenge for most design firms, often because of big egos and a lack of respect for the full range of skills required to achieve excellence. Too many firms have been led by individuals who could not tolerate equals, or, when they could, had too little respect for skills other than their own to tolerate full partners with balancing capabilities.

Case 8: Financial Management According to the Russian Politburo

The financial rewards of the design professions are rarely comparable to those of other professions and businesses. Regrettably, many design professionals do not recognize this fact.

Firm J grew and prospered, and its principals' tendency to spend grew with it. Personnel were hired in advance of need, offices were outfitted in a manner consistent with the firm's design tastes, and personal spending by the principals centered on slow whiskey and fast cars, sailboats, and women. This expensive lifestyle was financed with borrowed money and a failure to pay consultants money they were owed. In time, Firm J's credit ran out, it was nearly forced into bankruptcy, and it suffered a general dissolution of its reputation and practice.

Case 9: Losing Sight of the Big Picture

It is very easy to lose sight of long-term issues when working hard to meet current client deadlines. It should be remembered, however, that successful firms are always hungry, and they never forget that continuous marketing is a constant priority.

Firm K built a busy practice, whose principals focused all their energies on their current workload, even to the point of ignoring or turning down potential new commissions. When the projects all moved into construction and the fee volume dropped precipitously, a financial crisis ensued. The firm could not cut costs fast enough to respond to the drop in revenue and no new work had been lined up to fill the gap. It took the principals 18 months to rebuild, but the firm was so financially and psychologically weakened that it never recovered its earlier success.

Case 10: Sometimes the Batteries Run Low

Building and maintaining a successful practice requires consistent effort. It never gets easier, and the more ambitious you are, the harder it is. But even successful design professionals can burn out. After a period of success, they begin to focus on other priorities or just run out of energy.

Firm L was dominant in its county of practice. A large percentage of the major corporate, institutional, and private clients automatically considered them when they had a project. The firm was led by one principal, who was a talented designer and an effective leader; the other principals all had strong complementary capabilities but none the same as those of the senior partner. When the senior partner began to phase down and take more time off away from the office, no one could fill the void. Soon, the firm earned the reputation of being in decline, with a leader soon to retire. The firm survived only by being absorbed into another firm that could provide the absent leadership.

Lessons from Case Studies of Failure

A full list of lessons implicit in the case studies just described would require its own book, but the more important ones and their management implications can be summarized as follows:

- **Make a consistent effort to achieve excellence in all areas.** For a firm to achieve and maintain success, it must recognize that it has to be skilled at both the professional and the business aspects of architecture. In the simplest terms, a firm has to sell well, provide consistently good service on the projects it sells, and manage both its projects and its office in a way that generates a profit. There is no significant margin for error in today's competitive, demanding-client, low-profit-margin world.
- **Conduct a realistic self-appraisal.** To manage the basics well, the firm should have a plan that establishes goals, realistically assesses its own strengths and weaknesses, and then outlines logical steps to build on these strengths and overcome the weaknesses in the pursuit of the goals. This requires an *honest* self-appraisal—which is not easy, because too many design professionals begin to believe their own press releases.

- **Steadily follow a well-planned business development program.** Successful business development is usually directly related to a realistic plan, a strong reputation in a good market or markets, and ongoing efforts to develop new leads and sales. It is important to remember that once a strong reputation or momentum has been achieved, it must be maintained. Few firms are ever given a second chance. In addition, as illustrated in Case 3, a firm should not abandon an area of strength or even dilute its impact. As already noted, any expansion into new areas must be carefully governed and monitored by a realistic plan to eliminate weaknesses while building on existing strengths.
- **Be sensitive to changes in the marketplace.** A realistic plan and effective business development program must also recognize that the market is dynamic, not static. No firm can depend on one building type or a long-standing reputation to carry it into the future. Today, the pace of change in all things is accelerating, and firms must change, too, if they are to stay viable.
- **Structure an organization that can carry out the work.** The firm's organization must be structured to respond to the new work produced by business development. This means not only having the full range of technical skills required to provide excellent service, but also focusing these skills on the right problems. In Case 1, for example, the firm did not build a structure—one with new partners or a strong middle management—capable of

accommodating the additional load created by growth. The one- or two-leader firm is particularly vulnerable today as clients become increasingly demanding of personal commitment and error-free service.

- **Attract and hold key staff.** Any firm seeking to grow must create a structure that attracts and holds the best available person in every key position. The principals of the typical architectural firm should take a lesson from leading attorneys, accountants, advertising agencies, investment bankers, and other firms, where there is room for more than one "star"; and in the best of them, each major position is held by a specialist whose reward and status are based more on his or her contributions to the firm's success than on an arbitrary professional caste system.

  Principals should not be afraid to take on additional partners, officers, or principals. As service firms in other professions have repeatedly shown, the proper choice of additional partners to fill leadership openings can expand both the financial "pie" and the quality of the service. A partner in any category who pulls his or her weight costs nothing.

  Partnerships and other principal ties are primarily business relationships—ideally, but not necessarily—strengthened by personal ties of friendship and respect. Because they are business relationships, they can be severed with far more ease than most people assume. But these relationships should be made—or severed—primarily for business, not personal, reasons. When personal jealousies, family loyalty, or other emotional issues interfere in such decisions, the results rarely benefit anyone. One of the primary roles of a firm's leaders must be to minimize the inevitable petty personal differences that can sow the seeds of the firm's destruction.

- **Plan carefully for changes in senior leadership.** Probably the most dangerous period for any firm occurs during the transition of leadership from the founder(s) to the next generation, or, as is more common in a young firm, the departure of a partner. It is at this point, more than at any other, that a realistic plan and assessment of strengths and weaknesses must be made. The holes left by the departing leaders, as well as the actions necessary to fill them, should be identified.
- **Apply the "why not the best" principle.** The "why not the best" principle should be applied when hiring to fill all positions. Failure to clear out dead wood is almost as serious as neglecting to keep staff levels closely related to the volume of work available. Given the limited fees received by most design professionals, it is imperative that funds be spent on productive personnel. This does not mean, however, to follow a hire-and-fire philosophy, as then it will be impossible to form the bonds of loyalty and respect among principals and staff that are essential to the building and maintenance of a productive, stable staff of quality personnel. Always remember that the best staff have the most options and, without good reasons to stay in their present position, will be the first to exercise those options.

- **Manage personnel costs carefully.** Because salaries constitute almost two-thirds of most design firms' expenses and are the most easily adjustable segment, they must be the focus of financial control. Most firms—with or without such controls—make money during periods of rapid growth because personnel and other expenses usually do not catch up with volume. With controls applied to personnel, however, the other easy time to make money is when month-to-month volume remains steady and relatively little effort is required to keep all technical personnel billable. Unfortunately, few firms ever enjoy such conditions. Most experience wild swings in volume and need to expend a growing percentage of their resources on securing new work. These conditions, combined with narrow profit margins, leave no room for error or waste.
- **Recognize the importance of effective, conservative financial management.** Above all, a firm must make money to grow and prosper. To make a profit, the primary effort must always be directed at balancing volume and expenses. This requires coordination of business development, project scheduling, and staffing. The closer a firm comes to achieving a consistent balance, the more likely it is to make a profit. Financial management must, of necessity, be conservative. Owing to the cyclical nature of the building industry, it is essential that a firm accumulate cash reserves to weather the inevitable crises. There is no room for any personal behavior that wastes the firm's (and its creditors') resources on personal expenses. Too

many people are hurt by such actions. Effective financial management is impossible without formal controls on volume, expenses, and cash flow.

Final Points

Of course, even the strictest adherence to all of the precepts given here cannot guarantee that a firm will achieve success or avoid failure. After all, management is not the raison d'être of a design firm. Unfortunately, as the case studies illustrate, a weakness in any management area can cause failure, and only superior professional capability can ensure success.

12 Launching Your Firm

Now that you have the outline of a plan and a working knowledge of the basic issues covered in the preceding chapters, it is time to decide when (or, indeed, if) to launch your firm. As Massachusetts architect Earl Flansburgh wrote, "There is no good time to start a new firm, only better times." Obviously, it is usually easier to get started in a booming economy, when there is a lot of work, but many successful practices started during recessions. Brad's father's firm, Perkins & Will, was founded during the Great Depression. He considered it, on balance, a good time to start, because as the economy recovered, clients were willing to consider new, younger firms since so many established firms had gone out of business.

Two typical triggers usually are enough to get a new firm off the drawing board and into practice:

- The belief that the firm can get work
- The assumption that the principals have the resources to survive the limited cash flow of a start-up

If both these basics are in place, most new firms then must quickly implement the following steps:

1. Decide on whom, if anyone, you want to work with.
2. Decide on a start date.
3. Draw up a business plan that includes:
    - A vision statement and a list of goals for the first year
    - A description of the services you intend to offer
    - A list of sources from which work will come
    - A budget for the start-up costs and for the first 12 months
    - An initial cash flow projection to define the initial capital requirements
    - A list of the support you will need to provide your services at the desired level of quality
4. Obtain initial clients and identify the probable source of the next clients.
5. Verify that you have met the necessary legal (licensing, corporate registration, etc.) requirements.
6. Choose a name, design business cards and stationery, and plan other actions that will help set the right image.
7. Obtain start-up capital.
8. Decide where to locate.
9. Select advisers: legal, financial, insurance, general business.
10. Promote your practice: send out announcements, call friends and former colleagues.
11. Set up the office: equipment, a basic accounting system, telecommunications, files, stationery, and so on.

12. Identify back-up resources: administrative and technical.
13. Begin practicing.

Now let's consider these steps more closely.

Partners and Associates

One of the most critical decisions you have to make is whom, if anyone, you want to work with. As discussed in earlier chapters, it is unusual that an individual has every skill necessary to lead and build a successful practice. There are exceptions, of course, such as firms led by sole practitioners who have chosen to focus on smaller projects that can be successfully carried out by a single design professional. But most practices with more far-reaching ambitions have to consider the question of partners.

The classic leadership mix for a new firm unites individuals who—in combination—have:

- New business development skills to get work
- Technical skills to successfully complete the work
- Basic management skills to keep the practice solvent

Ideally, each of the firm leaders will appreciate the importance of, and participate in, all three of these basic responsibilities.

Launch Date

It is important to set a date to start up the office, for, as with most deadlines, it imposes a degree of discipline into the planning and preparations.

There is little conventional wisdom regarding the best time of year to start a firm. If your plan calls for an immediate major effort to see potential clients, August and December might not be good choices because many people are away. September and January, however, are both good times to find people back at work.

In any case, often external factors—the need to sign a lease on office space, a first client who wants you to begin work immediately, or even losing one's full-time job—will override the selection of an arbitrary date.

The First Business Plan

In every chapter of this book, we've emphasized that a firm's future should be built on the foundation of a plan, and the first-year plan is often the most important.

The first vision statement for Brad's firm has changed significantly over time. When they started, the principals wanted to be the project architects on all jobs. As the firm grew, this had to change. But what did not change was their commitment to remain focused on building types where their research, experience, and other sources gave them a knowledge base and real expertise to bring to each new challenge. The initial vision remains a core belief for the firm.

Definition of Services

It is important to formulate a clear statement of the services you intend to offer. Labels such as "Architecture" or "MEP Engineering" might be sufficient in a small town, where you have to be a generalist, but in most other locations, you should differentiate yourself and begin building a supportive image. If you have special skills or interests, make sure you emphasize them.

It is also imperative that you offer services that you can deliver—and well. This does not mean that you should hesitate to offer services that you have not done before, just be prepared to do whatever it takes to do them well.

Location

Many new, small firms are launched from the founder's home. Often this is the only financially viable alternative, but it comes at a cost. To be efficient, most of us need a clear boundary drawn between home and work. Moreover, you are more likely to be viewed as a serious practitioner if you have a "real" office.

First Clients and Marketing Plan

We strongly recommend that you launch only after you have the clear promise of work and a plan to get more work in the future. As described in Chapter 3, avoid taking unethical advantage of your former employer, but recognize that most new firms are planned while the founders are working for someone else. Marketing and sales are ongoing processes, and few firms can afford to wait to start these processes until the day they open their firm.

First Budgets

Two budgets are essential parts of the plan: one for the start-up costs and one for the costs for each of the first 12 months. These budgets, of course, should be tied into a realistic projection of cash flow and calculation of your capital requirements. (See the "Start-Up Costs Checklist" at the end of this chapter for more on this.)

The Opening

Stage the opening of your office as an event. Give a party and send announcements to all of your family, friends, past clients, professional contacts, and anyone else you can think of.

With these decisions made, and a plan and resources in place, you are as ready as most design professionals when they started. If your firm is successful, you will have a constantly rewarding and challenging career. Good luck.

Start-Up Costs Checklist

Expense	Estimated Cost	Actual Cost	Date to Pay
Business license/permit(s)			
Professional license			
Business opening announcement			
Rental deposit on office (if not in home, two months' rent)			
Telephone installation/deposit			
Answering service			
Utility deposits (if not in home)			
Internet service			
Insurance			
Health			
General liability			
Professional liability			
Valuable papers			
Life			
Theft			
Hazard or tenant			
Disability			
Auto			
Legal			
Initial consultation			
Form of business papers			
Accounting			
Initial consultation			
Format resolution			

Expense	Estimated Cost	Actual Cost	Date to Pay
Professional association dues			
Local			
State			
National			
Initial business brochure			
Letterhead/business cards			
Equipment/furniture			
Computer hardware			
Computer software			
CAD software			
Typewriter			
Drafting desk(s)			
Desk(s)			
Adding machine			
Lamps			
File cabinet(s)			
Flat file(s)			
Conference table			
Chair(s)			
Telephone			
Telephone answering machine			
Facsimile machine			
Car phone/pager			
Photocopying machine			
Diazo machine			
Coffee machine			

Expense	Estimated Cost	Actual Cost	Date to Pay
Reference library (code books, design books, this book, etc.)			
Library shelving			
Supplies			
Pens/pencils			
Markers			
Mylar			
Bumwad/tracing paper			
Vellum			
Drafting tape			
Paper clips			
Post-Its®			
Legal pads			
Telephone message pads			
Computer disks			
Light bulbs			
Measuring tapes			

Study Guide

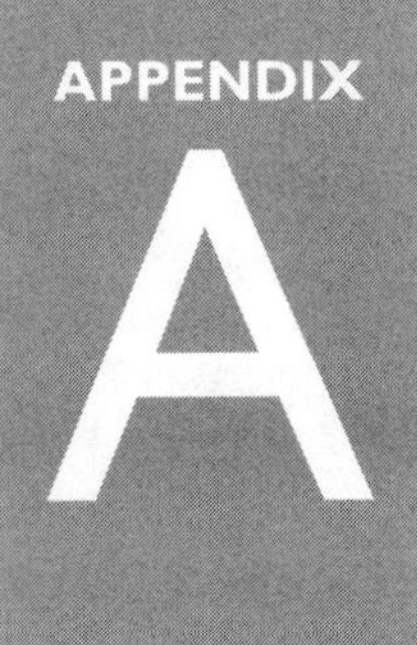

This book was written with the intent that it might also serve as a text in the practice or management course contained in most design curricula. To that end, and based on our experience teaching this course and lecturing in other similar courses, we suggest a number of projects that can be assigned to reinforce the lessons conveyed in this book. Specifically, we have found the following 13 study projects to be of value to new design professionals:

1. Define the type of firm they want to have in year 1, year 10, and year 20.
2. Write a job description for a prospective partner. Include general responsibilities, specific duties, professional requirements, and personal qualities.
3. Describe the qualities you would expect future potential leaders in the firm to have. Indicate how you would go about developing or reinforcing those qualities.
4. Think about, then write, your own obituary, as you would like it to be written about you. Consider both personal and professional aspects.

5. Design a brochure, using material from the Web or from other media, to describe your theoretical firm in its first few years, and after 10 years.
6. Using readily available sources—local newspapers, the chamber of commerce, the local planning departments, and others—identify 10 projects coming up in your geographic area for which no architect has been chosen.
7. Develop a proposal from your theoretical firm for a new day-care center (or other project to be defined).
8. As part of the proposal, develop a detailed schedule, labor projection, and fee computation for the project. Include fees for each of the other disciplines (structural engineering, landscape, etc.) that should be included on the team.
9. Prepare and present a PowerPoint® or other form of presentation for the project.
10. Fill in the standard form of contract, AIA B141, and add at least 10 clauses that you think should be included in a contract for this project.
11. Work with three of your classmates to define a team for the project, then outline the team's organization and structure. Include several different services that you feel would benefit the client.
12. Pick an ethical issue, research how it might occur, and discuss the shades of gray inherent to it.
13. Develop a mission statement and business plan for your theoretical firm.

Charting Your Course*

Master Strategies for Organizing and Managing Architecture Firms

By Weld Coxe, Hon. AIA; Nina E. Hartung; Hugh H. Hochberg; Brian J. Lewis; David H. Maister; Robert E. Mattox, FAIA; and Peter A. Piven, FAIA

"Things are so variable you can't just sit down and write a formula."
Overheard at the AIA Practice Management Conference in New York City, October 1985.

The search for the best ways to organize and manage architecture firms has occupied more and more attention over the past generation. The goal is always simple: Find the format that will enable the architecture firm to provide excellent service to the client, do outstanding work recognized by peers, and receive commensurate rewards in professional satisfaction and material returns. The answers, as the observation quoted above reflects, have not been so simple to find.

*Reprinted with permission from *Architectural Technology,* May/June 1986. *Architectural Technology* ©1986 The American Institute of Architects.

As management consultants with the opportunity to analyze literally hundreds of architecture firms, we have found the search for ideal management methods challenging. Each time we've observed a format that appears to work well for some or many firms, an exception has soon appeared, contradicting what looked like a good rule to follow. For example, some firms do outstanding work organized as project teams, others are very successful with a studio organization and still others get good results from a departmentalized project structure. One of the major puzzles for observers has been finding a relationship between the project delivery system used by firms (that is, "how we do our work") and how the organization itself is operated (that is, "how we structure and run the firm").

After years of study, and trial and error, a model has begun to emerge that holds promise for making some order out of these issues. At the heart of this new model is the recognition that although no one strategy fits all firms, there is a group of understandable principles with which almost any firm of architects can devise its own best strategy.

The model derives from observing that two key driving forces shape the operation, management and organization of every architecture firm: first, its choice of *technology,* and second, the collective *values* of the principals of the firm.

Technology, in this sense, refers to the particular project operating system or process employed by the firm to do its work. The choice of technology resolves such questions as: Are we going to work in teams or departments? Will we have one design director or do we all design our own work? *Values* refers to the personal goals and motivation of the principals in charge of the firm. The choice of values answers these questions: Why do we do what we do? What do we want to receive for our efforts?

Technology Shapes the Delivery Process

Recognition of the importance of technology in shaping architecture firms is particularly derived from work conducted by David Maister during his years as professor at the Harvard Business School. In studying other professional firms generally—especially law and accounting firms—Maister recognized a pattern in the key technologies they all use. He defines these technologies as:

- *Brains (expertise) firms,* which provide service to clients who wish to retain "the smartest kid on the block"—at almost any cost. These firms give their clients new ideas.
- *Gray-hair (experience) firms,* which customize ideas, but rarely are positioned at the cutting edge. Clients of these firms recognize that the problems they themselves face have probably been dealt with by other companies; the client therefore seeks an organization that can offer know-how based on past experience.
- *Procedure (execution) firms,* which serve clients who know that their problems can be handled by a broad range of firms and who are seeking a professional firm that can give them a prompt start, quick disposition and low cost.

Figure 1 is an illustration of Maister's model for positioning professional service firms. The diagram illustrates the relationship of these technologies and the best markets for firms that specialize in each.

	BACK ROOM ADDED VALUE	**FRONT ROOM ADDED VALUE**	
Execution-Intensive Programmatic Low Client Risk	"Pharmacy" (Familiar, Routinizable Work: Consultation Not Required)	"Nursing Ward" (Familiar, Routine Work: Consultation Service Sought)	**Procedure = Execution** **Gray Hair = Experience**
Diagnosis-Intensive Nonprogrammatic High Client Risk	"Surgery" (Complex, High Risk: Client Does Not Seek Involvement)	"Psychotherapy" (Complex Problem: Client Wishes to Be Involved, Advised)	**Brains = Expertise**
	Consulting Technical Skill Content of Work	**Consultation Interactive Skill Process**	

Figure 1. David Maister developed this "Model for Positioning the Professional Service Firm," based on analyses of all types of professional services. Within each field, Maister found that firms could be categorized by the skills they offered, and observed that the kind of work each performed reflected this. The model shown here uses various kinds of health care as an analogy to clarify these distinctions. Consider how firms specializing in each type of service would differ in: billing practices, staffing, marketing, use of systems, management style, training and recruiting, firm size, etc.

The impact of different technologies on the shape of an architecture firm is profound. For example, a firm where the partner-in-charge directly executes the project uses a technology different from that of a firm where the partners hand the execution of projects over to project managers. Similarly, a firm that organizes projects around a single design director has a technology different from one that allows each project team to make its own design decisions.

Applying Maister's work specifically to architecture-firm technology, three categories—similar to the generic categories above—emerge:

- *Strong-idea (brains) firms,* which are organized to deliver singular expertise or innovation on unique projects. The project technology of strong-idea firms flexibly accommodates the nature of any assignment, and often depends on one or a few outstanding experts or "stars" to provide the last word.

- *Strong-service (gray hair) firms,* which are organized to deliver experience and reliability, especially on complex assignments. Their project technology is frequently designed to provide comprehensive services to clients who want to be closely involved in the process.
- *Strong-delivery (procedure) firms,* which are organized to provide highly efficient service on similar or more-routine assignments, often to clients who seek more of a product than a service. The project technology of a delivery firm is designed to repeat previous solutions over and over again with highly reliable technical, cost and schedule compliance.

It is important to recognize that there is nothing judgmental being implied about the architectural quality of any of these technologies. At their most successful, firms specializing in each technology still exhibit strength in all areas of design, service and delivery. It is the emphasis that makes the difference. This emphasis may be shifted by the preference (strengths) of the architects in the firm, or by the marketplace.

Take the hospital market, for example. The modern hospital was first the province of hospital specialists (strong-idea firms). As the ideas these specialists developed were understood across the hospital industry and the architectural profession, the center of the hospital market shifted to strong-service firms, whose strength was the ability to offer close, experienced attention throughout the very complicated process of building or rebuilding the modern hospital. After proprietary health-care clients entered the market in recent years, a share of hospital work has gone to strong-delivery firms, which specialize in adapting the standard specifications of the proprietary owners to different situations.

Obviously, these technologies often overlap. Clients frequently want a kind of service that incorporates some aspects of more than one technology, and some architecture firms, similarly, deliver services that do not clearly fall within just one of these groups. Nevertheless, it is worth noting that there is a general progression in the way technologies evolve in every firm and every market. New ideas originate in strong-idea firms. As the ideas become understood and accepted in the marketplace, they are then widely applied by strong-service firms. Eventually, when the ideas can be routinized and are in demand by client after client, some or all of the work will move on to strong-delivery firms, where repetitive projects are turned out and efficiency is the key. Thus, it is important for firms to pay attention to how their technology matches the evolving market.

The different technologies, when they are working best, require notably different project-operating organizations, staffing patterns, decision structures, etc. Technologies in architecture firms influence:

- Choice of project process
- Project decision-making
- Staffing at the middle of the firm and below
- Identification of the firm's best markets
- What the firm sells
- What the firm can charge
- Best management style

Technology is the fundamental driving force that shapes the professional design process of the firm, and it is becoming recognized that all really successful firms have a clear and consistent project process. Those firms that try to be all things to all types of clients tend to have the most difficulty optimizing their work and/or their organization.

One immediate example is in staffing. Strong-idea firms will hire the best and the brightest right out of school and expect turnover after a few years. Strong-service firms seek career-oriented professionals and try to retain them so their experience is available to future clients. Strong-delivery firms, on the other hand, will hire paraprofessionals and use computers to apply standard details and procedures over and over again at the most efficient cost. The senior partner in charge/project manager of a strong-service firm, who is accustomed to giving individual attention to each aspect of complex projects, is rarely geared to provide the fast, efficient, routinized service desired by the strong-delivery client. Thus, the difference in staffing models makes each technology so distinct that it would be difficult to have all three models operating in top form in the same firm. The tables that accompany this article illustrate similar contrasts in strategies for all the different areas of the firm influenced by its choice of technology.

Values Shape Management Styles

The second driving force that shapes architecture organizations is the values of the professionals leading the firm. The fundamental differences in values become evident if one examines the word "practice," which is so often used by professionals to describe their organizations, in contrast to the word "business."

Practice, as defined by Webster, is "the carrying on or exercise of a profession or occupation . . . as a way of life." *Business,* on the other hand, is defined as "a commercial or mercantile activity customarily engaged in as a means of livelihood."

When the two definitions are compared from a management perspective, what stands out is the contrast between "a way of life" and "a means of livelihood." What is becoming evident is that many architecture firms are practices first and businesses second, while others are businesses first and practices second. Therein lies a whole new perspective about what goes on in such organizations. The basic difference is their bottom line:

- *Practice-centered* professionals, who see their calling as "a way of life," typically have as their major goal the opportunity to serve others and produce examples of the discipline they represent. Their bottom line is *qualitative:* How do we feel about what we are doing? How did the job come out?
- *Business-centered* professionals, who practice their calling as "a means of livelihood," more likely have as their personal objective a *quantitative* bottom line, which is more focused on the tangible rewards of their efforts: How did we do?

As with technologies, it must be emphasized that there is nothing more noble about either choice of values. The choice is an entirely personal, largely self-serving one, derived from how individual architects view their missions in life and what they hope to get out of their lives in return for working.

What is important about this distinction is the recognition that although all successful architects clearly strike a balance between practice values and business values, it makes a significant difference which of the two is primary. The choice can be expressed as a spectrum with practice-centered architecture firms at one end and business-centered firms at the other.

The different positions—practice-centered versus business-centered—will lead to very different choices in significant areas of organization and management. Practice-centered firms, for example, tend to prefer partnership structures, where the leadership is collegial and decision making is often by consensus. Business-centered firms, in contrast, work well in corporate models, where there is a clear hierarchy of roles and decision making is by chain of command. The practice-centered model is frequently preferred by principals who like to work as closer/doers—getting and carrying out their own work. The business-centered model is frequently preferred by principals who see marketing as a departmentalized function, with the work handed to operating departments to carry out.

Both values can produce equally successful results in client service, design quality and even profitability. The choice of values, however, can make significant differences in the best way to structure the firm. Values in architecture firms influence:

- Organizational structure
- Organizational decision-making
- Staffing at the top
- How the firm markets
- Identification of the firm's best clients
- Marketing organization
- Profit strategy
- Rewards
- Management style

What is most valuable about recognizing values as a key force shaping architecture firms is seeing how important it is that all the leading professionals in the firm share similar goals. Depending on these values, different organizational patterns will work best. Any effort to compromise values will inevitably weaken some of the choices of organizations, and consequently weaken the firm.

Matrix Integrates Technology and Values

When the two key driving forces described above—technology and values—are looked at in combination, they form a matrix within which the differences between firms, and the best strategies for different firms, become clear. The matrix (Figure 2) produces six basic types of firms, each of which will have a distinctive "best strategy" for each consideration described above. Examples of each of these best strategies are given in the accompanying tables (Figures 4–10). The model gives, for the first time, a clear picture of

TECHNOLOGIES		
Strong Delivery	A	B
Strong Service	C	D
Strong Idea	E	F
VALUES	Practice-Centered Business	Business-Centered Business

Figure 2. The best organizational and management strategies for architecture firms depend on the kinds of technologies it uses and the values subscribed to by firm principals. This matrix divides firms into six categories, based on these distinctions. Each category has its own "master strategy."

why some firms succeed doing things one way, while others can be equally successful doing things quite differently. Also clear is that it will be very difficult to optimize any firm that mingles too many of the different strategies. And when this recognition is combined with the understanding that the best clients and best markets for each different technology are quite distinct, it is possible to take a whole new view of how firms can best position their strengths to serve their clients.

In a recent test of the implications of this new model, the Coxe Group surveyed by questionnaire a sample of about 100 firms of different sizes, different markets and different organizational formats. After answering a series of questions to define its position on the matrix, each firm was asked to rate its level of satisfaction with the way the firm was currently operating. The results are illustrated in Figure 3. Those firms that showed the highest level of consistency in conforming to the best strategies for their position also reported the highest level of satisfaction with the way their organizations were working. The Coxe Group plans additional research to further validate the implications of the model, but this initial sample confirms the essential hypothesis. Those firms that have a clear notion of what they do best (their technology) and a common set of goals (their values) have always succeeded the best—for themselves and for their clients.

The charts on the following pages reveal rudimentary "master strategies" for each category of architecture firm. Once a firm decides which type of practice it is (e.g. an "A," "B," "C," D," "E," or "F" firm), it can follow the suggestions in the appropriate box to gain insight into the best ways to organize and manage the firm.

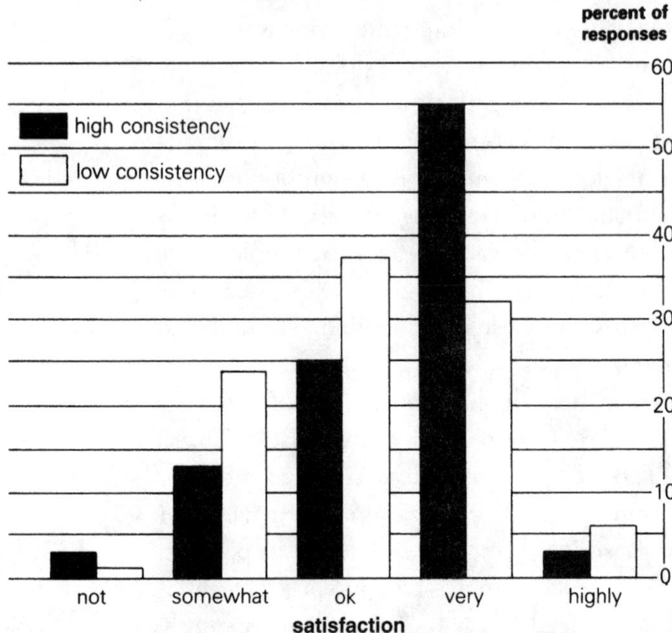

Figure 3. Principals of firms that fall most completely into a single category (as shown in Figure 2) report a far greater degree of satisfaction with the way their firms operate than respondents from firms that exhibit less consistency.

Strong Delivery	Projects are processed through departments or teams, headed by a principal in charge, in accordance with standard details and specifications developed through experience. The PIC makes the decisions. Success is achieved by delivering a good product over and over.	Projects follow an assembly-line process in which established standards are critically important. Since the product is standard, the client may deal with several job captains over the course of the project. Quality control is the key to client satisfaction.
Strong Service	Projects are delivered through project teams or studios whose principal in charge (the closer/doer) has a high degree of project decision-making authority. Strong, technically oriented people provide quality-control input, but project success relies on the authority of the closer/doer.	Projects are headed by project managers and delivered by departments whose department heads have quality control and project decision-making authority.
Strong Idea	Projects are delivered via highly flexible teams, organized around each job, which take their creative direction from the idea (design) principal.	Projects are delivered via stable teams or studios, often organized around different client or project types. Design principal(s) maintains project authority.
	Practice-Centered Business	**Business-Centered Practice**

Figure 4. Best Strategies for PROJECT PROCESS AND DECISION MAKING.

Strong Delivery	Closely held as a proprietorship or corporation by one or a few design professionals who manage a vertical organization. Decision making tends to be autocratic. Thrives as long as the principals stay closely involved.	"Investor"-owned by insiders or outsiders who delegate much of the operations and management. Decisions are largely based on a standardized process or SOP. Works well as long as the firm's process/product does not become obsolete.
Strong Service	Broadly owned by professionals structured as a partnership or as a corporation functioning as a partnership. Organizational decision making is by consensus. Functions best when owners share similar professional capability and goals.	Closely held proprietorship, partnership or corporation with owners making decisions by majority rule. Decisions are clearly oriented toward meeting the goals of major owners.
Strong Idea	Owned by a sole proprietor or a few equal owners who function as partners. Their ideas and creativity in projects drive the firm, and few organizational decisions are made.	A proprietorship or small partnership (or closely held corporation functioning as a partnership). Organizational decisions are tailored to maximize the application of one or a few original ideas.
	Practice-Centered Business	**Business-Centered Practice**

Figure 5. Best Strategies for ORGANIZATIONAL STRUCTURE AND DECISION-MAKING.

	Practice-Centered Business	Business-Centered Practice
Strong Delivery	Recruit experienced professionals who are committed to getting the job done efficiently. Financial compensation—base and bonus—tend to be higher than industry norm. Limited job security, except at top.	Hire and train paraprofessionals to do maximum amount of the work via standardized procedures. Invest in training, not salary and benefits, to keep costs low, efficiency high. Factory-like culture with compensation by job classification, publishable benefit package.
Strong Service	Recruit career-oriented professionals with strong sense of commitment to client. Reward via stability of practice, good benefits, pensions—average or below-average salary. Goal is to retain experience via low turnover.	Hire experienced professionals comfortable in corporate-like structure, as workload requires. Higher pay, limited benefits. People at top are entrenched; less loyalty to staff in event workload declines.
Strong Idea	Young bright professionals are attracted to the firm to be associated with one of the leaders ("gurus") of the profession. Typically receive below-market salary, minimal benefits and move on after a few years unless tapped to an inner circle.	Recruit young bright professionals interested in learning from the firm. Compensation often below industry norm—attraction is working on interesting projects. Turnover is encouraged as staff develop experience, want higher rewards.

Figure 6. Best Strategies for STAFF RECRUITMENT AND DEVELOPMENT.

Strong Delivery	Best clients are volume developers and organizations interested in reliable, proven, repeat-type solutions. Sell the firm's proven track record and knowledge and understanding of principal(s) about how to get through the system and agencies. Past clients return because of proven track record and rapport with the principal(s).	Best market is one-time or repeat client unconcerned with originality and/or clients looking only at bottom line. Sell proven product, standardized design, assembly-line ("it will only take a minute and we'll have it all done") package deal.
Strong Service	Best markets are institutions and agencies with complex projects that seek reliable solutions and expect to be involved in their project's evolution. High repeat business from well-satisfied past clients. Sell closer/doer experience, technical skills and commitment to remain on top of the job with personalized approach tailored to the client.	Best markets are major corporations and agencies with large, mainstream projects where the client expects to delegate execution of the project after making the selection. Sell proven track record, known or demonstrably competent project manager and organization's strength.
Strong Idea	Best clients are those with unique, one-of-a-kind problems, or "patrons" with individual or corporate egos to be satisfied. Clients are always the top decision makers, who may bypass input from their organization. The sales message is the reputation of the "guru" leader, and a track record of successful innovation, both design and technical, and/or solutions to uncommon problems.	Best markets are usually clients seeking leading-edge solutions that have been successfully tested by others, e.g., developers or lower-risk corporations and institutions. Clients respond to "sizzle" and messages like "innovation that is cost effective."
	Practice-Centered Business	**Business-Centered Practice**

Figure 7. Best Strategies for SALES MESSAGE AND TYPE OF CLIENTS.

Strong Delivery	Principal(s) sells one-on-one; may frequently proactively take opportunities to past clients. Effective advertising and public relations campaigns keep the principal's and firm's name in front of the market. Marketing staff supports these efforts.	Marketing is carefully planned and managed. Sales representatives find and sometimes close leads. Bidding opportunities are welcomed. Advertising promotes a standard product/service. Often rely on heavy entertainment of prospects. Blanket coverage of conventions.
Strong Service	Marketing relies on closer/doer principals strong at finding and courting clients. Facilitative marketing manager (who may be a principal) encourages broad staff participation in marketing, produces high-quality brochures, publishes a client newsletter, seeks regular publications in both professional and user-oriented publications. Good record of design awards, particularly by trade or user groups.	Centralized marketing and sales department, under a strong marketing director, is responsible for preparing the marketing plan. Frequent use of "bird dogs" to find leads, publication of articles oriented to meeting client needs, targeted direct mail, client seminars, some advertising. Sales are closed by one or a few principals who delegate work to project managers.
Strong Idea	Marketing is generally unplanned, relies almost entirely on reputation developed via books and/or articles, professional society awards, entry in premier design competitions, frequent speeches and often a faculty appointment. Marketing staff, if any, responds only to inquiries.	Marketing is actively planned, particularly efforts to get to know specific clients, seek publicity, publish articles in leading magazines and produce effective brochures. A marketing coordinator will keep the program moving.
	Practice-Centered Business	**Business-Centered Practice**

Figure 8. Best Strategies for MARKETING APPROACH AND MARKETING ORGANIZATION.

	Practice-Centered Business	Business-Centered Practice
Strong Delivery	This firm specializes in producing a relatively standard product over and over again. It will do best charging lump-sum fees—its profits come from efficiency. Maximizing efficiency—reducing the costs of production—produces high monetary rewards for the principals.	This firm also seeks high monetary rewards, but achieves them by maximizing volume. Its standardized product and assembly-line process for delivering it thrive on volume. Thus, the firm can often bid low to keep volume up. Lump-sum fees are essential.
Strong Service	Given the choice, this firm will price all its work hourly, producing steady cash flow with moderate profits. Rewards here relate to security for many in the firm—increase in salaries, increase in benefits, share in profits, and growth to ownership.	For this firm to maximize return, the task is to focus on profitable activities, minimizing nonbillable time, carefully controlling overhead. This firm can do well on lump-sum fees, hourly rates without an upset or cost plus fixed fee. Rewards are high monetary returns for the few at the top.
Strong Idea	The essential reward for this firm is, simply put, fame. What is most important is wide recognition of the importance of the ideas because fame will bring new opportunities to develop new ideas. Economically, this firm will do best if it charges high rates based on the value—not the cost—of what it delivers.	This firm, having business values, will seek monetary rewards as well as fame. It will strive to capitalize monetarily on the innovative ideas it develops via value-added premiums, royalties and the like. It will not consider itself successful unless it makes money, as well as builds a reputation.

Figure 9. Best Strategies for PRICING AND REWARDS.

Strong Delivery	Authoritative owner leads firm and establishes a working environment that attracts professionals willing to subordinate themselves to, and implement, the defined management policies.	Owners delegate operations authority to managers who structure rigid processes to keep the "assembly line" working.
Strong Service	Broadly based ownership with many equals. Can thrive on weak leadership as long as all are committed to the goals. Consistent organizational management provided by a facilitative general manager.	Owner(s) establishes leadership direction and assigns strong management authority to a CEO, who is likely to be the most influential (or majority owner) among them.
Strong Idea	Strong leadership based on ideas/values and projects precludes the need for structured management, relying rather on administrative support.	Strong leadership based on ability to draw ideas/creativity from others. Management is a coordinating and administrative function.
	Practice-Centered Business	**Business-Centered Practice**

Figure 10. Best Strategies for LEADERSHIP AND MANAGEMENT.

PART 2

Ownership Transition

13 Introduction to Ownership Transition

Every firm needs, but often overlooks, an effective plan to recognize leadership, expand ownership, and/or perpetuate the firm. The means to accomplish those goals is the activity called *ownership transition*. This book will help you, the design professional, to understand the essentials of ownership transition: what its elements are, how to plan for it, and how to develop and implement a successful ownership transition program. Throughout the book you will find terms and phrases that may be either new to you or are used in a new context. Refer to the definitions provided in the Glossary at the end of the book as you encounter them.

This book was written for design professionals: architects, interior designers, landscape architects, planners and urban designers, graphic designers, engineers, and others who are active in designing the built environment and the objects in it. Design professionals are similar to other people in most ways, and their businesses are similar to other businesses in most ways as well. There are, however, certain distinguishing features about design professionals and what they do that should be noted as we consider ownership transition.

One distinguishing feature is that design professionals provide services, not products. The services they provide—architecture, interior design, landscape architecture, planning, engineering, graphic design—are the result of their innate talents, augmented by knowledge gained through education and practical experience. For those design professionals who practice a "learned profession"—especially architects and engineers—the achievement of prescribed levels of education and practical experience is necessary to secure the state-sanctioned registration that is required to practice.

Beyond the education, experience, and licensure necessary to offer a professional service, perhaps the most important difference between providing services and products relates to the assets required to do either. In general, product-based businesses require substantial fixed, or *hard*, assets to produce the product being offered to the marketplace: property, equipment, inventory, and so on. Professional service firms need people. In professional service firms, the so-called real assets (the assets that produce value) walk out the door every night; it is imperative that they walk back in the next day. That difference is particularly important with respect to the individuals whose continuing efforts are required by the firm to ensure its success, presently and in the future. A successful ownership transition plan can attract and retain the people that the firm will need, to practice successfully now and to make ownership transition possible in the future.

What Is Ownership Transition?

The process by which the current owners put, or begin the process of putting, another group of owners in place is called *ownership transition*. Owners provide capital, marketing, management, quality, and leadership to their firms. If the current owners wish their firm to continue to survive and thrive, it is imperative that they ensure that those elements will be provided to the firm in the future. Ownership transition can happen in an unplanned, abrupt way, such as when a single owner dies suddenly. The transition has the best potential for achieving the multiple objectives the current owner(s) may have when it is planned and, subsequently, carefully implemented. Some of those objectives are described in the following subsections.

Why Is Ownership Transition Necessary?

Growth

As firms grow, most find that they cannot simply add staff at the bottom. They need to add principals at the top as well, to secure and manage client relationships and to provide necessary project management, expertise, and internal leadership. It is possible to employ professionals who enjoy, and are compensated for, principal-level responsibilities without having equity ownership. However, since responsibilities at the highest level are ordinarily associated with ownership, we will use the term *principal* and *owner* in this discussion interchangeably. Firm growth spurs the need to expand ownership. Ownership expansion generally occurs in three ways: (i) by elevating current employees who are qualified candidates to principal status and transferring ownership to them; (ii) by recruiting individuals from outside the firm to become owners; and (iii) by affiliating, through

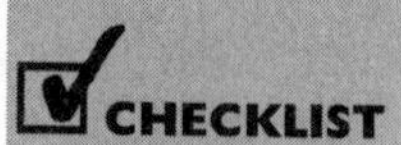

Why Is Ownership Transition Necessary?

1. Growth
2. Expansion
3. Retirement
4. New expertise
5. Continuity
6. Contact with the marketplace

merger or acquisition, with another firm that already has individuals suited for ownership.

Expansion

Firms that wish to expand geographically or into markets within their geographic sphere of influence can do so effectively only if such expansions are led by entrepreneurial professionals—those who can do what principals do.

Retirement

Ownership transition becomes an important matter when principals begin to think about their own retirement or, equally important, about how to realize the (usually increased) value of the capital investment they have made in their firms. Certain things become very clear at those junctures. Unless principals liquidate their firms, suffering the economic penalties that usually occur, retiring principals prepare for the successful continuation of their firms. The firm will not be able to continue successfully without other capable principals to lead and manage the firm. Further, without a new generation of principals in place, there will be no one to whom the retiring principal can transfer (i.e., sell) ownership.

New Expertise

Firms that seek to develop new expertise or enter new markets, and that do not have on-staff employees with that potential, frequently seek to acquire the necessary skill sets by bringing in new, principal-level candidates. As a condition of joining the firm, these candidates will want principal status, and they will need it to be effective in the marketplace and in the firm. The process of ownership transition can facilitate the transfer of ownership to some candidates, while giving the firm's owners time to evaluate the newcomers.

Continuity

Ownership transition fosters continuity of a firm. Many design professionals develop viable practices over the course of their careers and hope to have their firms stay in business beyond their own tenure. Transferring ownership to the next generation ensures continued service to valued clients, a stable workplace for valued employees, and a firm that continues into the future.

Keeping in Touch with the Marketplace

The marketplace plays a major role in what design professionals are able to accomplish. If there are no buyers for professional services, there can be no service providers. Design professionals must connect with the marketplace—the buyers of services. They must establish and maintain relationships with their clients so that their firms will enjoy opportunities to provide services. Such services have the potential to result in successful relationships, successful projects, and financial reward.

Sometimes, as they get older, design professionals postpone thinking about retirement in any specific way, or consciously opt not to retire. Their clients generally retire at the conventional retirement age, usually between 65 and 70. Their clients' successors frequently choose to hire and work with their own peers, not those of their former superiors. With certain notable exceptions, especially among the design "gurus," this syndrome commonly results in design professionals losing touch with the marketplace as they approach normal retirement age. A firm that loses touch with the marketplace loses its raison d'être and, ultimately, will no longer sustain itself. Ownership transition allows the next generation of professionals in a firm to move into leadership roles, with increased visibility and responsibility for marketing. Bringing new members into the ownership circle often helps the firm to maintain its understanding of and connection to the marketplace.

14 Ownership Transition Options

Transferring ownership from current owners to new owners can be accomplished through several different types of transactions. The alternatives described in this chapter have very different results for the founders of the firm, as well as those who are currently employed by the firm who might become owners in the future.

Internal Transfer

The most effective way for an owner to assure his or her firm's continuity, recover his or her investment in the firm, and eventually retire is to implement a plan that transfers ownership from the owner to current employees who are capable of running the firm successfully.

The advantages of *internal transfer* include: (a) the opportunity to continue the firm as an ongoing entity; (b) access to a pool of buyers who have become integrated into the firm's way of working; (c) assurance of a reasonable financial return for the owner, usually in the range of 1.00 to 1.50 times accrual-basis net worth; (d) ongoing control of the firm until the selling owner's percentage is reduced to less than 50 percent; and (e) maintenance of the selling owner's personal compensation and perks, subject to the establishment of a compensation and benefit arrangement that includes, and is acceptable to, the new owners.

The disadvantages of internal transfer include: (a) the lack of available and suitable candidates internally; (b) the need to begin sharing information and control; and (c) the need to involve, foster the success of, and ultimately rely upon the contributions of others for the success of the firm, particularly with respect to the ability to secure new work.

Bring in a Leader

The future success of the firm, and the ability of the current owner(s) to retire gracefully, depends on having people—leaders—in place to run the firm successfully. When the firm does not have such potential leaders in place, or the current owners do not see that potential, one alternative is to search for a leader outside the firm.

The advantages of bringing in a leader from outside the firm include: (a) the opportunity to continue the firm, if the transfer is successful; and (b) potential redirection/rejuvenation of the firm. The disadvantages include: (a) the risk associated with unknown personalities; (b) the need to share, almost immediately, information and governance of the firm with a newcomer; (c) the high levels of compensation and perks that may be required to attract such a person; and (d) the possible need to redirect the firm's marketing and project execution to accommodate the interests of the new leader(s).

The firm will likely need to provide compensation and benefits at market-rate levels to attract and retain the new leader. With a successful new leader in place, however, the current owner can reasonably expect to receive at least 100 percent of accrual-basis book value for his or her interest in the firm.

TIP

Bringing in leaders from outside the firm is frequently unsuccessful because of cultural incompatibility; therefore, this is rarely done.

Merger

If qualified candidates for ownership transfer are unavailable internally or externally, or if the conditions surrounding such a transfer are perceived to be excessively risky, the owner(s) may consider merging with another entity. In a *merger of interests*, no cash changes hands at the time of the merger, but the merging owner(s) will create the opportunity to have their financial interest in the merged company redeemed at a later date, probably at 100 percent of accrual-basis book value.

A merger has the advantages of: (a) providing for continuity of the firm, albeit in a new configuration; (b) permitting the owner's eventual retirement and return of capital; and (c) maintaining control of the owner's own work. However, a merger would require the owner to: (a) begin working with new partners in an unknown and untested relationship; (b) begin sharing information, governance, and control with new partners; and (c) compromise on many issues, particularly those related to finances and marketing.

Acquisition

Owners frequently consider the possibility of selling their firms to another firm when the need for maximizing financial return is paramount, other options are deemed inappropriate or unlikely to be

TIP

The primary reason that acquistions are not successful is lack of cultural compatibility between the acquiring and acquired firms.

successful, or other strategic issues unrelated to ownership become important (e.g., market expansion). The advantages of acquisition by others include: (a) assurance of the firm's continuity, albeit in a different form; and (b) the probability of higher personal return on equity, possibly in the range of 1.5 to 3.0 times accrual-basis book value. The disadvantages are significant; they include: (a) relinquishing control of the firm to the acquiring firm immediately; and (b) living within the acquirer's financial and cultural framework while employed. However, the opportunity exists in the other direction, as well. If qualified candidates do not exist within a firm, the firm's current owners may see potential successors in another firm with whom they might feel compatible. By acquiring such a firm, they would not only better assure their succession (thus making their own retirement feasible), but could acquire other benefits, as well, such as broader and/or deeper market share, enhanced staff quantity and/or quality, physical facilities, accounts receivable, and others.

In the event of the sale of the firm, a current owner planning on near-term retirement (e.g., three to five years) will probably receive higher value for his or her ownership interest in an outside sale.

Worst-Case Scenario

Three owners of a design firm in the Southwest, aged 65, 67, and 70, were the sole owners of the firm. Although at least three generations of potential owners had come through the firm, none had been considered for ownership, and hence left to pursue other avenues of professional development. With no prospective candidates left to consider for ownership, the owners decided to seek an interested outside buyer. None could be found.

However, if that same individual expects to continue to practice for a longer period, the combination of his or her salary and profit distribution over a longer period of time, even coupled with lower divestiture compensation, would yield higher total compensation.

Employee Stock Ownership Plan (ESOP)

ESOPs are legal entities established by federal legislation to foster employee ownership. Congress created this vehicle to encourage those in control of companies to extend ownership to employees. It enacted legislation that gives lending institutions a tax incentive that permits them to lend money to ESOPs at favorable rates. Firm owners who desire to take advantage of this opportunity create an Employee Stock Ownership Trust (ESOT)—the legal entity—and the Plan, which describes the workings of the Trust. The firm's employees become member owners in proportion to their compensation. Typically, a shareholder sells a portion of his or her shares to the Trust for fair value, as established by a third-party evaluator. Since sale of a minimum of 30 percent of the firm allows tax-free treatment to the seller, it has become the conventional minimum amount sold. The ESOT borrows from a lender to pay the selling shareholder; the firm pays a proportionate share of its profits to the ESOT; the ESOT uses those distributed profits first to redeem its loan and then to build value.

Despite Congress's purpose—to encourage broader ownership through employee stock ownership plans—in practice, these plans have been used primarily as personal financial devices to redeem, fully or partially, the ownership positions of key

Ownership Transition Alternatives

	Liquidate	Transfer Internally	Bring in a Leader	Merge with an Equal	Be Acquired
Value	75–90% accrual-basis book value	100–150% accrual-basis book value	Eventual transfer @ 100% accrual-basis book value	Withdraw @ 100% accrual-basis book value	150–300% accrual-basis book value
Governance/ Control	Maintain to end	Maintain until sell below 51%	Share control	Share control	Give up control
Design	Maintain control to end	Probably maintain as desired	Share, if a designer	Probably maintain control of own work	Possibly negotiate retention of design
Financial Implications	Maintain salary and perks	Need to satisfy buyers	Need to compensate at market	Need to compromise with partner	Live in acquirer's financial frame
Marketing	No change	Need to involve and foster success of new partners	Redirect to support new leader	Change to meet combined need	Acquirer's decision
Effect on Staff	Staff may leave as they sense end	Positive, especially if right person	Probable demoralizer	Could be positive depending on partner	Positive or negative depending on acquirer's culture
Timing	Continue as is	3–6 months to effect	3–6 months to identify and effect	3–6 months to identify and effect	6–9 months to identify and effect
Risk	Little to none	Little financial risk	Depends on individual	Modest if right partner	No financial risk

shareholders, who exchange the appraised value of all or part of their interests for cash, or for a *qualified replacement property*, the value of which is not taxed until it is sold. Qualified replacement properties are financial instruments such as stocks, bonds, notes, and other evidence of indebtedness, including bank certificates of deposit, issued by U.S. companies actively conducting a trade or business, including insurance companies and financial institutions.

The essential advantage of establishing an ESOP is to provide cash (or a qualified replacement property) to the selling owners while permitting them to retain essential control of the company, either by selling only a minority interest or by selling nonvoting stock (which would require recapitalizing the company) or by being trustee of the Plan. The ESOP can also serve as a form of employer-funded retirement vehicle for all employees, and can be used in conjunction with other ownership transition programs.

The disadvantages of establishing an ESOP include: (a) creation of a retirement vehicle and corresponding annual benefit payment beyond that which is reasonable for the firm, and legally permissible; (b) the need to sustain the annual cash flow required to repay principal and interest on the loan *and* redeem the positions of retiring ESOP participants at the then-appraised value of the company; (c) potential lawsuits by disgruntled employees; (d) failure to advance the goal of transferring leadership; and (e) less available ownership for individuals with leadership capability and ownership aspirations.

Liquidation

If there is no other reasonable way to continue the firm, the owner(s) have no choice but to liquidate the practice. In the extreme, liquidation represents the transfer of the firm's business from the current owner or owners to no owners because the firm ceases to exist. Additionally, absent an ongoing entity to provide for follow-on insurance coverage, there would be a need to purchase a professional liability insurance "tail," or assume the risk of potential uninsured and unfunded claims.

Liquidation ordinarily means that the firm's owners continue to practice until a decision is made to retire, at which point the owners gradually stop seeking and accepting new commissions, complete projects in progress, reduce staff, collect accounts receivable, and then close the door and retire. In effect, they gradually phase the practice down and out, effectively or formally liquidating the firm.

The process of liquidation involves converting the firm's assets to cash, and paying its liabilities, in hopes of realizing a positive surplus. In theory, firms should be able to liquidate cleanly at 100 percent of accrual-basis book value. Unfortunately, it is virtually impossible to liquidate without financial penalty. It becomes difficult to gradually reduce expenses as revenue declines, especially with respect to the direct and indirect costs of staff. Payment for leased premises and equipment may not be co-terminus with the effective date of liquidation. Accounts receivable may become more difficult to collect once the firm is no longer providing services. Furniture and equipment may not bring reasonable prices when sold. The common parlance for the condition is "fire sale."

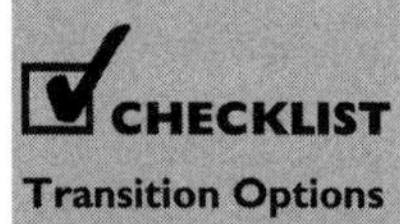

Transition Options

1. Internal transfer
2. Bring in a leader
3. Merger
4. Acquisition
5. Employee Stock Ownership Plan
6. Liquidation

The advantages of liquidation include: (a) the right to maintain control of the firm up to the point of liquidation; and (b) maintenance of compensation and perks, so long as they are affordable by the business. Disadvantages of liquidation include: (a) the probability of staff defections along the way; and (b) the significant negative impact on the firm's value. Liquidating owners usually recover only a fraction of the company's accrual-basis book value, sometimes as little as 50 percent.

15 Determining Candidate Selection Criteria and Communicating Founders' Expectations

What Do Owners Contribute to Firms?

Firms need specific, very important contributions from owners that only owners can provide. These contributions, defined below, can be thought of as owners' responsibilities.

Capital

The owners are responsible for providing the capital necessary to start and operate the firm. Start-up capital is required at the firm's initiation for organizational expenses (leasehold improvements, furniture, fixtures and equipment, stationery, and marketing materials) and initial operating expenses that are incurred and must be paid for pending receipt of cash for services performed. Capital is vital to support the increasing need for more sophisticated technology.

Once the firm is up and running, additional capital may be required to fund unusually rapid growth—growth that cannot be funded out of profitable operations, and to provide cash for ordinary operating needs when collections fail to meet current needs. These additional capital needs are frequently met with bank loans in the form of lines of credit for which the owners assume the responsibility and the risk. When capital is required, either at formation or later, the firm's owners are the only ones who can be expected to provide it. They are the financial stakeholders. Although others in the firm clearly have a stake in the firm's well-being, ultimately, the owners bankroll the firm. If the owners operate their firms successfully, they are entitled to reap the rewards of ownership, including a return on the investment they have made.

Marketing

Professional design firms exist to provide professional services to clients on projects. It is the owners' responsibility to secure those clients and projects—that is, to market and sell. Although nonowners are frequently involved in supporting the marketing effort, it is the owners' responsibility to feed the firm. Typically, clients buy services from representatives of the firm who they perceive as able to commit the firm's resources to the project at hand. Those are the owners (or key employees vested with such authority by the owners).

The ability to market and sell can be a personal characteristic or a learned ability. In some firms it is the single most important criterion for ownership. Since the firm can only do, and generate revenues from, the work it sells, marketing is the lifeblood of the firm. Those individuals with the ability to obtain clients and projects—the "rainmakers"—are legitimately understood to be making a significant contribution to the firm's well-being, perhaps the most significant contribution. An important corollary is that those who have the ability to market and sell will be owners, if they want to be, if not in their present firm, then elsewhere.

Management

The owners must ensure the successful management of the firm. They must maintain the viability of the firm so that it continues to fulfill client expectations regarding the execution of their projects. Owners must manage the firm so that it produces a profit that is sufficient to remain competitive in the marketplace and ensure its bankability and continuity. They must manage it so that it provides a return, at the level they deem appropriate for their investment and risk. As in the case of marketing, the owners can seek the assistance of others in the firm at many levels, but it is the owners' responsibility to ensure that the firm is managed successfully. They make the critical management decisions regarding every aspect of the practice: its finances, operations, human resources, and marketing.

TIP
Understanding others' personal styles allows us to develop the ability to influence them.

Quality

The owners must establish and assure the level of quality that is consistent with their clients' expectations and their own professional values. Satisfied clients generate future revenues, especially through repeat and referral work. Equally important, the firm's reputation in the community is exemplified by its completed projects, which will stand in the future as examples of what the firm is capable of producing. Although implementation, review, and control of quality may be delegated, the essential determination of the level of quality desired in completed work cannot be left to nonowners. The firm's reputation for service is of equal importance. Since the firm's projects are achieved by serving clients, the owners must be attentive to the quality of the firm's services. It is the owners' right and responsibility to establish the level of quality that must be achieved—in design quality, in technical quality, and in quality of service.

Leadership

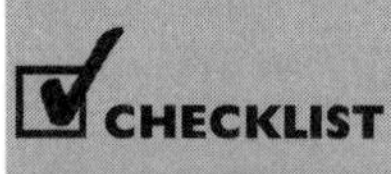

Responsibilities of Ownership

1. Provide capital
2. Market and sell
3. Manage successfully
4. Establish quality
5. Exercise leadership

The owners must provide the leadership that is necessary to move the firm toward the realization of their vision. Owners lead the firm by creating and sharing the vision they have for their firm with employees, clients, and the community at large. Owners demonstrate leadership by setting examples, performing, motivating, encouraging, mentoring, and rewarding employees, so that they perform in ways that help move the firm toward the vision. Owners provide inspiration, direction, and motivation for their firms. Employees who display similar characteristics and abilities will likely become candidates for ownership in the future.

Candidate Selection Criteria

Owners who contemplate transferring ownership in the firm to others must identify successors who will make the firm successful. There is no ultimate ownership transfer objective that will not be served by this criterion. We have already cited the essential elements that owners provide to their firms: capital, marketing, management, quality standards, and leadership. But these are ownership requirements, not selection criteria. Selection criteria are the personal and professional qualities that the current owners seek in their potential successors, which all *relate* to the essential elements that owners provide to their firms. The selection criteria are the "why" a person is selected for ownership. The responsibilities of owners are "what" owners do after selection. They are necessarily related. Owners must believe that candidates who meet the "why"—the selection criteria—will become successful owners, fulfilling the "what"—the responsibilities. With good reason, the following selection criteria are frequently considered when evaluating potential new owners (also referred to as *candidates*).

Professional Maturity

The candidate demonstrates high professional standards and actively works to help others develop similar attitudes, with the overall result that matters are handled appropriately throughout the firm. Professional maturity refers to the attitudes, behaviors, and expressions that demonstrate the professional wisdom that comes from maturity, and not to specific professional/technical skills, discussed below. When evaluating professional maturity, owners should ask themselves: "Does the candidate address issues directly and professionally? Is the candidate's manner confident and assured? Does he or she convey appropriate information and opinions? Does his or her demeanor and behavior reflect well on the firm?"

Professional/Technical Competence

The candidate consistently demonstrates high skill levels (in one or several professional/technical areas) by doing, by guiding, and by establishing performance standards and motivating others to achieve them.

The candidate should conform to the basic professional/technical, business, and other tenets by which the firm practices. Candidates who seek design, technical, or managerial excellence have to set the standards, put appropriately skilled people in place, and guide them to assure that the established standards are followed.

Compatibility of Values

The candidate possesses, demonstrates, and reinforces strong professional and business values that are compatible with those of the firm's current principals. It is essential that the firm's principals and the candidates have compatible values. If the current principals are *practice-centered*, they are likely to engage in their profession as a way of life and to value success qualitatively, asking "Did we achieve the level of quality we sought?" If, on the other hand, the principals are *business-centered*, they are likely to undertake their work less as a lifestyle manifestation and more as a way to earn a living; they are likely to value success in quantitative terms, asking "Did we achieve our financial goals?" Roughly stated, design professionals with strong practice-centered values are more likely to make critical decisions, especially project decisions, with the achievement of quality (as they define it) as the primary objective. Design professionals with strong business values are likely to make the achievement of financial goals their primary objective. A candidate whose values are inconsistent with those of the ownership group is likely to be continually uncomfortable with the principals' key decisions, and if elevated to principal is likely to make his or her partners uncomfortable, if he or she insists upon adhering to a personal point of view.

TIP

Ensure that the candidates selected for ownership share the basic values of the current owners, otherwise the members of the new ownership group will have different personal objectives with respect to organization, leadership, decision-making, and especially, financial return. Opposing views will lead to future conflict.

Business Understanding

The candidate understands the importance of a sound business foundation and business practices, makes decisions with the objective of achieving the proper balance of professional and business objectives, and guides others accordingly. Regardless of the dominant value set of the principals, the firm will be both a practice and a business. Decisions made by the principals and by others down the line will reflect aspects of both value sets. On each project the principals will not only have professional objectives, such as achieving quality in design, they will also have business objectives, such as adhering to schedule and budget. In exercising their daily business responsibilities, candidates for ownership must demonstrate not only that they understand the need for balance, but also that they understand and agree with the balance that the current principals desire.

Attitude toward, and Understanding of, Risk

The candidate understands the concept of risk taking and the role it plays in moving the firm forward. He or she is able to balance short- and long-term priorities. The candidate must recognize that the firm's need to explore new opportunities may expose it (and him or her) to risks that are personally discomforting; based on that recognition, the candidate must commit to making the best decision for the overall well-being of the firm. Opportunities will be available to the firm continually. Capitalizing on opportunities will require choices of some kind, and those choices will have attendant risks.

An example of a common situation requiring risk analysis is the marketing opportunity inherent in an unsolicited (or even solicited) request for proposal.

Although many view such a solicitation as an opportunity to be considered for new work, fewer understand the risks involved in pursuing it. Most understand the easily identified short-term cost of preparing the response; fewer assess the risks inherent in diverting the firm's resources from those likely to be more productive in the long term. Every firm decision involves choice, and every choice involves risk, some minor, some major. The candidate must understand this concept and always act in the interest of the firm when analyzing choices.

Marketing and Selling Skills

A principal's most important contribution to the firm is likely to be acquiring and satisfying clients. This is especially true in smaller firms with a limited number of principals. The "acquiring" part involves marketing and selling. Candidates must develop skills and refine personal styles so that they inspire confidence and are successful in bringing in work—through developing relationships with prospective clients, maintaining and nurturing relationships with existing clients, and appropriately representing the firm in marketing and selling situations. In the final analysis, the principal must be a "closer." Prospective clients for design professional services will want to buy from professionals who can commit their firms' resources—the owners. The principals must be able to "close"—to get the prospective client to say, in effect, "I want *you* (and your firm) to be my architect, interior designer, or engineer." In larger firms, the principal must encourage subordinates to take the lead in maintaining relationships with existing and former clients, and must ensure that marketing receives necessary attention at all times. New work, after all, is the lifeblood of the firm.

TIP

Because new work is the lifeblood of the firm, the current owners must have confidence that some or all of the new owners must be able to sell.

Client and Project Management Skills

After the job is sold, the principal must be able to lead the project team to achieve both the client's and the firm's goals. If the firm intends to grow, the principal must not become overly protective of his or her role in client relations, but must work to help others to develop client and project management skills, including selling, negotiating, and planning skills. Typically, the principal who sells the project becomes the principal-in-charge (PIC) of that project, especially in small to middle-sized firms, and frequently in large firms, as well. Usually, the PIC sells the project, negotiates the contract for services, assembles the project team, and establishes the project objectives. Frequently the PIC will establish the initial concept for the project and assume responsibility for client interface and communication at the front end of the project. His or her role is one of leadership, to ensure that the client's and the firm's goals are achieved. Satisfied clients enhance the firm's reputation and bring repeat and referral work. In addition, successful projects build individual and collective knowledge, experience, and confidence within the firm, and provide the money necessary to reward the contributors and build the firm.

Leadership Skills

The candidate must be a leader. In larger firms with larger ownership groups, it may not be necessary for *all* candidates to be leaders, but certainly *some* must be. One useful definition of leadership that is particularly appropriate in architecture, interior design, and engineering firms, is that a leader is one who conceives a vision for a desired future, communicates it to others, and motivates them to help achieve it. Candidates must demonstrate that they have leadership skills and consistently perform as leaders. Their leadership in the firm should be apparent to staff, clients, the profession, and the community at large.

Strategic Thinking

TIP

Prospective owners must have the capacity to think strategically.

Typically, professional, technical, and clerical/administrative staff focus their efforts on achieving the relatively short-term (tactical) objectives to which they are assigned, particularly related to projects. Principals, however, must focus on long-range (strategic) *and* short-term (tactical) objectives. This dual focus is vital to the firm's interest. If principals don't do the strategic thinking, it won't get done. Candidates for ownership must recognize that some component of principals' time must be devoted to strategic issues and strategic planning—the determination of where the firm is going and how it will get there.

Strategic planning can be understood to comprise two key elements: a coherent vision for the future and an action plan to implement that vision. Since principals must determine the course of the firm, they must be able to think strategically. While a candidate's strategic thinking skills may not have been fully engaged prior to being selected for ownership, each candidate must have the capacity for developing strategic planning skills and the willingness to engage in strategic planning.

Governance and Relationship Skills

Firms are governed by their owners. Candidates for ownership must understand, support, and be willing to assume, without reservation, a role in the firm's governance. This means understanding the nature of governance in the firm—the who, what, when, where, and how: Who will be involved in governance matters? What subjects and issues will fall in this realm? When and how will they be addressed? What will be the dynamic of the governance discussions? How will decisions be made?

Since it is likely that governance will be a team effort by the owners, the candidate must be willing to improve teamworking skills so that he or she can be effective in executing his or her governance responsibilities. Effective teamwork is achieved through having clear goals; encouraging broad participation in discussions; and having the ability to express feelings, to address causes of problems rather than symptoms, to seek consensus and appreciate deviations, to trust other team members, and to exercise creativity by seeking better ways to do things. In the best of worlds, candidates for ownership will have demonstrated an understanding of these elements and will have used them in other situations involving teamwork. At the very least, they should demonstrate an understanding of the need for and an interest in developing personal teamworking skills, prior to selection for ownership.

Personal Style and Interpersonal Skills

Principals must work effectively with others, inside and outside the firm, with partners, staff, consultants, and clients. Therefore, candidates for ownership should be aware of their personal style to ensure successful interaction with those constituencies. Regardless of firm size, the success of the firm is achieved through interaction with others. People have different personalities and different personal styles; one instrument, the Myers-Briggs Type Indicator, identifies sixteen. Because individuals operate out of their essential preferential styles, each behaves differently. They play out their roles and responsibilities in the workplace in accordance with their personalities. While it is extremely helpful to understand one's own style, it is also important to understand the personal styles of those with whom one interacts. By doing so, we develop more ability to influence those with whom we interact to make decisions in our favor.

The potential for success in interpersonal interaction is significantly enhanced when differences in personal style are understood and skills are developed to enhance interpersonal relationships and exchanges. For these reasons, each candidate should have a personal style that fosters successful relationships, and each must be willing to improve his or her interpersonal skills for the benefit of the firm.

Commitment to the Professional Development of Others

It is a long-recognized premise of effective management, proven in practice, that the further down the organizational chart one can delegate decisions and actions, and have them executed properly, the more effective the organization will be. This premise not only suggests the advocacy of delegation, but it also implies the need to develop the skills of those to whom responsibilities will be delegated. Candidates must be willing to delegate responsibility *and* be committed to promoting the professional development of those to whom they delegate.

Ethics

Candidates should demonstrate ethical behavior and they should take appropriate action when the performance of others in the firm suggests less than adequate compliance with the norms of personal and professional ethical standards. Although personal ethical norms are likely to be unstated, professional norms are frequently explicit. The American Institute of Architects (AIA), for example, publishes a Code of Ethics and Professional Conduct that articulates the canons, standards, and rules by which AIA members are expected to behave. Furthermore, it maintains a National Ethics Council, to hear and adjudicate claims of unethical behavior that are brought to its attention. Members found to have been guilty of unethical behavior according to the AIA Code can be censured or have their membership in the Institute suspended or terminated.

TIP

For more information about the AIA Code of Ethics and Professional Conduct, refer to *The Architect's Handbook of Professional Practice,* published by the American Institute of Architects in Washington, D.C.

Contribution to the Profession and the Community

If the current owners are actively involved in their profession and community, they will want their successors to demonstrate similar interests. Therefore, candidates should understand the importance to the firm's success of such extracurricular contributions, and they should be willing to commit significant energy to such professional and community activities. The reasons for becoming involved in these arenas are multiple.

Professional involvement can nurture relationships with others in the field, which may lead to joint ventures. It can improve technical knowledge that enhances one's expertise and provides an opportunity to participate in advancing one's role in society.

Professionals who become involved in community activities are presented with opportunities to gain information and develop relationships, which may lead to new work. Community involvement opens arenas in which professionals can develop personal presence and presentation skills. And, like professional involvement, community involvement enables professionals to play a significant role in the betterment of the community itself.

Investment in the Firm

TIP

Candidates must be willing to assume the financial obligations of ownership.

The candidate must understand the fundamental investment needs of the firm, recognize and respect the financial return such investment engenders, and, above all, be prepared to make the necessary investment as an equity principal. Such commitment is made manifest through contributing personal funds, assigning a portion of future personal compensation, and accepting the financial risk inherent in signing personal guarantees for bank loans, leases, or other debt instruments. The owners must capitalize the firm by investing personal funds when the firm is initiated, deferring compensation as required to meet current cash needs, making additional capital contributions, and personally assuming the risk of repaying funds borrowed to meet short-term cash needs. In short, candidates must be willing to assume the financial obligations of ownership to be selected as principals.

Role Model

Principals set the example for others in the firm. Therefore, candidates should consistently exhibit behavior they expect others to emulate. Candidates should demonstrate the behavior and level of performance that contribute to the firm's success so that their employees will follow their lead, modeling their own actions accordingly.

Trust

Although it appears last in this list, in the final analysis trust is frequently the most important criterion for owners considering candidates for ownership. In executing their daily responsibilities inside and outside the firm, the owners affect the well-being of the firm and their fellow owners. Although it is certainly true that this will be more significant in general partnerships, it is true regardless of the legal form of organization. Owners make decisions every day that affect the firm's welfare. They seek to establish relationships with prospective clients whose projects can have a substantial impact on the nature, direction, and reputation of the firm. They negotiate contracts involving the establishment of fees and the scope of services required to earn them. They make project decisions that can put the firm at risk with respect to professional liability. They hire and fire people who have the capability to support or detract from the firm's efforts. They make capital and operational decisions causing the outlay of vast sums. By virtue of their ownership, they have the ability to expose the firm and their fellow owners to serious economic and professional liability. Therefore, owners must be able to trust each other; current owners must have confidence that they will be able to trust each new owner to "do the right thing" even without supervision.

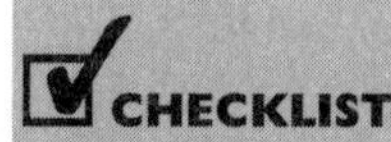

Criteria for Selection

- Professional maturity
- Professional/technical competence
- Compatible values
- Business understanding
- Attitude toward, and understanding of, risk
- Marketing and selling skills
- Client and project management skills
- Leadership skills
- Strategic thinking
- Governance and relationship skills
- Personal style and interpersonal skills
- Commitment to the professional development of others
- Ethics
- Contribution to the profession and the community
- Investment in the firm
- Role model for others
- Trust

Communicating Expectations to New Owners

The firm's current owners usually have an intuitive understanding of their responsibilities. At the very least, they have performed in ways that exhibit a set of de facto "decisions" about those responsibilities. The current owners have capitalized the firm and assumed the responsibility for its ongoing capital needs. They have marketed and managed the firm.

Problems may arise, however, when the current owners expand ownership to the next generation, whose members do not share the same intuitive understanding of the requirements of ownership. The current owners may find it difficult to articulate what the firm needs from its owners and to establish criteria and expectations for new owners. This frequently occurs because they have never been explicit about their own contributions.

Current owners may think it unnecessary to be explicit about selection criteria for new owners, believing that they "will know one when they see one." Although they usually want new owners to behave and perform in particular ways, current owners sometimes have difficulty understanding the importance of clearly expressing these expectations. Current owners should be clear about their expectations for new owners' behavior and performance.

Here is a specific example: Two owners of a medium-sized firm identified a key project manager as someone they thought should be brought into ownership. They had not established specific criteria for new owners against which to measure the candidate. Instead, they relied on a "gut sense" that the candidate was making managerial and technical contributions to the firm, mostly on projects, at a level that they felt was appropriate for owners. They "intuited" the benefit to the firm of expanding the ownership by offering shares to the candidate. The current owners did understand, however, that they must be clear about the performance and behavior that they expected from the candidate as an owner, which was substantially different from what they expected of him as a nonowner. In short, they wanted to foster the candidate's success as an owner, and they understood the importance of clearly expressing their expectations to achieve it.

At a meeting with the candidate, the owners presented information to the candidate that was intended to convey a complete sense of what their offer of ownership entailed. The owners delivered two documents at the meeting: a memorandum outlining the essential business elements—matters of firm valuation, transfer mechanism, governance, decision-making, roles and responsibilities, compensation and benefits, and a statement expressing their expectations of the candidate as an owner—organized into the following five areas of firm needs:

- *Capital:* The candidate will accept the valuation and payment mechanisms established by the firm for transfer purposes; will assume a proportional share of financial risk, including providing cash capital as required and assuming personal responsibility for bank loans; and will be responsible for contributing to the firm's profitability at levels established by the owners.
- *Marketing:* The candidate shall demonstrate principal-level marketing behavior; shall develop a personal network of people in positions to directly or indirectly influence decisions regarding new work for the firm; shall participate actively in civic, cultural, and professional groups; and shall cultivate a "book of business" for the firm.
- *Management:* The candidate shall develop and demonstrate holistic, principal-level management behavior; shall be responsible for firmwide

staff planning, understanding total firm projections, forecasting staff needs, and providing oversight; shall manage more projects, assuming personal responsibility for managing 25 percent of firm revenue; and shall assume responsibility for CAD oversight.

- *Quality:* The candidate shall be the firm's quality control "czar;" shall share specific project quality control responsibilities with another (named) principal; and shall organize and assign responsibility for monthly staff seminars on the subject of quality.
- *Leadership:* The candidate shall actively participate in planning, mentoring, and similar leadership activities; shall adopt principal-level dress and behavior; shall act like an owner, representing the firm's interests and ensuring appropriate employee behavior in the studio; and shall develop and display broad perspective regarding firmwide productivity, especially regarding other managers' projects.

TIP

It is important that current owners identify those they believe have the greatest potential for development as the next generation's leaders.

In this example, the expectations expressed by the principals were specific to the particular firm, its personalities, and its circumstances. Such expectations would only coincidentally be appropriate for others. Although expressing such expectations might appear so basic as to be unnecessary, in fact they are not. They give new owners a clear sense of how they will be expected to behave and perform, how they will be evaluated, and how their future will be considered by those in control. When new owners understand what success "looks like," they will be better able to achieve it. Ultimately, the individual's success will be an important contribution to the firm's success.

16 Valuing the Firm: How Much Is It Worth?

As a founder contemplates the ownership transition process, one of the most significant issues he or she must face is: What is the firm worth? The following discussion introduces valuation concepts and provides a framework for founders to use as they consider the value of their firm.

What Is Value?

Value is sometimes defined as the amount that an informed buyer will pay a willing seller in the absence of duress. When considering a publicly owned corporation, value is relatively easy to identify. Publicly held firms are required to publish and distribute basic financial information and other data about themselves. With that information, current and prospective owners can make informed decisions about buying and selling, which they can then act on by trading company shares through the stock market(s) on which the company is listed. Each such transaction represents a sale by a seller and a purchase by a buyer at a mutually agreed price established through the trading procedures of the market. As the absolute indication of what an informed buyer paid a willing seller, the last sale in a given company determines its value at that moment. No such market exists for privately held firms—firms owned by individuals who generally operate and control them in their own interest.

It is difficult to make direct comparisons between privately held and publicly traded companies. Small to medium-sized design firms typically pay taxes on a cash basis, while managing compensation on an accrual basis. In cash-basis accounting, revenue is recognized when it is received, and expenses are recognized when they are disbursed, as contrasted with accrual-basis accounting in which revenues are recognized when they are earned and expenses are recognized when they are incurred. Earnings are distributed through compensation: salary, risk payments (bonuses), benefits, and retirement plans. Additional working capital needs are typically funded either through borrowing or by adding accrued net profits to retained earnings (profits kept in the firm and not distributed).

In addition, because of the relatively low cost of entry into the design services marketplace, and because of the highly personal nature of the services provided by those who own and run design and planning firms, there is virtually no public market for such firms in this country. Even though a public market does not exist for privately held firms, the owners of those firms occasionally need to establish the value of their firms. Without a public market in which value is determined through day-to-day trades and reported publicly, the determination of value for privately held design and planning firms is dependent upon knowledge of the private marketplace, where valuation is determined as a function of the conditions in which exchanges of ownership normally occur:

- Death of the owner(s) and the ensuing transfer by the estate to others
- Internal transfer of some or all of the ownership to others within the firm
- Merger of the firm with another firm
- Sale of the firm to another firm, or the purchase of a firm
- Development of an Employee Stock Ownership Plan (ESOP)
- Liquidation of the firm

CHECKLIST

Events That Require Valuation

- Liquidation
- Internal sale
- Merger
- External sale
- Divorce settlement
- Estate settlement
- Employee Stock Ownership Plan

How Is Value Determined?

Without a public market to establish the firm's value on an arm's-length and ongoing basis, there are three ways to determine value. Each of the valuation methods listed below has distinct advantages and disadvantages.

- *Survey:* One can conduct a survey, or refer to a survey conducted by others, that researches and tabulates the values of other firms. The publisher of one such valuation survey includes formulas for value developed from the data collected. At best, such surveys can indicate the ranges and averages of valuations for all the firms listed. At worst, the data can be inadequate, inaccurate, inconsistent, inappropriate, or irrelevant.
- *Formula:* One can establish a formula for valuation that can then be applied to purchases and sales in the future. If the formula appropriately reflects the firm's actual condition and applicable

TIP

Privately held companies often determine value by referring to surveys, establishing a formula, or hiring an expert to appraise the firm.

circumstances at the time of valuation, the formula can produce a reasonable valuation. If, however, the formula does not include parameters that take into account the particular circumstances and conditions affecting the firm at the time of the valuation, or the formula includes those parameters but applies them inappropriately, then the results can be unreasonable, misleading, or totally erroneous.

- *Evaluation by an appraiser:* Some firms retain an appraiser who is experienced in the evaluation of businesses. If the appraiser is skilled in preparing business valuations and is knowledgeable about the company and the disciplines and marketplaces within which the company operates, then the valuation is likely to be reasonable and appropriate for the particular purpose and circumstances. If, however, the appraiser is unskilled or does not understand the company or the marketplace and circumstances in which it operates, then any valuation produced is likely to be suspect.

Components of Valuation

Three components of a firm's financial situation are usually examined in developing a valuation: net revenues, net income, and net worth.

Net revenues are revenues that are earned by the firm's employees and that support the firm's own staff, and exclude revenues that are used for consultants or other nonsalary project expenses, such as travel, accommodations, reproductions, or communications. A firm's net revenue is the financial representation of the work volume that the firm has produced in the accounting period (typically a month, quarter, or year). Examination of net revenues over a three- to five-year period will yield a good picture of the workload enjoyed and output produced by the firm. By extension, net revenues can serve as an indicator of what the firm might enjoy and produce in the future. When using net revenues as a basis for determining value, buyers and sellers generally use a *weighted average* that gives greater weight to more current years, and lesser weight to earlier years, as delineated in "Determination of Weighted Averages," page 308.

Net income, or operating profit, is the arithmetic difference between revenues and expenses and is the financial indication of the firm's ability to operate successfully. Profits enable the firm to grow, reinvest in itself, reward its valuable contributors, and provide a return to the owners who have invested their money in the firm. In examining net income, it is important to adjust reported net income to properly account for profits that have been distributed in the form of bonuses, contributions to profit-sharing plans, additional principals' compensation, or other redistribution of profits earned. Examination of adjusted net income over a three- to five-year period will yield a picture of the profit earned by the firm and, by extension, what an informed buyer could reasonably expect it to earn in the future. As with net revenues, buyers and sellers who use net income as a basis for determining value generally use a weighted average that gives greater weight to more current years and lesser weight to earlier years. (See "Determination of Weighted Averages," page 308.)

Net worth (also called *book value*, *shareholders' equity*, or *partners' capital*) is the arithmetic difference between the firm's assets and liabilities, and represents the

TIP

It is essential to adjust reported net income to account for profits that have been distributed as bonuses, pension or profit-sharing plan contributions, or other redistributions of earnings.

CHECKLIST

Components of Value

The normal bases used to determine value are:

- Net revenues
- Net income
- Net worth

underlying value of what the owners own. Whereas the net revenue and net income components are used to give the prospective buyer a sense of potential future revenues and earnings streams, net worth is the monetary expression of the underlying value of the firm today, and permits both buyer and seller to consider the relationship between price and value. Unlike the use of net revenues and net income that record the firm's operations over a span of time, net worth is a picture of the firm's financial condition at a specific point in time and therefore does not require calculation of a weighted average.

Purposes of Valuation: How Valuation Is Used in the Ownership Transition Process

In establishing the value of a professional services firm, it is extremely important to understand that there are several values that can be calculated, depending on the condition of sale and the purpose for which value is determined—book value, liquidation value, value for purposes of internal sale as an ongoing entity, value for purposes of external sale as an ongoing entity, value for purposes of merger. In addition to the obvious need to establish value for internal or external ownership transfer, determination of value is frequently required for a marital settlement upon the divorce of an owner, estate settlement upon the death of an owner, formation and annual valuation of Employee Stock Ownership Plans, or the departure of an owner from the firm's employ, voluntarily or involuntarily.

Book value, often expressed as *net worth, shareholders' equity*, or *partners' capital*, is a common benchmark for valuation. Most firms have such a line item in their financial statements or can determine it easily. It is a representation of the entire financial position or condition of the firm, expressed as a single dollar amount that is the difference between the reported value of all the firm's assets (including accounts receivable) less its liabilities (including accounts payable and other payables). Book value is, in a sense, a snapshot of the firm's history distilled at a single point in time, usually at the end of a firm's fiscal year, and is often verified by a review or audit by the firm's outside certified public accountants.

Liquidation value is a figure that is lower than book value in most cases. It indicates the likely value that will be received for an entity that is not a going concern. It is usually lower than book value due to the owner's inability to obtain full value when disposing of assets.

In liquidation, the current owners are unwilling or unable to realize their value in the firm by selling their ownership interests to others, either within or outside the firm. Their remaining option is to cease operations and liquidate the company. In such circumstances, the owners attempt to recover the value of all assets and pay all liabilities, leaving the remaining worth at the time of liquidation for distribution among themselves. Ordinarily, the resulting value in such situations is generally less than the book value described in the preceding paragraph. There are at least two reasons:

1. A firm choosing such a course of action is rarely able to fully recover all its assets. It is typical that some receivables become uncollectible, and fixed assets are frequently unmarketable.

2. In addition, the firm becomes unable to complete work under contract and cease operations efficiently. Firms frequently incur both direct and indirect expenses relative to revenue that exceed the expenses that would have been incurred to complete such work if the firm had maintained normal operations. In a firm liquidation, it is not unusual to suffer a penalty in the range of 20 percent to 40 percent of accrual-basis book value, and sometimes even more.

Internal sale value is generally at or above book value. It acknowledges value beyond the balance sheet "net worth," and confirms the added value of a going concern to its owners. In an internal transfer, the current owners identify capable and qualified people in the firm who are willing to buy ownership interests from the current owners and participate in governing the firm with them. In unusual circumstances, candidates are given the opportunity to acquire the entire ownership interest and assume total responsibility for the firm immediately. In either circumstance, the firm will be maintained as an ongoing entity and will continue its operations. Because the buyer(s) will realize the financial benefit of the firm's reputation in the marketplace, will have access to the firm's backlog and current workload, and will usually benefit from the continued participation of the founders in marketing and management, they may pay a premium above book value. That premium—the amount that exceeds accrual-basis book value—may be understood as the value of the firm's "goodwill," which is rarely, if ever, reported on the books. The reality in the marketplace today is that prices paid in internal transfers are very close to book value. Normally, values for internal

TIP

Goodwill is rarely, if ever, reported on the financial statements.

sale range from 1.0 to 1.5 times accrual-basis book value, assuming reasonable capitalization and profitability, with one recent survey revealing an average multiple of 1.1.

TIP

In a good economy, values for internal sale can range from 1.0 to 1.5 times accrual-basis book value.

External sale value is generally higher than internal sale value, reflecting the fact that external buyers for various reasons—quick entry into a market, acquisition of a competitor, acquisition of wanted skills, access to more funding, and so on—are willing to place and pay higher value on the entity than internal buyers.

In an external sale, the current owners identify, or are identified by, an outside firm that is interested in acquiring the firm's clients, projects, people, financial assets, backlog, and access to market. In an external sale, the acquirer assumes responsibility for the selling firm's liabilities and ongoing operations, including its payroll and other normal operating expenses. In rare cases, the owners of a firm, recognizing the need for ownership transfer and lacking capable internal candidates, may acquire a firm that has more depth. Whether the firm is acquiring or being acquired, it is extremely rare for an external buyer to buy less than majority control of the firm; frequently the buyer wants to buy 100 percent of the ownership, not just majority control. Since the sellers are yielding control of their firm to the buyer, together with the financial and other benefits that are incident to such control, external sales usually provide a higher return to the sellers than internal transfers, if the sellers expect to depart relatively soon—that is, within three to five years. In a good economy, values for external sale can range from 1.5 to 3.0 times accrual-basis book value, again assuming reasonable capitalization and profit.

TIP

In a good economy, values for external sale can range from 1.5 to 3.0 times the accrual-basis net worth of the company.

Merger value, or value for the purposes of a merger of interests, is generally established at book value. Since the objective in a merger of interests is for the merging firms to pool their resources, the merging firms seek a way to establish a common financial basis to do so. Book value is one of the bases most commonly used.

Determining Value

Since value is determined in the marketplace as buyers and sellers come to terms on specific transfers, how do prospective buyers and sellers seeking to transfer ownership within a firm develop an understanding of the appropriate value that should apply to their specific situation?

Surveys. As previously mentioned, one way to determine value would be to refer to surveys to learn the values at which ownership in other, hopefully similar, firms was transferred. However, such research will only provide information about other situations that may or may not reflect one's own. One survey, the Zweig White & Associates Valuation Survey, includes several formulas for determining value that were derived from the data in the survey. (The Zweig-White Z3 Value, for example, includes factors for value per employee, value/net revenue, value/gross profit, value/book value, and value/backlog.) Owners interested in determining the value of their own firms can apply valuation formulas from such surveys to their own situation to get a rough idea of the value at which interests in their firm might be transferred.

Outside evaluation (or appraisal). When the valuation must be trusted by both sides and/or must withstand scrutiny and challenge, an expert can evaluate the firm for the purpose intended—that is, for internal transfer, merger, external sale, court proceeding, and so on, based on the condition of the marketplace and the specifics of the firm at that point in time. The process involves:

1. Understanding the details of the practice and how it compares to others in the marketplace.
2. Gathering and plotting the firm's financial history and the key indicators derived therefrom.
3. Calculating the value for the purpose described.

Methods of Determining Value

As previously indicated, there are two distinctly different markets for the acquisition of design firms: internal, through transfer to qualified candidates within the firm, and external, through merger with or acquisition by another firm. Since the objectives of internal and external buyers differ, they may choose different formulas for determining value. Although outside buyers may acquire firms for many reasons, they generally will expect a direct return on their investment. This tends to favor formulas based on a multiple of earnings, since future earnings are required to repay the investment. The sellers in such cases are making a one-time transaction and are giving up control, hence they frequently seek to maximize value.

Inside buyers are generally concerned with securing a continuing role in the firm and, especially, in its governance, rather than an immediate return on investment. Since sellers to inside buyers frequently stay active in the firm, while selling over a period of time, they tend to look at value in both present and future terms. This tends to favor a valuation method based on net worth. Compensation agreements also substantially affect internal valuation approaches.

The applicability of the methods discussed below and in the examples that follow depends on the specific circumstances for which the value is being established.

Multiple of Earnings (or Earnings Capitalization) Formula

The most common method of valuing conventional businesses is by a *multiple of earnings*, which projects a firm's future earnings based on its historical earnings. Average annual earnings for the most recent three- to five-year period are calculated and multiplied by a price/earnings ratio. In this approach, if a firm's net average earnings are determined to be, say, $100,000, a buyer paying a multiple of four times those earnings ($400,000) would expect to recover the $400,000 investment in four years. (Accountants and certain financial specialists use the term *capitalization rate*, which is the inverse of multiple of earnings, and which would be .25 in this example.)

TIP

Compensation agreements substantially affect internal valuations.

Such formulations work well in valuing publicly held businesses where profits and taxes are accounted on a consistent basis with other companies, and where there is a past history of similar buyers receiving similar returns on investment. Few privately held design firms calculate, or pay taxes on, profits in the conventional sense. In such firms, net income is distributed to owners annually in the form of compensation and bonuses. In addition, the owners of closely held firms can provide benefits and perquisites to owners that would otherwise be compensation or taxable profit.

In a valuation based on multiple of earnings, the earnings that would otherwise appear on the books must be adjusted to account for salaries paid to owners significantly over or under salaries paid in the marketplace for comparable responsibilities, exceptional perks, bonuses, and contributions to pension and profit-sharing plans, all of which can be considered distributions of profit. (As an example, compare the "Adjusted Income Statement (Accrual Basis) at December 31, 2000," on page 304 with that on page 300.)

In the current marketplace, valuations based on a multiple of earnings for the purpose of internal transfer range from 1.5 to 3.0 times weighted average adjusted net income, and 3.0 to 6.0 times weighted average adjusted net income for external transfers (outside sales).

Multiple of (Net) Revenues

Firms can be valued on the basis of a percentage of *net revenues*. This method allows buyer and seller to establish and agree on an easily identified financial basis. This method is particularly useful when the firm has had a record of marginal or irregular profitability up to the date of purchase. Perhaps more important, revenue-based valuations are generally less volatile (and less subject to manipulation) than valuations using other bases. Although it is possible to use gross revenues as the base, it has become conventional to use net revenues (net revenues = gross revenues minus amounts expensed for consultants and other nonsalary project expenses) because of the varying degrees to which design firms use and pay for consultants to execute the work. (As an example, see the "Income Statement (Accrual Basis) at December 31, 2000," on page 300.)

TIP

In a good economy, values for internal sale can range from .1 to .4 times weighted average net revenues.

In principle, the multiple of revenues method is similar to multiple of earnings, albeit with a different financial base. A firm earning a 10 percent profit on net revenues that is valued at four times earnings could also be valued at 40 percent of net revenues. The percentage of net revenues method tends to be fairer to incremental sales and/or estates, provided that all other factors of firm operation are basically consistent from year to year. The most appropriate application of the multiple of net revenues valuation method is the same as for multiple of earnings methods. In practice, the multiple of net revenues formulation facilitates arriving at a weighted average value to use as the basis for calculation, and has the advantage of not requiring restatement or adjustment of the base to arrive at a basis for the calculation, as is frequently the case when using a multiple of earnings.

In the current marketplace, valuation on the basis of a multiple of net revenues for internal transitions ranges from .1 to .4 times weighted average net revenues, and .2 to .8 times weighted average net revenues for external transfers.

Factored Book Value

Book value approaches to valuing a practice have the advantage of dealing with intrinsic worth, rather than with assumptions about future earnings or return on investment. This has a particular advantage in the presentation of an offer to a prospective buyer, because the price requested will have been based on the real, verifiable value of the firm. Furthermore, book value tends to reflect the cost of being in business, since it is largely made up of the working capital required to operate the firm. Book value, also called owner's equity or net worth, is a standard balance sheet number, and generally can be established with relative accounting ease and verified by the firm's certified public accountant. (As an example, see "Balance Sheet (Accrual Basis) at December 31, 2000," page 301.)

Whether looking at earnings, revenues, or worth, it is essential to look at accrual-basis accounts. As previously stated, accrual-basis accounts record revenues when they are *earned* regardless of receipts, and record expenses when they are *incurred*, regardless of when they are disbursed. This is especially important when looking at book value. In firms that are relatively stable with respect to volume and profit, cash-basis revenues and profits may approximate revenues and profits that are accounted on the accrual basis. That is never the case with book value, where accounts receivable (the value of work performed and billed, but not collected) and work in process (the value of work performed but not yet billed) can aggregate three to four months' billings. In essence, the accounts receivable and work in process plus the value of furniture, fixtures, and equipment (less corresponding payables and other liabilities), constitute the capital employed in the practice. If the volume of the practice grows, billings will grow, accounts receivable will grow, and so will the accrued book value of the firm (provided, of course, that there have been no extensive borrowings to finance the expansion). Since it is not necessary for design firms to keep more cash on hand than is needed for normal, ongoing operations, if business volume shrinks, receivables will be collected in due course and excess cash not needed to fund operations can be distributed as additional compensation or expensed in some other way. Again, the accrued book value represents the new, diminished scale of the practice.

Another important consideration in calculating book-value-based valuations is in the handling of the liability for deferred federal income taxes (defined as the taxes that the firm would pay if it recorded taxable income on the accrual basis of accounting, less the amount actually paid on the cash basis of accounting). In preparing (corporate) financial statements, accounting rules require recording as a liability on the balance sheet the value of corporate income tax that the owners would pay if they liquidated the firm and collected its receivables. Since it is almost always the case that the owners would distribute such receipts as compensation that would be deductible as a business expense of the firm and on which they would pay personal income tax, the line item for deferred federal income tax represents a liability that would likely never be paid in an ongoing concern, and therefore is often added back to book value to create a pretax net worth for valuation purposes. As an example, see "Adjusted Balance Sheet (Accrual Basis) at December 31, 2000," page 305.

Thus, the most significant advantage of valuations based on book value is that, all other things being equal, they accurately reflect the net cost of being in business. The limitation of valuations based strictly on book value is that they do not make allowances for over- or undercapitalization or for profitability, especially when there is "goodwill"—such as ongoing client relationships, expertise, reputation in the marketplace, or other factors that can be expected to provide continuing business to the firm. Since any premium over book value can be understood to connote goodwill, a common, and useful, way to address the matter of goodwill is to apply a multiplier. In the current economy, valuation for internal transition based on book value ranges from 1.00 to 1.50, with 1.25 times accrual-basis book value being quite common. In the current economy, valuation for external transition based on book value ranges from 2.0 to 3.0 times accrual-basis book value.

To help you understand the financial and related numerical information that follows, we have created a hypothetical firm, XYZ Design, to which we will refer throughout the text.

CASE STUDY

XYZ Design, PC

XYZ Design is a 20-year-old, 20-person firm located in a medium-sized Midwest city. Founded by Frank Young and Frances Zimmer, who are currently 55 and 50 years old, respectively, and who were raised and schooled in the city, the firm has developed a regional practice serving healthcare and related institutions in the city and in the towns that fall within a 90-mile radius. Devoted to providing superior client service and excellent, but not cutting-edge, design, the firm gets the great majority of its commissions via repeat work and referrals from satisfied clients, and about 20 percent through proactive marketing. The firm is organized as a professional corporation in which the principals have assumed the primary responsibility for design, marketing, and overall firm management, and have delegated substantial project management and production responsibilities to employees. At the end of 2000, the firm's income statement and balance sheet appeared as shown in "Income Statement (Accrual Basis) at December 31, 2000," page 300, and "Balance Sheet (Accrual Basis) at December 31, 2000," page 301. A summary of key values for the firm's most recent four years' operations is shown in "Abbreviated Financial Statement," page 306.

Income Statement (accrual basis) at December 31, 2000

Revenues	
Gross Revenue	$3,200,000
(Consultant Expense)	(900,000)
(Other Direct Expense)	(100,000)
Net Revenue	$2,200,000
Expenses	
Direct Salary Expense	$750,000
Indirect Salary Expense	600,000
Other Indirect Expense	775,000
Total Indirect Expense	1,375,000
Operating Profit	$75,000
Key Indicators (before adjustments)	
Payroll Utilization Rate	.56
Operating Profit/Net Revenue	.03
Overhead Ratio	1.83
Net Revenue/Direct Salary Expense	2.93

Scenario 1: Internal Transition

Although they are able to operate the firm comfortably at its principal-to-staff ratio of 1:9, Frank and Frances, the owners of XYZ Design, have begun to look ahead to the possibility of retiring in 10 to 15 years. Frank would like to begin selling his stock now, while Frances is not yet ready to begin selling down. They have identified two key staff members, Andrew and Barbara, with whom they work effectively and comfortably. Frank and Frances hope these two will be able to run the firm successfully, and so have decided to consider them as candidates to buy interests in the firm.

Balance Sheet (accrual basis) at December 31, 2000

Assets		
Current Assets		
Cash	$10,000	
Accounts Receivable	800,000	
Work in Process	40,000	
Prepaid Expenses	10,000	
Total Current Assets	$860,000	
Fixed Assets		
Furniture & Equipment	$90,000	
(Depreciation)	(50,000)	
Leasehold Improvements	50,000	
(Amortization)	(30,000)	
Net Fixed Assets	$60,000	
Total Assets		$92,000
Liabilities		
Current Liabilities		
Note Payable—Credit Line	$50,000	
Note Payable—FF&E (Current)	10,000	
Accounts Payable—Consultants	250,000	
Accounts Payable—Trade	20,000	
Accrued Salaries and Expenses	30,000	
Total Current Liabilities	$360,000	
Long-Term Liabilities		
Note Payable—Long-Term Portion	$80,000	
Deferred Federal Income Tax	50,000	
Total Long-Term Liabilities	$130,000	
Total Liabilities		$490,000
Owners' Equity (NW)	$430,000	
Key Indicators		
Average Collection Period (Days)	90	
Working Capital	$500,000	
Required Working Capital @ Collection Rate × Net Revenue	$550,000	

Frank and Frances retained a management consultant to assist them in developing an ownership transition program, in collaboration with the firm's attorney and accountant. They asked the consultant to help them understand: (a) the value of the firm for the purpose of internal transfer; (b) the way in which the value can be made affordable to Andrew and Barbara; and (c) the other considerations that must be addressed in order to present a reasonable offer to the candidates.

The consultant met with the owners to discuss their goals and objectives for the transition and their expectations regarding value, to learn about the firm's management and operations, and to gather existing ownership and financial documents that he knew would be required to do the work. The consultant informed the owners that he would employ the following approach to determine valuation:

1. Consider three methods: multiple of net revenue, multiple of adjusted net income (profit before distributions and taxes), and multiple of adjusted net worth.
2. Choose the most recent three- to five-year period and ascertain that the firm has not gone through major structural changes—such as mergers or acquisitions—because there is a reasonable likelihood of there being changes in the economic cycle within that time frame.
3. Develop weighted averages for revenues and income.
4. Apply multipliers, the ranges for which are based on empirical data for ownership transfer in privately held design firms that are available through consultation and research.

5. Develop specific multipliers within each range by developing a "Profile Factor" for the firm to convert qualitative assessments into quantitative terms by comparing the firm's operations with others.
6. Examine and evaluate the results and reach a tentative conclusion.
7. Test the conclusion for affordability. Construct alternate scenarios to ascertain that the transfer is affordable at the calculated value, and can be reasonably achieved.

The consultant compiled the firm's financial data for the most recent four years and displayed them in the form of income statement and balance sheet summaries with key financial indicators.

He then adjusted the firm's income statements to reflect the value of profits that had been distributed and expensed as bonuses and as a contribution to the firm's profit-sharing plan. An example of the

Worst-Case Scenario

Two owners of a Mid-Atlantic engineering firm wanted to extend ownership to two key engineers in the firm. They engaged a consultant to help them understand the value that might apply and how ownership could be transferred. The consultant's review of the firm's current balance sheet and income statements revealed that the firm had positive net worth, but had been operating at marginal profitability levels for the past few years. Although reasonable values could be established based on the firm's net worth and net revenues, without a significant change in the firm's operations, the prospective buyers would be unable to pay for what they committed to buy. The owners decided to defer any transition until they could operate more profitably.

adjustment is shown below in the "Adjusted Income Statement (Accrual Basis) at December 31, 2000."

Adjusted Income Statement (accrual basis) at December 31, 2000

Revenues	
Gross Revenue	$3,200,000
(Consultant Expense)	(900,000)
(Other Direct Expense)	(100,000)
Net Revenue	$2,200,000
Expenses	
Direct Salary Expense	$750,000
Indirect Salary Expense	600,000
Other Indirect Expense	775,000
Total Indirect Expense	$1,375,000
Operating Profit	$75,000
Adjustments	
Owners' Salaries Over-/Undermarket	$ 0
Bonuses to Principals and Staff	150,000
Profit Sharing Plan Contribution	50,000
Total Adjustments	$200,000
Adjusted Income	$275,000
Key Indicators (after adjustments)	
Utilization Rate	.625
Operating Profit/Net Revenue	.125
Overhead Ratio	1.57
Net Revenue/Direct Salary Expense	2.93

Adjusted Balance Sheet (accrual basis) at December 31, 2000

Assets		
Current Assets		
Cash	$10,000	
Accounts Receivable	800,000	
Work in Process	40,000	
Prepaid Expenses	10,000	
Total Current Assets	$860,000	
Fixed Assets		
Furniture & Equipment	$90,000	
(Depreciation)	(50,000)	
Leasehold Improvements	50,000	
(Amortization)	(30,000)	
Net Fixed Assets	$60,000	
Total Assets		$920,000
Liabilities		
Current Liabilities		
Note Payable—Credit Line	$50,000	
Note Payable—FF&E (Current)	10,000	
Accounts Payable—Consultants	250,000	
Accounts Payable—Trade	20,000	
Accrued Salaries and Expenses	30,000	
Total Current Liabilities	$360,000	
Long-Term Liabilities		
Note Payable—Long-Term Portion	$80,000	
Deferred Federal Income Tax	50,000	
Total Long-Term Liabilities	$130,000	
Total Liabilities	$490,000	
Owner's Equity (NW)	$430,000	
Adjustment for Deferred Federal Income Tax	50,000	
Adjusted Net Worth		$480,000
Key indicators		
Average Collection Period (Days)	90	
Working Capital	$500,000	
Required Working Capital @ Collection Rate × Net Revenue	$550,000	

Abbreviated Financial Statement

	2000	1999	1998	1997
Gross Revenues	$3,200,000	$2,800,000	$2,500,000	$2,750,000
Net Revenues	2,200,000	1,900,000	1,650,000	1,600,000
Adjusted Income	275,000	228,000	173,250	160,000
Adjusted Net Worth	480,000	460,000	400,000	420,000

The consultant also adjusted the firm's balance sheets to add back to Net Worth the value of Deferred Federal Income Tax that was recorded as a liability in accordance with standard accounting practice but that is not a liability that will come due and be payable, as long as the firm continues as an ongoing concern (as described on page 298). An example of the adjustment is shown in "Adjusted Balance Sheet (Accrual Basis) at December 31, 2000," page 305.

The "Abbreviated Financial Statement," prepared by the consultant is shown above.

Using the data for XYZ Design's most recent four years, the consultant calculated the weighted average net revenue and weighted average adjusted net income. He chose a weighting mechanism that recognized the importance of the current status of the firm, and placed a constant diminishing emphasis on each year in the past on a uniform basis. One such example using a constantly descending series is determined by the formula:

$$\sum_{0}^{n} x^{n} = 1.00.$$

Application of the formula to the number of years being considered produces the table of values shown in "Weighting Constants," page 307, and used in "Determination of Weighted Averages," page 308. Each year in the series bears a uniform ratio in its relative importance to the preceding year, the effect of which is a series whose sum is unity (1.00).

Applying the weighting factors shown below in "Weighting Constants," the consultant calculated the weighted average net revenues and weighted average adjusted income for the last four years, as shown in "Determination of Weighted Averages," page 308.

Understanding that the reasonable ranges for internal ownership transfers in the current marketplace ranged from .1 to .4 times Weighted Average Net Revenues, 1.5 to 3.0 times Weighted Average Adjusted Income, and 1.0 to 1.5 times Adjusted Net Worth, the consultant developed the "XYZ Design Profile Factor" for the firm, as shown on page 309, to determine where the value for XYZ Design should fall within the reasonable range.

Weighting Constants

	Number of Years					
Ratios for each year	**1**	**2**	**3**	**4**	**5**	**6**
1st Year	1.00	.618	.544	.518	.509	.504
2nd Year		.382	.296	.268	.259	.254
3rd Year			.160	.139	.132	.128
4th Year				.072	.067	.065
5th Year					.034	.033
6th Year						.016

Profile Factor

Using information obtained from and about the firm, the consultant assessed the firm's operations and condition and developed a Profile Factor to convert the assessment into numerical terms, as described in the following table. Note that the rating

Determination of Weighted Averages

Determination of Weighted Average Net Revenues

Year	Net Revenue	Weighting Factor	Weighted Net Revenue
2001	$2,200,000	.52	$1,144,000
2000	1,900,000	.27	513,000
1999	1,650,000	.14	231,000
1998	1,600,000	.07	112,000
	Weighted Average	1.00	$2,000,000

Determination of Weighted Average Adjusted Income

Year	Adjusted Net Income	Weighting Factor	Weighted Adjusted Income
2001	$275,000	.52	$143,000
2000	228,000	.27	1,560
1999	173,250	.14	4,255
1998	160,000	.07	1,200
	Weighted Average	1.00	$240,015

Worst-Case Scenario

The sole proprietor of a 10-person consulting firm wanted to reduce his efforts in the firm's interest over a few years by offering to sell the firm to his most senior employee. He met with an attorney, who did not have significant experience in dealing with design professionals, in general, nor in ownership transition in design firms, in particular. The proprietor related his objectives, and described the firm's clients, staff, and capabilities, and its annual revenues, which approached $1,000,000. Based on that information, the attorney prepared a Term Sheet that established the firm's value at $1,000,000, which the prospective buyer was expected to pay over 10 years, after which he would own the firm. The proprietor presented the Term Sheet to the candidate without other information or discussion. The offer was rejected.

XYZ Design Profile Factor

Category	*Subrating*	*Rating*
Business Development		
. . . systems & organization	3.0	
. . . market strength	3.0	
. . . reputation	2.5	
. . . diversification of client base (one market, broad geography)	2.0	
. . . diversification of selling base	2.0	2.50
Project Delivery		
. . . quality of projects & service	3.5	
. . . technology application	2.5	
. . . senior staff involvement (principals control)	2.0	2.67
Human Resources		
. . . turnover level	3.0	
. . . quality of staff	2.5	
. . . training & development	2.0	
. . . culture	2.5	2.50
Financial Performance		
. . . profitability	2.5	
. . . current financial indicators	2.5	
. . . financial stability	2.0	2.33
Leadership & Management (beyond principals)		
. . . capability and quality	2.5	
. . . strength of second tier	2.0	
. . . commitment to transition	3.0	2.50
Average of All Ratings		2.50
PROFILE FACTOR: (2.50/5.00)		0.50

*

EXPLANATION

In a prototypical firm of average profit and generally average rating with respect to the criteria on which the Profile Factor is based, values determined in each of the three methods will coincide; variances from average in most real situations give different results among the three; these results are then analyzed and combined as appropriate to yield a tentative conclusion.

in the Profile Factor can range from 0 to 5, with 0 representing an assessment of "very poor," 3 being average (a routinely modestly successful firm), and

5 being exceptionally strong. (It is very rare for a 0 or a 5 to appear in the development of a Profile Factor.)

Using the Profile Factor, the consultant calculated the valuation for internal transfer based on each of the three methods, as follows:

1. Multiple of Net Revenue

Concept: Apply a multiple, determined by applying the Profile Factor to the range of net revenue multiples at which design firms like XYZ Design transfer ownership, to the weighted average net revenue for the last four years.

Formula:

$$V_{NR} = \{\text{Base} + [\text{Profile Factor} \times (\text{Range})]\} \times (\text{Wtd. Avg. Net Revenue})$$

Range for internal sales: 0.1 to 0.4
Weighted average net revenue: \$2,000,000
Calculation for internal valuation:

$$V_{NR} = \{0.1 + [0.50 \times (0.4 - 0.1)]\} \times \$2{,}000{,}000 = \$500{,}000$$

2. Multiple of Earnings

Concept: Apply a multiple, determined by applying the Profile Factor to the range of earnings (adjusted income) multiples at which design and planning firms transfer ownership, to the weighted average adjusted net income for the last four years.

Formula:

$$V_E = \{\text{Base} + [\text{Profile Factor} \times (\text{Range})]\} \times (\text{Wtd. Avg. Adjusted Net Income})$$

Range for internal sales: 1.5 to 3.0
Weighted average adjusted income: \$240,000

Calculation for internal valuation:

$$V_E = \{1.5 + [0.50 \times (3.0 - 1.5)] \times \$240{,}000$$
$$= \$540{,}000$$

3. Multiple of Net Worth

Concept: Apply a multiple, determined by applying the Profile Factor to the range of net worth multiples at which design and planning firms transfer ownership, to the current accrual basis net worth, adjusted to reflect factors such as deferred income taxes, if any.
Formula:

$$V_{NW} = \{\text{Base} + [\text{Profile Factor} \times (\text{Range})]\} \times (\text{Adjusted Net Worth})$$

Range for internal sales: 1.0 to 1.5
Adjusted net worth at 12/31/99: \$480,000
Calculation for internal valuation:

$$V_{NW} = \{1.0 + [0.50 \times (1.5 - 1.0)]\} \times \$480{,}000$$
$$= \$600{,}000$$

Having learned from the owners that they wanted to realize a modest premium on book value, and having tested the value for affordability (see Chapter 17, "Making the Purchase Affordable: Ownership Transfer Mechanisms"), the consultant recommended that an appropriate value for the purpose of internal ownership transfer would be \$600,000, formulated as a multiple of 1.25 times the firm's accrual-basis book value.

Scenario 2: Merger

Although they have been able to operate the firm quite comfortably at its current principal-to-staff ratio of 1:9, Frank and Frances, the owners of XYZ

Design, have begun to look ahead to the possibility of retiring from ownership in 5 to 10 years. Although they have an extremely supportive staff with whom they work effectively and comfortably, they are *not* confident that any of them will be able to contribute to the firm at an ownership level, run the firm successfully, and eventually buy them out.

However, a recent opportunity presented itself. XYZ Design had participated in a joint venture relationship on a project with another, somewhat smaller firm, Design Group, Inc., a 10-person firm with net revenues of $1,000,000 and a book value of $240,000. In the course of working together on the project, the owners of XYZ Design began to think that merging with Design Group might not only improve the firm's competitiveness in the marketplace with respect to obtaining clients and executing projects, but might provide the future leadership they thought would be required for them to retire gracefully. The owners of Design Group indicated their receptivity to considering a merger.

The firms exchanged ownership, financial, marketing, project, administrative, and other documents. The principals of both firms met several times and compared many aspects of their practices, including:

- Goals and objectives for the future
- Roles and responsibilities
- Clients and projects
- Marketing organization and process
- Firm organization and governance
- Staffing and salaries
- Project structure and process
- Financial condition and operations
- Administrative policies and procedures

The principals of both firms sought reactions to the prospect of merger with several clients and other influential people and concluded that a merger would probably be well received. Having already learned that they worked well together, they decided that a merger would likely be successful and would give them all a better platform from which to realize their personal objectives for the future. They agreed that if they could work out the financial exchange, there were no other "deal-breakers." After reviewing their plans with their respective accountants and attorneys, they decided to proceed on the basis of a *merger of interests*.

In a merger of interests, little or no cash is exchanged. Each firm contributes its assets and liabilities to create a new firm that combines the assets and liabilities of both. In the case of XYZ Design and Design Group, XYZ Design contributed its $480,000 book value, and Design Group contributed its $240,000 book value, creating a new, larger firm with a book value of $720,000 in which each original owner owned exactly the same value after the merger as before. The owners of XYZ Design had equally owned 100 percent of the firm's $480,000 net worth, or $240,000 each, and the owner of Design Group owned 100 percent of his firm's $240,000 net worth. After the merger, the two former owners of XYZ Design would own $480,000—two-thirds of $720,000—or $240,000 each, and the former owner of Design Group would own one-third of $720,000, or $240,000.

Although it was not necessary in this case, in certain circumstances it may become necessary for firms entering into a merger to make modest value adjustments in their respective values if there is a material difference in their ratios of net worth to net revenues, which would reflect differences in their capability to produce revenues on their respective capital bases.

Scenario 3: Acquisition by Others

Architects & Engineers, Inc. (A&E), a larger firm that was active in the same institutional markets as XYZ Design, and familiar with its clients and projects, approached the owners of XYZ Design and asked if they would consider an affiliation. The owners of XYZ Design thought that a relationship with A&E might provide an opportunity to work on larger, more challenging projects, might make them more competitive for the kinds of projects they already sought, and might provide a better exit strategy for themselves. They responded positively and met with representatives of A&E, who described their interest as being one of acquisition to facilitate their firm's geographic expansion into areas in which XYZ Design was traditionally strong. They had learned enough about XYZ Design to surmise that the owners might have difficulty in achieving an internal transition soon enough to meet their financial objectives in the relatively limited time remaining before their intended retirements, and therefore might be receptive to an offer that would provide a different exit strategy.

A&E's CEO met with the XYZ Design owners to discuss A&E's interest and present information about his firm. Among other things, they discussed:

- A&E's firmwide organization and how XYZ Design would fit within it.
- XYZ Design's owners' roles and responsibilities in the A&E organization and on projects.

- How XYZ Design's staff would be integrated into the firm.
- How XYZ Design's clients would be maintained.

The XYZ Design owners were sufficiently interested in the possibility of acquisition by A&E to be willing to provide additional information about their firm. After A&E signed a confidentiality agreement restricting its disclosure and use of information provided by XYZ Design, its representatives were given a comprehensive information package, including information about XYZ Design's clients, projects, prospects, staff, and finances. A&E thoroughly reviewed the documentation, and asked for and was given answers to specific questions that arose during their examination. A&E analyzed XYZ Design's financial operations and condition to determine the price that A&E would be willing to pay and at which A&E thought the owners of XYZ Design might be willing to sell. Based on A&E's past history in acquiring firms, their understanding that the XYZ Design owners would be ceding control of the firm, and their knowledge of the marketplace, A&E offered to buy 100 percent of XYZ Design for $1,200,000, on a *pretax* basis, in an exchange that would involve an asset purchase plus elevated compensation for the selling owners. "The Buyer's Value Analysis," page 316, demonstrates A&E's analysis.

Having done their own analysis, the XYZ Design owners considered $1,200,000 to be a fair price, but only if it were paid as an *after-tax* stock purchase. However, understanding that the purchase would be more affordable to A&E on a pretax basis, and therefore more likely to be consummated, Frank and Frances agreed to accept an acquisition based on an asset purchase plus elevated compensation, but only

Buyer's Value Analysis

Assumptions

Average Net Revenue:	$2,000,000	
Average Net Income	240,000	
Net Worth	480,000	
Valuation @ 2.5 × NW	$1,200,000	
	Capital Transaction	*Cash + Extended Compensation*
100% value	$1,200,000	$1,200,000
Purchase		
Buyer pays	1,200,000 for stock	240,000 for fixed assets
Buyer owes	0	960,000 as compensation
Buyer's tax cost @ 25%	300,000	60,000
	1,500,000	1,260,000
Profit Distribution		
Buyer earns per year	240,000	240,000
Buyer pays seller	0	240,000 per year for 4 years
Buyer's payback	6.25 years	5.25 years, including initial payment

if the value could be increased by 20 percent to $1,440,000. By so doing, A&E would be able to save $225,000 in taxes, and Frank and Frances, the sellers, would realize the same net gain that they would in an after-tax stock purchase. Their analysis appeared as shown in "Seller's Value Analysis," page 317.

The XYZ Design owners presented the counter-offer to A&E's representatives, who accepted it. The principals negotiated the specifics of a *Memorandum of Understanding* (sometimes called a *Term Sheet*) that

Seller's Value Analysis

	Capital Transaction	*Cash + Deferred Compensation*
100% value	$1,200,000	$1,500,000
Purchase		
Buyer pays at close	1,200,000 for stock	300,000 for fixed assets
Buyer owes	0	1,200,000 as compensation
Buyer's tax cost @ 25%	300,000	75,000
Buyer's total cost	1,500,000	1,575,000
Profit Distribution		
Buyer earns per year	240,000	240,000
Buyer pays seller	0	240,000
Buyer's payback	6.25 years	6.6 years, including initial payment
Sale		
Sellers receive	1,200,000	300,000
Sellers' capital gains tax @ 20%	(240,000)	(60,000)
Sellers' net	960,000	240,000
Sellers' additional compensation	0	1,200,000 over 5 years
Sellers' income tax @ 40%	0	(480,000)
Sellers' net	0	720,000
Sellers' total net for sale	$ 960,000	$ 960,000

documented their agreement (subject to corroboration of facts through a due-diligence examination) with respect to:

- Price to be paid
- Method and schedule of payment
- Settlement date
- Offers of employment to XYZ Design's staff

Worst-Case Scenario

As they approached normal retirement age, but continued their marketing and project responsibilities, the founders of a large landscape architecture and planning firm brought a group of key second-generation designers and managers into ownership by selling a small number of shares at reasonable values and on reasonable terms. The second-generation owners continued to exercise their project responsibilities, while gradually beginning to assume marketing and firmwide management responsibilities, although the time they had to do the latter was limited.

As the founders got closer to retirement, they lacked the confidence that the second-generation owners would be able to run the firm successfully by themselves, and therefore would be unable to buy the balance of the founders' equity. The buyers themselves shared some of this lack of confidence. At about the same time that the owners decided to consider selling to a larger firm (hopefully, a firm with which their planning and landscape capabilities would be complementary, and one that proved to be a good cultural fit), such a firm approached them with identical objectives. A consultant assisted both firms in assessing the likelihood of success for the acquisition, and in understanding how to accomplish the merger. The firms negotiated and agreed on the conditions that would apply, including price, payment terms, roles, responsibilities, and compensation for key individuals. The day before the agreements were to be signed, the buying firm was itself purchased by an even larger, publicly owned firm, and the deal fell apart.

- Due-diligence period and content
- Announcements to staff, clients, the profession, and the public
- XYZ Design principals' ownership position in A&E
- XYZ Design principals' terms of employment
- XYZ Design principals' roles and responsibilities
- XYZ Design principals' compensation and benefits
- Bonuses related to achievement of agreed-upon performance measures

The A&E and XYZ Design principals executed the Memorandum of Understanding and proceeded with the due diligence necessary to assure themselves that the data presented during the negotiations were factual.

Extenuating Circumstances and Exceptions

The essential data on which valuation determinations are made are financial. The data are reported in two financial documents: the firm's Income Statement and Balance Sheet. But the determination of value depends on and assumes other conditions, as well, some of which are not reported in the financial statements. At the very least, these include ongoing operations, reasonable capitalization, normal backlog, and continued participation of the key people.

There are conditions and situations that serve as red flags for a buyer, suggesting that the valuation should be reexamined and adjusted, as appropriate. They include:

- Over- or undercapitalization
- Unusual backlog, under or over the norm of other firms in the same market and relative to the firm's own history

- Ongoing litigation
- Pending liability matters and insurance concerns
- Real estate or other assets with market values exceeding book value
- Under- or overinvestment in technology
- Unusual operational procedures
- Unusual staff turnover
- Disadvantaged, women, or minority business enterprise (DBE, WBE, or MBE) status

Over- or Undercapitalization

Most professional design firms attempt to operate with sufficient working capital so that the firm's operations and capital growth needs can be funded without the need for additional capital infusion, but also without maintaining excess cash balances. Generally, an appropriate balance can be struck if the firm monitors its collection rate carefully and is profitable at a level that permits it to reward its investors and performers, as well as retain sufficient monies to fund desired capital investment and growth.

A firm that is undercapitalized will not have sufficient working capital to fund ongoing operations and desired capital investment and growth. In such circumstances, a buyer considering a partial or total purchase of the firm would quickly observe that some or all of the firm's future earnings would be needed to increase working capital levels and would not be available for distribution to the owners. The informed prospective buyer would therefore likely discount the value of the firm by an amount that accurately reflected the capital insufficiency.

On the other hand, the selling firm may have retained more cash than it needs to operate, building the firm's value rather than paying out profits currently. In this circumstance, the firm's future earnings will likely be available for distribution, but its current value may be unattractive or unaffordable, especially if the seller is seeking a multiple of accrual-basis book value.

Backlog

Backlog, which is the sum of revenues that are contracted for but not yet earned, rarely appears on financial statements, yet is extremely significant. Because the firm is constantly working off backlog, no professional service firm can exist without it nor continue for very long without filling the pipeline. It normally takes several months from the date services are performed to receive the cash represented by those services. Therefore, firms try to maintain backlog levels representing several months' net revenues to maintain a constant flow of revenues.

A prospective buyer of a firm with below-normal backlog amounts would be legitimately concerned about that firm's prospective revenues and would likely reduce his or her estimate of the firm's value. Conversely, a firm with backlog amounts that substantially exceed the norm usually presents a significant benefit to the buyer. Assuming the firm has, or can develop, the capacity to deliver the services required, strong backlog amounts predict strong future revenues—a benefit that the seller is well advised to take into account in considering the value of the firm.

TIP

Consider a future royalty or similar earn-out arrangement to compensate the seller if the firm is likely to benefit from circumstances that cannot be guaranteed or even accounted for at the time of the sale.

What about the value of work that has been marketed and for which a preliminary commitment has been expressed, but not yet contracted? The actual execution of a contract for the work would substantially increase the firm's value to a prospective buyer. Yet because there is no certainty that the contract will actually be signed and that services will be performed, a buyer would probably balk at increasing the firm's value based on that possibility. One reasonable solution that can compensate the seller appropriately without penalizing the buyer is to structure a royalty to be paid to the seller if and when the firm realizes this type of revenue after a transition has occurred.

Litigation

Firms occasionally learn of project circumstances that have the potential to negatively affect the firm's finances. Sometimes these circumstances result in a liability claim; sometimes they do not. If the firm is uncertain about the potential liability, it may choose not to report it at all.

When outside accountants are engaged to prepare financial statements, whether by compilation, review, or audit, they usually ask if there are any matters, such as pending or threatened litigation, that could impact the firm. If a specific liability has been identified, the accountant may choose to record that liability on the firm's balance sheet. If the specific amount of a liability is unknown, however, it cannot be recorded as a liability, but may be found to be deserving of a note to the statements.

Prospective buyers are advised to examine the firm's financial statements for unusual liabilities or notes to the financial statements that would suggest the presence of future events with potentially negative consequences. Buyers should also look beyond the balance sheet: Ask the seller for lists of pending claims and actions; question the seller about current threats and disputes; and get assurance that no such liabilities exist.

Real Estate

Many design professionals have learned that monies spent in rental costs and leasehold improvements would be better spent if instead of renting spaces they purchased a building or condominium office space and leased the space to their firms. Because the tax benefits of real estate ownership flow through to proprietors or partners differently from corporate shareholders, design professionals who practice in corporate entities and who purchase real estate, frequently establish separate entities, usually partnerships, to own the real estate, both to shield the real estate from creditors of the service firm and for financial and tax reasons, as well. In such cases, the assets and liabilities of their practices will look very different from those of practices that do not own real estate. For example, if the real estate asset has been largely or fully depreciated and is free and clear of any corresponding liabilities, such as mortgages, it may be substantially undervalued relative to its real value in the marketplace. In any case, both buyer and seller should either segregate the ownership of any real estate from ownership of the practice or ensure that its real value is properly accounted for in the valuation of the practice.

Prospective buyers should request copies of titles for all real property owned, as well as copies of leases and related obligations for leased space.

TIP
Except in rare circumstances, it is better to keep ownership of real estate, even real estate used for the company's operations, outside the practice.

Technology

It was only a decade ago that a design practice could be initiated with little more than the apocryphal sawhorses, hollow-core door, and T-square. With the advent and proliferation of computerization, design practices require more initial investment, and reinvestment, in technology to remain viable. Currently, such investment is on the order of $3,000 to $5,000 per person, per year. Firms that have not kept up with the need to remain technologically competitive in hardware, software, and training are likely to require extraordinary infusions of capital or, in the alternative, increased levels of debt, to restore the firm to an appropriate level of technological competence.

In evaluating a practice, a buyer should determine whether the firm has kept pace with technological innovations in the field and assess whether, as a consequence, the evaluation should be adjusted. Additionally, the prospective buyer should assure that required licensing agreements for hardware and software are in place, as well as any arrangements for technology sharing or communications.

Operational Procedures

Occasionally, a firm will develop practices, processes, or procedures that give it an edge in competing with others for work. When that practice, process, or procedure is proprietary, the firm can enjoy a healthier financial return than its competitors. The procedure may involve inside knowledge of a client's business, a particularly efficient method of addressing a client's problem, or a firmwide practice that allows it to operate more efficiently regardless of the client type. In rare cases, the procedure may have characteristics that make it applicable to a wide range of conditions, and therefore marketable to others.

The buyer should understand the way the firm operates and determine whether it is employing any unusual procedures that would tend to increase (or decrease) its value in the marketplace.

Turnover

Design practice has become more technologically intensive, but it remains heavily labor-intensive. It is dependent on the people who do the work, whether with computers or without, and the firm incurs its greatest operating expense to pay their salaries. It is not too simplistic to say that without competent professional, technical, clerical, and administrative staff who are experienced in the firm's processes and procedures, the firm will be unable to work efficiently and effectively.

Employees leave from time to time for personal or professional reasons; this is understandable and, up to a certain point, tolerable. However, high turnover rates are usually indicative of a problem of some kind within the firm. Therefore, the appraiser or buyer encountering this phenomenon should look behind the numbers to learn what causes the unusual turnover rate and whether it is likely to inhibit the firm's ability to practice effectively in the future.

Minority Status

As a consequence of governmental action to redress prior discrimination against cultural, racial, and gender minorities, various local, state, and federal agencies have legislated set-asides for firms whose controlling owners are members of a disadvantaged group: minority-owned business enterprises (MBEs), women-owned business enterprises (WBEs), or disadvantaged business enterprises (DBEs). Identification and registration as one of these categories does not guarantee a revenue stream for the firm.

Nevertheless, as a consequence of the set-asides, these businesses can gain a competitive advantage in certain markets, primarily on public sector projects. Accordingly, the appraiser or buyer should ascertain whether the firm is minority-owned and registered, whether it has availed itself of the special considerations for such firms, whether it has received any benefit from this special status, whether it is likely to do so in the future, and whether the acquisition will affect the status.

The essential work in establishing a firm's value is a function of basic financial indicators and relationships, especially net revenues, profitability (earnings), and accrual-basis book value (net worth). However, other conditions that are not necessarily reported in the Balance Sheet or Income Statement have the potential to dramatically affect the firm's well-being and, ultimately, value. The appraiser or buyer must be sure to take these conditions into account, not only to present an honest appraisal and estimate of the particular practice, but also to present an opinion that reflects the evaluator's good-faith estimate of the value at which the firm is likely to change hands.

Making the Purchase Affordable: Ownership Transfer Mechanisms

17

Firms whose principals are contemplating ownership transition are sometimes faced with the problem that the high value of the firm based on the firm's net worth leads to a high purchase price for the buyer—a price that is unaffordable without assistance of some kind. If the firm assists the buyer to facilitate the purchase, then the firm may need to provide unusually high levels of compensation to the buyer (either in base salary or profit) to enable the buyer to have sufficient funds for the purchase, after paying income taxes on the compensation. The problem is exacerbated when the firm has had, and/or anticipates, low levels of profitability.

This chapter discusses several alternative strategies that may be employed by firms to make the purchase of an ownership interest more affordable to candidates, and therefore more likely to be achieved.

After-Tax Transaction for Stock

Assume that a firm practicing in a corporate form intends to transfer ownership internally, with an initial transfer of 10 percent of the value of the firm to a new owner. Referring to XYZ Design, after the firm's consultant calculated the value of the firm for the purpose of internal transfer (as described in Chapter 16), he made assumptions regarding XYZ Design's financial future from the weighted averages already developed, and used those assumptions as a basis for determining the methods by which the value could be transferred from the sellers to the buyer, as shown in "Internal Transfer Mechanisms," opposite.

TIP

The purchase price must be affordable to the buyer. If it is not, the buyer or buyers will probably opt not to buy and no transfer will occur.

If, as indicated, the value of 100 percent of the firm for purposes of internal transfer were $600,000, then the value of a 10 percent interest would be $60,000. In a transfer structured as an after-tax stock purchase, a candidate offered a 10 percent interest in the firm would pay $60,000. That buyer might use his or her own funds, borrow some or all of the amount required for purchase, or perhaps be permitted by the seller to pay a down payment and sign a promissory note for the balance.

Having become an owner of the firm, the 10 percent buyer would become entitled to his or her 10 percent share of the firm's (assumed future) profit of $200,000, or $20,000, that became available for distribution to the owners. The firm would write a bonus check in that amount. Assuming local, state, and federal income taxes at approximately 40 percent, $8,000 would be deducted for taxes, leaving $12,000 after taxes. At $12,000 per year, after taxes, the buyer's "payback" would be the $60,000 purchase divided by $12,000, or five years, exclusive of interest cost on borrowed funds or opportunity cost on the use of one's own funds.

The seller would receive $60,000 for the 10 percent position being sold and would incur a capital gains tax liability at 20 percent, or $12,000, netting $48,000.

Internal Transfer Mechanisms

Assumptions

Net Revenue	$2,000,000	
Adjusted Income	240,000	
Profit Available to Owners	200,000	
Adjusted Net Worth	480,000	
Valuation	600,000	

	Capital Transaction	*Cash + Compensation Reallocation*
100% value	$600,000	$120,000 assumed cash basis
		480,000 assumed accrual basis
10% value	60,000	12,000 cash
		48,000 accrued
Purchase		
Buyer pays	60,000 for stock	12,000 for stock
Buyer owes	0	48,000
Profit Distribution		
Buyer's annual profit	20,000	20,000
Buyer receives	20,000	0
Buyer defers	0	20,000
Buyer's tax @ ±40%	(8,000)	0
Buyer's net	12,000	0
Buyer's payback	5 years	3 years, including initial payment
Seller receives	60,000	12,000 for stock
Seller's tax @ 20%	(12,000)	(2,400)
Seller's net for stock	48,000	9,600
Seller's additional compensation	0	48,000
Seller's tax @ ±40%	0	(19,200)
Seller's net from additional comp.	0	28,800
Seller's total net proceeds	$48,000	$38,400
Value difference to offset additional tax		$15,000

After-Tax Stock Purchase Plus Compensation Exchange Method

Now assume that in order to make the transfer more affordable to the buyer, the owners of XYZ Design opt to transfer a portion of the agreed value through a stock transfer, and the remaining value through internal compensation exchange. Again referring to "Internal Transfer Mechanisms" on page 329, assume that the firm has the very same key financial indices. In this example, however, assume that the firm establishes the value of its stock on the cash basis, at 20 percent of its full accrual value. Then, referring to the column headed "Cash + Compensation Reallocation," the transfer could proceed as follows.

The value of 10 percent would total $60,000, of which 20 percent, or $12,000, would be the cash-basis value of the stock, and $48,000 would be the excess of accrued value over cash-basis value.

The seller would sell the cash-basis stock for cash—cash for cash. The buyer who was offered a 10 percent interest in the firm would pay $12,000 for his or her 10 percent share of the firm's stock, obviously finding the $12,000 more affordable than the aforementioned $60,000. However, since the full value of a 10 percent interest at that point in time remains $60,000, the buyer would owe the seller—the individual seller or the firm—$48,000.

Having become an owner of the firm, the buyer would be entitled to his or her 10 percent share of the firm's (assumed future) profit of $200,000, or $20,000, that is available for distribution to the owners. In this case, however, the buyer would agree in advance to forgo receipt of that profit until his or her accrued position had been paid for, and therefore would not incur a tax liability. Now, the buyer's payback, including payback for the initial stock purchase, would be three years—the $60,000 purchase divided by $20,000 per year.

The seller would receive $12,000 for stock, on which he or she would pay a capital gains tax of $2,400, netting $9,600 after tax. And, since the buyer would not receive the $20,000 bonus in each of the next three years, the seller could be paid the $48,000 over the next three years, which, after income tax of $19,200, would net the seller $28,800 on that portion and $38,400 overall, compared with $48,000 that he or she would have received after tax in a capital transaction.

TIP

Sellers should explore all the reasonable options for transferring value; the most obvious method may not be the most advantageous.

An obvious question is: Why would a seller agree to take less than the agreed value? There are three possible answers:

1. To make the sale affordable, and therefore possible
2. To save the additional money that the firm would have had to pay the buyer for the buyer to pay the seller with after-tax dollars
3. In the case of a stock repurchase by the firm, to save the corporate tax the firm would have to pay to buy back stock with after-tax dollars

Even understanding the benefit to the firm to allow the buyer to buy with pretax dollars (since the firm then does not have to compensate the buyer at a level that he or she will have enough after tax to pay the seller), it is unreasonable to expect a seller to realize less money. This can be resolved by increasing the valuation, in this case by $15,000. The buyer is still benefited by being allowed to purchase an interest in the firm largely with pretax dollars, and the seller nets exactly the same amount he or she would have if the transaction had been accomplished entirely as an after-tax transaction for stock.

Deferred Compensation Method

Another way to solve the problem of unaffordable price is to have the firm declare deferred compensation payable to the selling owner, prior to the sale of stock to the buyer. The declaration of the deferred compensation creates an obligation on the books of the firm (a liability), and this obligation reduces the value of the firm and thus the price of the stock to the buyer, as indicated in the example. The deferred compensation would be paid to the selling owner over an agreed period of time, usually three to six years.

The period when the selling owner begins to receive deferred compensation payments usually begins later in the program, not at the time of the buyer's purchase. If the deferred compensation is paid to the selling owner at a time when he or she owns a significant share of the firm, then it will be paid out of profits of the firm, a large portion of which would likely otherwise go to the owner as bonus monies while he or she is actively participating in the firm. The result is that the seller ends up paying for his or her own deferred compensation. To avoid this result, deferred compensation is often paid at a future point in time, when the seller has reduced his or her participation and ownership interest in the firm and is entitled to less regular compensation. Deferring the payment also may result in lower taxes to the seller, since he or she may be in a lower tax bracket later because he or she is earning less income as his or her participation in the firm decreases. Of course, the seller assumes greater risk by postponing the payment of deferred compensation to a time when he or she has less control of the firm. That risk can be reduced by including provisions in the deferred compensation agreement that the firm must pay the deferred compensation prior to making certain other payments and distributions, such as owner bonus payments.

Use of deferred compensation as a part of the ownership transition process can provide a significant tax benefit to the firm. Unlike the payment to the founder when the firm redeems stock (which is not a deductible expense to the firm), the payment of deferred compensation is deductible by the firm and thus serves to reduce the firm's taxable income. However, deferred compensation is taxable to the seller at ordinary income rates (including payroll taxes), whereas the payment to the seller for the purchase of his or her stock would be taxable at capital gains rates. The difference in taxes to the founder can be as much as 20 percent. In order to compensate the founder for the loss of capital gains tax treatment, which he or she would realize if the transaction were structured as a sale of stock, the deferred compensation amount is often increased by all or a portion of

CASE STUDY

Deferred Compensation

Frank and Frances decide to offer Barbara a 10 percent ownership interest in the firm, to be purchased from Frank, who is closer to retirement and wants to begin selling down his ownership interest. Based on the management consultant's valuation analysis, the firm is valued at $600,000, thus a 10 percent interest would cost $60,000 ($600,000 × 10 percent). Contemplating that the price would be burdensome for Barbara, the consultant recommends establishing a deferred compensation plan for Frank, making the purchase more affordable for Barbara while at the same time rewarding Frank, as the founder, with a fair amount for his share of the firm.

the difference between the taxes payable at the ordinary income tax rates and at capital gains tax rates. Even with this increase, deferred compensation is still beneficial to the firm from a tax standpoint.

Two points are particularly important to remember in considering ownership transfer mechanisms that seek to reduce the cost of purchase to the buyer via deferred compensation. First, deferred compensation is often paid at a later date when the founder/seller has either reduced or discontinued his or her involvement in the firm. Second, the deferred compensation obligation is usually payable as a fixed obligation of the business and is not dependent on earnings. However, there is ultimately only one source of funds to support an ownership exchange—the firm's earnings. In the deferred compensation example, some portion of the firm's future earnings will be needed to pay the seller's deferred compensation.

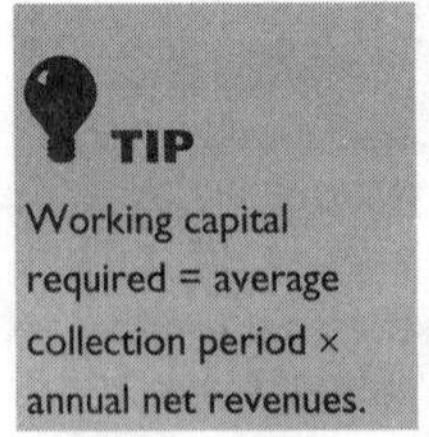

Also, every firm needs sufficient working capital to operate, essentially to "float" its accounts receivable, that is, to provide money to pay for salaries and other direct and indirect expenses, pending receipt of payment for the services it provided and paid for. Most design firms operate at working capital levels that closely approximate the amounts that are required to operate—they are neither substantially overcapitalized nor undercapitalized. If a firm reduces net worth by creating a liability to a seller, it will be reducing its working capital as it pays down that liability. In that circumstance, the owners will have to restore the firm's working capital to levels that meet the firm's operating needs, via capital contributions, profit retention, or debt.

A deferred compensation declaration of this kind should be supported by board resolutions and other

CASE STUDY

Deferred Compensation (Continued)

Frank's long-term goal is to be fully retired in 10 years. The value of the firm has been established as $600,000, so the cost of a 10 percent ownership interest in the firm would be $60,000 ($600,000 × 10 percent). The consultant recommends that the firm establish deferred compensation to Frank in the amount of $480,000. The result is that the value of the firm is reduced to $120,000 ($600,000 – $480,000), because the firm's liabilities have increased by the amount of the deferred compensation. With the value of the firm reduced to $120,000, a 10 percent ownership interest will cost Barbara $12,000 ($120,000 × 10 percent).

Barbara will pay the seller of the stock (either Frank or the firm) $12,000 in exchange for a 10 percent ownership interest in the firm. At the same time, the firm will enter into an agreement with Frank to pay him $480,000 as deferred compensation over an agreed-upon period of years, beginning either now or in the future when he begins to withdraw from daily involvement in the firm.

The deferred compensation will be ordinary income to Frank, and therefore will be taxed at ordinary income tax rates. If Frank had sold his stock at the fully appreciated value of $600,000, then the gain would have been taxed at capital gains rates, which are currently lower than the tax rates on ordinary income. To compensate Frank for the extra tax he will have to pay on the gain, the firm will increase the principal amount of deferred compensation paid to him by 20 percent, which is an approximation of the increased amount of taxes he will pay. Therefore, Frank will receive a total of $576,000 in deferred compensation ($480,000 × 20 percent = $96,000 + $480,000 = $576,000), which will be taxable as ordinary income to him.

Frank and the firm enter into a deferred compensation agreement under which Frank will receive $576,000 as ordinary income, paid through the firm's regular payroll over a period of five years. Deferred compensation payments will begin five years after Barbara's purchase, when Frank will begin to reduce his time spent on the firm's business.

appropriate data, since the taxing authorities may wish to characterize it for tax purposes as a distribution of dividends, with the result that the payment would not be deductible to the corporation.

Owner Transfer for Partnership or Limited Liability Companies

A partnership or limited liability company (LLC) with the same financial profile would proceed differently. Unlike new corporate shareholders who buy, and then own, proportional interests in the firm's net worth, new partners in partnerships and members of LLCs simply acquire the rights to their portion of the firm's future profits. The current partners/members do not sell their capital (which comprises the firm's net worth), nor do the new partners/members buy the existing capital. However, a firm going through an ownership transfer will continue to need an appropriate amount of working capital to continue its operations, generally the amount necessary to float the uncollected receivables. Therefore, those coming into ownership will need, and are generally required, to build up their capital accounts in proportion to their ownership interests. Then, as the "buyers" build up their capital accounts, the "sellers" will be able to draw down their capital accounts proportionally. For a discussion of different types of legal entities, including partnerships and LLCs, see Chapter 21, "Choosing the Form of Entity."

Again referring to "Internal Transfer Mechanisms," page 329, now assume that XYZ Design is a partnership with the very same average key financial indices: net revenues, $2,000,000; adjusted net income, $240,000; profit available to owners, $200,000; net worth (capital), $420,000; and valuation, $600,000.

The candidate who was offered a 10 percent ownership interest would need to contribute his or her portion of the cash capital of the firm, say $12,000, with his or her after-tax dollars. The candidate would also have to build up his or her accrued capital account by deferring profits to which he or she becomes entitled. As in the previous example, as the new owner builds up his or her capital account by deferring withdrawal of profit, the existing partners will be able to draw down their capital accounts until the capital accounts of all partners are in proportion to their ownership interests in the firm.

Zero-Based Transfer

As we have seen, ownership transfer is driven by the firm's profitability. The buyer's access to profit allows him or her to pay for what he or she has bought. However, owners of firms sometimes desire to bring new people into ownership when the firm has not had a history of profitability. In such cases, the sellers would have to communicate a picture of economic distress, likely causing prospective purchasers to question the economic viability of the transaction. Although design professionals seek ownership for many reasons beyond pure economic return, few are so altruistic that they would willingly enter into an ownership transaction if they were unable to reasonably contemplate a return or payback of their investment.

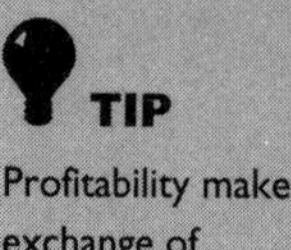

TIP
Profitability makes the exchange of ownership possible.

Referring again to XYZ Design, imagine that the firm had not earned a profit for several years, but that Frank and Frances were nonetheless interested in bringing Barbara, a key employee, into ownership. Without the ability to demonstrate that Barbara would be able to earn out and pay for the 10 percent interest they intended to offer, Frank and Frances could not see how they could present a reasonable scenario for the transition. Their management consultant suggested they consider what is known as a *zero-based transfer.*

The consultant suggested that Frank and Frances form a new company (which we will call NewXYZ) to be owned 45 percent by Frank, 45 percent by Frances, and 10 percent by Barbara. At the point of formation, XYZ Design would transfer the fixed assets (furniture, fixtures, and equipment) that NewXYZ would need to operate, would value them as shown on the XYZ Design Balance Sheet, and would take back a note from NewXYZ. NewXYZ would then own an asset offset by a liability in the same amount, yielding a net worth of zero. Considering NewXYZ's starting value of zero, Frank and Frances would not be selling anything of value and would not charge for it, and Barbara would not have to pay for it. Barbara would become a 10 percent owner of an entity without initial value.

NewXYZ would begin operating, picking up and continuing the work that had been initiated by XYZ Design, and paying the salary and other direct and indirect expenses necessary to operate. The obvious question that arises is: Where will NewXYZ get the funds to pay the expenses necessary to operate? Since XYZ Design's accounts receivable will continue to be collected, XYZ Design will lend NewXYZ the funds necessary to begin practicing, which NewXYZ will pay back out of its (hopefully) successful operations going forward. Frank and Frances will have a priority call on the equity that NewXYZ develops.

Barbara will have the rights and responsibilities of a principal in the firm and, if she is successful in helping make the firm successful, she will also have an increasingly valuable equity stake as the firm grows and increases in value.

18 Designing the Ownership Transition Program

Important Considerations

Once the decision has been made to transfer ownership to others in the firm, the current owners must make several critical "business" decisions in order to form a comprehensive understanding about what they wish to offer (the "deal"), and then communicate that offer to the prospective candidate(s). Without that understanding, it is highly likely that they will forget one important element or another and, in the worst case, offer something that they later find they cannot deliver. By answering the following questions, the current owners will establish the framework for the offer they will make to the candidates.

1. Objectives of Ownership

Will the firm be structured: (a) as a vehicle through which the owners can practice their professions while retaining primary responsibility for their personal financial goals (i.e., high current income approach as in law firms, medical practices, etc.); or

(b) as a collective vehicle that endeavors to build common equity for all (i.e., institutional/corporate approach)?

The answer to this question allows a buyer to understand whether he or she will be able to realize a current return on his or her investment after he or she has paid for it, or whether profits will be retained in the firm to build the firm's value, which will allow a return only when shares are sold at a later, perhaps much later, date.

2. Control

Will all (new) owners have an equal voice in firm affairs or will there be a difference between a "control" group and a "participation" group (i.e., those who control the destiny of the firm and make its critical decisions versus those who simply participate in the firm's profits)? In small to medium-sized firms, it is common that there is only one class of owners. Larger firms sometimes offer small ownership positions to larger numbers of people. In the latter case, the firm is usually controlled by a smaller group, whose members own a majority share of the firm.

For example, the (usually small) group of owners who own all the equity in a large firm may feel that it would be advantageous for the firm to offer ownership to a large group of employees who they do not want to govern the firm. In that situation, the owners could make a very small percentage of the authorized shares available for purchase, which would result in a large number of employees owning a very small amount of the firm's total equity. Since the number of shares controlled by such new shareholders would be very small, by intention, they would not be able to affect elections to the firm's board of directors nor its essential decisions.

3. Participants

Who will be invited into ownership, and in what initial increments? If there is one candidate that the current owners have identified, this question is readily resolved. However, when there is a group of prospective candidates in the firm, and the firm neither needs, nor can afford, to bring in as many new owners as there are candidates, then hard decisions must be made regarding who will be invited and in what increments. The options include: (a) inviting only the most deserving into the control group, excluding all others; (b) inviting some into the control group and others into a group of participating, but not controlling, owners; and (c) inviting all as participating, but not controlling, owners.

4. Valuation

What do the present owners consider a fair value for their interest in the firm? This is the critical valuation question, as discussed more completely in Chapters 16 and 17.

5. Method of Paying Out Sellers

Do the sellers want payment currently or do they prefer that payment be deferred to a later date or to retirement? Unless there is need for additional working capital in the firm, most owners prefer to take payment currently, that is, as it is paid in. Additional capital may be required if the firm intends to grow beyond its ability to fund that growth out of earnings, or if the firm plans to acquire other firms in the future. Both situations will require more capital than the firm may have—capital that can be provided, at least in part, by the capital contributions of new owners. If, however, the firm is planning for the withdrawal of one or more of the current owners, then the capital the new owners contribute as a condition of the transfer will help to fund the withdrawal: The capital coming into the firm from the new owners will replace capital being withdrawn by the current owners, as they sell down their interests in the firm.

6. Method of Buying In

TIP

New owners must be able to access their share of the firm's profits to be able to pay for their interests in the firm.

How will the buyers pay for their interests in the firm? It is extremely rare for new owners to have sufficient personal financial resources to pay for their ownership interests in cash. New owners may not have a great deal of personal wealth that would support a bank loan to fund the cost of purchasing an ownership interest in the firm. Consequently, they need to be assisted in some way. Those ways include: (a) accepting a cash down payment and a note for the balance to be paid annually, hopefully out of profits; (b) having the firm guarantee a bank loan if the sellers require cash, which is rarely done; or (c) other mechanisms, such as those described elsewhere in this chapter.

7. Vesting

When will buyers be considered "vested" in their share of profits or losses and in their share of the firm's capital if they die or withdraw before their interest is fully paid? "Vesting" here does not refer to formal, IRS-approved vesting that is common for tax-sheltered plans, but refers to the buyers' "ownership" of their portion of the firm's profits and capital.

There is only one reasonable answer to this set of related questions. Regarding access to profit, if the new owners are not vested in their share of the firm's profits when they become owners, then they will not be able to earn the money they need to pay for their interests. If they have borrowed from a bank or from the firm, they will not be able to redeem the note. If they have used their own funds, losing the opportunity to earn money on those funds, they will have to "pay themselves back." Although design professionals seek ownership for reasons other than financial, few are so altruistic that they will assume the financial and other risks of ownership without a reasonable financial return. Therefore, all new owners should share in their portion of the firm's profit. Unlike access to profit, however, new owners should own their share of the firm's capital only when they have paid for it.

8. Decision-Making

After ownership has been transferred to new owners, how will the owners make decisions for the firm? Design professionals want to become owners to participate more fully in the essential direction and decision-making process of the firms in which they work. Such decisions are made by the owners. Those coming into ownership will want to participate in decision-making, and the current owners will be well advised to make that happen, since their own futures will depend upon the ability of the new owners to understand the decision-making process and participate in it effectively.

Partnerships are governed by their partners; corporations are governed by their directors, who are elected by the shareholders. Limited liability companies are governed by their "members" (a legal connotation comparable to shareholders/directors). The common practice in many small, closely held firms is for all partners or corporate shareholders (who are often also the corporation's directors) to share responsibility for firm management and operate on a one-person, one-vote basis. Many small to medium-sized firms operate by consensus and never take votes. Decisions are made only when everyone agrees to support them. However, since the selling owners will likely own more of the firm than the buying owners, and therefore will be more at risk, it may be necessary to establish a decision-making protocol in the legal documents to ensure that those who are more at risk will not suffer at the hands of those with only small amounts of ownership. For example, the firm's ownership documents might stipulate that decisions be made by majority vote of the directors, except for decisions exceeding a low-end threshold dollar amount, which would be made by majority vote of shares.

9. Compensation

What will the policy be with respect to base salaries of owners and distribution of firm profits? Who will determine the policy? More than any other matter, compensation disagreements have the greatest potential for fostering dissension among the owners.

TIP

More than any other matter, compensation disagreements have the greatest potential for fostering dissension among owners.

Owners' compensation (salary and bonus) will likely be determined by the ownership group or its appointee, who will be in a position to control such decisions. Since the new owners may be fearful of future actions that affect their compensation, the sellers should consider mechanisms to ensure that compensation issues will be addressed fairly. One

Worst-Case Scenario

Nearing normal retirement age, the majority owner and design leader of a graphic design firm engaged a consultant to assist in exploring the possibility of bringing two or three key designers into ownership. The candidates identified as prospective owners had already begun assuming some of the project responsibilities normally assigned to principals and were deemed ready to assume primary responsibilities on projects. The firm was sufficiently profitable for an exchange to occur. In considering the specific terms of an offer, the owner decided to retain design control of the firm's work. One of the two lead candidates left the firm, and the other refused the offer.

successful solution is to create a ratio between the salaries of current and new owners, such as current owners: x percent = new owners: $x - y$ percent, indicating that the average salary of new owners will be less than the average salary of the current owners.

10. Benefits

Will there be any special benefits or "perks" for new owners? Owners in professional firms—in fact, in any small to medium-sized firm—are in a position to compensate themselves in ways other than salary by providing or accepting various benefits and perks in addition to or in lieu of salary. Typical examples include automobiles, parking, membership dues, attendance at conferences, and others. Senior owners who have significant responsibility for attracting clients and maintaining client relationships may do more business entertaining than the new owners, especially at the beginning of a transition, and may wish to differentiate their use of business expenses from new owners. The current owners may simply choose to provide certain benefits to themselves that would otherwise have to be paid for with their own after-tax dollars. It may be reasonable, or simply may be the current owners' choice, to provide different levels of benefits and/or perks to different owners. Regardless of the decision, it is important to be crystal clear about entitlement to such benefits for new owners, to avoid misunderstandings and disagreements among owners arising from perceived inequitable treatment.

11. Withdrawal

How will the firm deal with: (a) death and permanent disability; (b) retirement, and at what ages; and (c) early withdrawal? Universally, redemption of ownership for reasons of death and disability is at full value. Because it sometimes happens that owners who attempt to maintain their ownership beyond normal retirement age lose their connection to the marketplace and thereby encumber the firm, owners should consider the benefit to the firm, and the possibility of a requirement, of withdrawing from ownership, but not from employment, at normal retirement age, however they choose to define it.

On the other hand, the firm's ability to succeed, and the ability of the remaining partners to retire, can be harmed by owners who voluntarily withdraw from ownership before normal retirement age. Owners should therefore consider assessing an appropriate economic penalty against a voluntarily withdrawing owner, such as 5 percent of value for each year prior to normal retirement that the withdrawal occurs. (See Chapter 20 for a discussion of typical stockholder agreement provisions that address these issues.)

12. Involuntary Separation

Which mechanism will make it possible to ask an owner to withdraw, and how will such an owner be compensated? Ownership groups should not be encumbered by the presence of an owner who turns out not to meet the demands of ownership or who disrupts the effectiveness of the group. That said, it is dangerous to permit or encourage factionalism. Frequently, unanimity or a supermajority is required to ask an owner to withdraw. The shares of an owner who is asked to withdraw are normally redeemed at full value.

13. Additional Owners

Which mechanism will be employed to invite new owners into ownership or to expand the interests of minority owners? The same supermajority that is employed to ask owners to withdraw is frequently employed to invite new owners into ownership or to expand the interests of majority owners. For small ownership groups it would not be unreasonable to require unanimity.

14. Qualifications of Owners

What legal and other criteria must be met for people to be considered for ownership in the firm? What are the expectations for owners' time commitments, performance, and behavior? Current owners frequently expect that the new owners will come into ownership fully formed and able to contribute exactly what is required. After all, they themselves did, didn't they? Reality is elsewhere, and osmosis works better in the chemistry lab than in professional practice. If the current owners expect certain behavior or performance from new owners, they have a

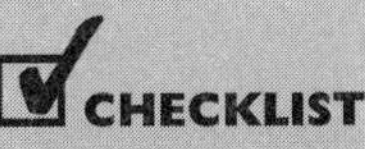

Important Considerations

- Objectives
- Control
- Participants
- Valuation
- Methods of paying out sellers
- Methods of buying in
- Vesting
- Decision-making
- Compensation
- Benefits
- Withdrawal
- Involuntary separation
- Additional owners
- Qualifications of owners
- Other firm name, organization, and so on

Worst-Case Scenario

The partners of a midsize design firm brought three key staff members into ownership on reasonable terms. One year later, one of the founders called the firm's management consultant and expressed concern that one of the new owners was not performing at the principal-level that had been expected. When asked, "Did you discuss what you expected?" the founder said "No."

right to, and should, ask for it, but they should also be prepared to assist in the development of the new owners to help them achieve the levels of performance that are expected. Examples of reasonable expectations include full efforts in the firm's interest, maximum time commitment, contribution to fees sold, project performance within agreed budgets, and maintenance of professional credentials, including any requirements for continuing education.

15. Other

What other conditions, if any, should apply to the matter of ownership? Should the name of the firm or its form of organization change? This question should prompt the current owners to think about issues that perhaps have seemed natural and have not been addressed, but that now may require direct attention.

Getting the Ownership Transition Program Started

19

Assembling the Team

To develop a successful ownership transition program, the founder needs a team to assist and facilitate the process. The team will usually consist of four members: an attorney, a management consultant, a certified public accountant (CPA), and the most important member of the team, the current owner (also called "founder" in this discussion) or all the owners, if there is more than one. Whenever possible, it is best to have professionals who are experienced in ownership transition for service firms and specifically for design firms. The current owners' active participation as a team member is essential, since their desire and vision will drive the program.

TIP

The ownership transition team may begin with the management consultant, the attorney, or the accountant, depending on who has an existing relationship with the owner.

Although all of the members of the team will assist in the development of the program, certain tasks are usually delegated to specific consultants. This depends on the particular skill set and experience level of the consultant. Where possible, it is best to work with a team of professionals who have worked together in the past. This will assure a clear understanding of the delegation of tasks and

CASE STUDY

Beginning the Process

Referring again to XYZ Design, Frank and Frances have begun to assess candidates for ownership. Andrew has been with them since the formation of the firm and is a loyal, hard-working project manager. Three years ago Frank and Frances hired Barbara, who had been with a larger firm, with the understanding that if things worked out, Barbara would be offered ownership. Frank would like to begin phasing down his active participation in the firm and be close to retirement in 10 years. He would like to start selling some of the ownership in the firm to key employees, but doesn't know how to begin the process.

responsibilities and will ensure a good working relationship. As a general rule, the management consultant will often be the coordinator of the team. The consultant will also assist the founder in designing the program and determining the method of valuation and candidate evaluation.

At a minimum, the attorney will prepare the necessary legal documents for the program, including the Term Sheet. An attorney who has experience in the development of ownership transition programs will also be able to assist the founder and the consultant in designing the program.

The certified public accountant will usually assist in the preparation of financial statements and the determination of the value of the firm. The accountant will also assist in analyzing the tax consequences of the transaction and prepare cash-flow projections if those are needed to assist the parties in determining the feasibility of the program.

Laying the Foundation

The current owner should provide certain information to the team prior to meeting with them. This information provides the foundation for the team to understand the firm's financial picture, current business, and legal framework. The following information is usually assembled by the current owner and is sent to the team a week or two before their initial meeting:

- Financial statements and tax returns for the past three to five years.
- Organizational documents. If the firm is a partnership, this will include the partnership agreement. If the firm is a corporation, this will include the certificate of incorporation, the bylaws, a list of current stockholders, and a Stockholder Agreement if one exists.
- Employee census, including each employee's number of years with the firm, number of years in the profession, and annual compensation.

Designing the Program

Once the current owner has identified the team members and provided them with relevant background information, he or she will meet with the team to discuss the key issues related to ownership transition. Several questions are common to most ownership transition programs. The current owner's answers to these questions will articulate the values of the firm and the goals for the ownership transition program. The answers will also determine the substantive terms of the ownership transition program. The questions common to most ownership transition programs are:

- Why has the owner decided to undertake an ownership transition program? For example, planning for future retirement or need for a new generation of owners. See Chapter 13, "Introduction to Ownership Transition," section titled "Why Is Ownership Transition Necessary?" on page 251.

- How should the firm be valued? See Chapter 16.
- What are the criteria for selecting candidates for the program? For example, marketing ability, leadership skills, and management capability. See Chapter 15.
- What is the appropriate rate of transition of ownership from the founder to candidates? This requires the founder to identify three critical points: the time of initial transfer, the time at which he or she is comfortable giving up control of the firm, and the time when he or she desires to retire completely from ownership. See "Establishing a Rate of Transition" on page 356.
- How will the new owners be compensated? For example, increased salary, added bonus, and owner benefits.
- To what extent will the new owners participate in firm management? For example, board membership, committee membership, and administrative responsibilities.

Evaluating Candidates

The management consultant will sometimes interview those persons who the founder feels may be potential candidates for ownership. The purpose of the interviews is to provide appropriate criteria to help the founder evaluate candidates and to assist the founder in articulating the responsibilities of ownership. The interviews can be done before the

CASE STUDY

Where to Begin

Referring again to XYZ Design: Frank and Frances sought the advice of a management consultant experienced in ownership transition in professional design firms to discuss their intention of bringing in new owners. They identified Andrew and Barbara as good candidates for ownership, and provided factual information about the firm and its employees, and financial statements for the past few years.

The management consultant selected as part of XYZ Design's ownership transition team interviewed Frank and Frances to learn about their firm's management and operations, their objectives and concerns regarding ownership transfer, and their views about Andrew's and Barbara's strengths and weaknesses. He then interviewed the candidates separately, both to evaluate them independently of the owners' impressions and to gauge their interest in becoming owners of the firm.

After analyzing the results of the meetings, the consultant advised the owners that Andrew, who has been with the firm from the beginning, is content to remain as a project manager and has no desire for ownership, despite his longevity with the firm. By contrast, Barbara has an entrepreneurial outlook and appears to have the necessary aptitude and desire to become an owner.

Term Sheet is prepared, but are probably more meaningful when coupled with the discussion of the Term Sheet by the founder and the management consultant to the buyers. The objective evaluation of the consultant can be very valuable for a number of reasons. An experienced consultant will be able to compare the potential candidates to other candidates in successful programs and thus assess the likelihood of the candidates becoming successful members of the ownership group. The consultant also brings a level of objectivity that the founder cannot be expected to have. The consultant may recommend that one or all of the potential candidates are good choices or that none of the potential candidates would work out. In the latter case, the owner might choose to look outside the firm for potential candidates, or identify and develop better candidates from within the firm.

Establishing a Rate of Transition

EXPLANATION

Giving Up Control

An owner should begin to relinquish control over the firm before he or she is completely retired, and ideally when he or she has reached the halfway point in selling down his or her interest, to convince candidates that their participation in the firm will be meaningful, to enable new owners to learn to lead and manage under the owner's guidance, and to allow new owners to establish themselves as leaders of the firm.

The selling owner needs to determine the rate at which candidates will be allowed to purchase ownership in the firm. This is sometimes referred to as the *buy-in rate*. The rate at which the owner sells stock to candidates is called the *sell-down rate*. There are several factors to consider in determining the transition rate for the program. Because the firm will want to create a balance between the sell-down rate and the buy-in rate, the starting point for the determination of the buy-in rate will be the rate at which the founder wishes to sell down his or her interest. To determine the sell-down rate, the seller should first determine how long he or she wishes to participate significantly in the firm's operations. Once that decision has been made, then a rate of sell-down or divestiture can be calculated. For example, if the owner decides that he or she wants to decrease his or her participation steadily over a period of 10 years, then the firm has a decade in which to identify and sell shares to candidates who would replace that owner.

Sometimes an owner will want to keep control of a firm until he or she is effectively retired. While this is understandable, it is not a good idea for the firm because it can slow the leadership development process for new owners. By the time the seller has reached the halfway point in his or her sell-down phase, he or she should have transferred control of the firm, and the new owners should be well established in their roles as firm leaders. If the seller decides to retain control until the date of retirement, it is vital that the next generation of owners be prepared to assume their leadership roles in advance of the founder's retirement, to ensure that the firm does not suffer from a vacuum of leadership upon the owner's departure.

Another important factor in determining the transition rate is the maximum amount of ownership that the firm wants any one candidate to have. Prior to ownership transition, the current owner or owners will own 100 percent of the stock of the firm. In a situation where there is one owner, then all of the stock is owned by that founder. If there are two owners, then the stock would be owned by those two owners, equally or in some other proportion. As new candidates are brought in as owners, the goal is often to have all candidates own an equal amount of stock when they have completed all of their purchases over a period of time. For example, if a firm will have a maximum of six owners, then each owner would own one-sixth of the outstanding stock.

Although there is no precise method of determining the maximum amount of ownership to be granted to any one candidate, the starting point is usually an estimate of the total number of owners that the firm can support. The guiding principle in determining the maximum number of owners that the firm can support is the fact that the new owners of the firm must be better compensated as owners than they were as nonowners. This means that the firm must either become more profitable with its existing level of practice or expand its practice to create more income available for distribution. If it does

TIP

A good rule of thumb is that a firm can support one owner for every 7 to 11 employees.

not become more profitable, the founders will be required to share a significant part of their income with the new owners.

A good rule of thumb is that a firm can support one owner for every 7 to 11 employees in the firm, the exact number depending on its profitability. This means, for example, that a 25-person firm could support two or three owners. As stated above, the ultimate answer lies in the ability of the firm to compensate owners at levels greater than their compensation as nonowners. Of course, if the firm expands in size and number of employees, then it could afford additional owners. For example, if the firm increases in size from 25 to 35 employees, then using the same rule of thumb of one owner for every 7 to 11 employees, it could likely support 3 to 5 owners.

TIP

Generally, 5 percent is the minimum amount of stock to offer to a candidate. Less might not be sufficiently meaningful and more might not allow for additional offerings to others.

Once the maximum number of owners is determined, and assuming that the goal is to have all owners ultimately own an equal share of the company, the total ownership percentage for any one owner can be readily determined. If, for example, it is determined that a firm can support five owners, then the maximum amount of stock that each owner would own would be 20 percent (100 percent divided by 5 = 20 percent).

Having established a sell-down rate for the selling owner in the above example of 10 years and a maximum amount of stock to be owned by any one owner at 20 percent, the firm then needs to decide over what period of time the candidates would be allowed to buy in. Often the initial offer of ownership to a candidate will be significant, but not excessive. The minimum amount of stock offered initially should generally be at least 5 percent, although successful programs have started with as little as 1 percent. In future offerings, additional increments of 5 percent or more can be offered to a particular candidate until he or she has reached the desired maximum. In addition, it is preferable that offerings be spaced at least two years apart. This will allow the firm a reasonable period of time to observe and evaluate the new owner's performance to determine if increased ownership is merited. Also, if the new owner is purchasing his or her stock over time, then it would be wise to wait until he or she has completed one round of purchase before offering additional stock and starting another round of payments.

It is rarely the case that the seller's sell-down rate will be on a straight-line basis. For example, it is unlikely that all of the potential new owners will be identified and available for ownership transition at the beginning of the program. In addition, some new owners may not perform up to expectation, with the result that they will not be offered additional stock or their stock will be repurchased as they leave the firm. However, so long as the firm has established the guiding principles described above, it can work toward a goal that can be adjusted for actual results during the transition period.

EXPLANATION

The documents described here are the ones normally used for a corporation. If the firm is a partnership or an LLC, then the Partnership Agreement or LLC Operating Agreement would contain the provisions found in the Stockholder Agreement and related corporate documents.

Deciding on the Terms

It is best to summarize the terms decided by the sellers in one document, usually called a Term Sheet. In one or a series of meetings, the team will discuss the issues described above and explore alternatives, and the founder will identify his or her concerns and interests. Once the issues have been resolved, the team will suggest specific terms of the program to be offered to the candidates. The attorney will then prepare a Term Sheet (sometimes called a *Memorandum*

TIP

Using a Term Sheet is beneficial because it avoids spending time and money on developing the program documents until the candidate has confirmed his or her interest.

EXPLANATION

Term Sheet

A typical term sheet contains the following items:

- The percentage of ownership and corresponding number of shares of stock in the corporation being offered to each candidate. This will include the initial amounts being offered in the first phase of the program and an estimate (but not a guarantee) of the percentage of future ownership to be offered in subsequent years.
- The identity of the seller. The seller will either be the firm or the founder.
- The identity of the buyers. The candidates will be identified as buyers in the term sheet.
- The purchase price for the stock being offered to the buyers. The purchase price is usually based on the total value of the firm multiplied by the percentage interest of ownership being offered.
- The terms of payment for the stock being purchased. The buyer may pay for the stock in one lump payment or in installments over a period of time.
- The title and position within the firm, if any, being offered to the buyers.
- The compensation for the buyer, including base salary, bonus, and any owners' benefits.
- $$ The candidates' participation in the governance of the firm.

of Understanding or an *offering letter*) that embodies the agreed-upon terms. The Term Sheet is not intended to be a legally binding document, but rather a description of the material terms of the program that the founder is offering to the candidates. Using a Term Sheet is preferable to preparing all the program documents initially, because the founder may use the Term Sheet to canvass the candidates' interest level before spending substantial time and money in the further development of the ownership program, including the preparation of final legal documents to complete the program.

Presenting the Term Sheet

The founder and his or her management consultant usually present the term sheet to the candidates in an in-person meeting, to determine if they are interested in the program on the terms presented. After the term sheet is presented to the candidates, the candidates are encouraged to meet with their own financial and legal advisers to discuss the terms and decide whether to participate in the ownership transition program. The selling owner will request that candidates indicate their interest in the program within a reasonable time, usually within a few weeks of the in-person meeting.

Documenting the Program

After the candidates have expressed an interest in participating in the ownership transition program, the attorney will prepare the necessary legal documents for the program. These documents usually include the following, which are discussed in detail in Chapter 20:

- *Offering Memorandum.* The Offering Memorandum is a document that discloses all the material information about the firm and its business. Material information includes the history, structure, and current operations of the firm.
- *Stock Purchase Agreement.* The stock purchase agreement is the contract between the seller of the stock (the founder or the firm) and the buyer of the stock.
- *Secured Promissory Note and Security Agreement.* If the stock is being purchased in installments over time, the buyer's obligation to pay for the

stock will be evidenced by a promissory note, and the buyer will pledge his or her stock back to the seller to secure that obligation. If the buyer is purchasing the stock for cash, then it is not necessary to have a secured promissory note and security agreement.

- *Stockholder Agreement.* This is an agreement among the owners (founder and new owners) of a firm that is intended to keep ownership of the firm within the group whose members are active in the firm's business. The agreement contains restrictions on the transfer of stock and describes the events that trigger an obligation or option on the part of the firm and the other owners to repurchase stock, the method of valuing the stock at the time of repurchase, and the terms of payment for the shares of stock that are repurchased. The Stockholder Agreement may also contain other terms such as special voting rights on key issues and restrictions upon competitive activities by a former stockholder after his stock is repurchased.
- *Indemnification Agreement.* If the firm is a corporation, it is recommended that all stockholders enter into an indemnification agreement, whereby each stockholder agrees to be personally responsible for his or her proportionate share of obligations of the firm that are personally guaranteed by other shareholders.

Presentation of Program Documents to Candidates

Once the program documents have been prepared by the attorney, the selling owner and other members of the team review them and suggest modifications as necessary. The program documents are then presented to the candidates in a meeting with the founders and the other team members. At the meeting, they discuss the program in depth and review the documents. The candidates have the opportunity to ask the owner and the other team members questions about the program. The candidates then are given a reasonable amount of time, usually three weeks to a month, to review the documents with their own legal and financial advisers and to provide any comments on the documents for consideration by the owner. After the selling owner and candidates agree on the form and content of the documents, the documents are executed, stock is issued or transferred, the buyer pays for the stock or makes an initial payment and signs a promissory note for the balance, and the first phase of the ownership transition program is complete. In subsequent years, the founder, the new owners, and possibly other candidates, may agree to the purchase and sale of additional interests in the ownership of the firm, using similar documentation.

TIP

An ownership transition program usually takes three to six months to complete.

Using the process described above, the time to develop the ownership transition program and to close the first round of ownership is usually three to six months. This assumes the full cooperation of all parties. There are a number of reasons why the development of the program could take longer: the failure of the selling owner to be responsive to the team members; the candidates' request for extensive revisions to the program documents; or protracted negotiations between the founder and the candidates. Any or all of these reasons can extend the time frame. In some cases, ownership programs can take more than a year to develop and close the first round of ownership transition.

TIP

Ownership transition should occur in a series of transactions, ideally spaced several years apart.

Next Steps

After the candidates have purchased their initial shares of stock and the initial phase of the program has been accomplished, the owner and his or her team should revisit the program every year or two, depending on the proposed rate of transition. It takes time to evaluate the new owners' performance as leaders and owners of the firm and for the founder to determine whether the new owners will be offered the opportunity to participate in future offerings. Therefore, it is a good idea to stage the phases of ownership transition in multiple intervals of at least two years. If candidates are buying their ownership interests over time, it is preferable to have them complete the payment for one round of ownership before proceeding to the next round.

20 Documenting the Ownership Transition Program

As noted in Chapter 19, there are several documents that the firm's attorney must prepare to document an ownership transition program. Many programs feature an Offering Memorandum, Stock Purchase Agreement, Secured Promissory Note, Security Agreement, and Stockholder Agreement. In some instances, a program will also include an Indemnification Agreement, Deferred Compensation Agreement, and an Employment Agreement. These agreements are discussed in detail in this chapter.

The document descriptions given here assume the business is operated as a corporation, but the same principles apply to businesses operated as partnerships or limited liability companies. For a brief discussion of program documents for partnership and limited liability companies, see "Ownership Transition Documents for Organizations Other Than Corporations: Partnerships and Limited Liability Companies," at the end of this chapter. For a discussion of the advantages and disadvantages of

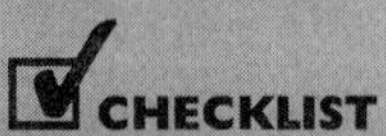

CHECKLIST

Ownership Transition Program Documents

- Term Sheet
- Offering Memorandum
- Stock Purchase Agreement
- Secured Promissory Note
- Security Agreement
- Stockholder Agreement
- Indemnification Agreement
- Deferred Compensation Agreement
- Employment Agreement
- Company's Financial Statements
- Company's Organization Documents

These documents are the ones normally used for a corporation. If the firm is a partnership or an LLC, then the Partnership Agreement or LLC Operating Agreement would contain the provisions found in the Stockholder Agreement and in some cases the Indemnification Agreement.

different entity types, see Chapter 21, "Choosing the Form of Entity."

Offering Memorandum

An Offering Memorandum presents all *material information* about a firm and its business to a prospective buyer. Material information is information that a prudent investor would want to know before investing in the firm; that is, information that could cause the potential investor to change the decision to invest.

In the ownership transition process, ownership of a corporation is expanded when the founder or the firm sells shares of stock to new owners. All sales of stock are controlled by federal (U.S. government) and state laws regulating the offer and sale of securities. The goal of these laws is to protect buyers by disclosing all material information that a prudent investor would want to know about the firm issuing the stock before making a purchase.

Large public corporations are required to register their stock with the U.S. Securities and Exchange Commission (SEC), but most design firms are privately owned by the firm's key professional employees. These privately owned (also called privately held) firms are generally not required to register their stock with the SEC, but must nevertheless comply with certain federal and state requirements in offering and selling stock in the firm, including the requirement for adequate disclosure of material information about the firm to prospective purchasers.

Regardless of whether the firm or an existing stockholder is selling stock, the recommended method for disclosing material information about a firm whose stock is being offered is by preparation of an Offering Memorandum (also called a Private Placement Memorandum or PPM). An Offering Memorandum is similar to a prospectus for a publicly traded company. The Offering Memorandum presents material information about the firm, its legal and financial structure, and its business and management, and gives disclaimers or warnings about the risks of investing in the firm. All of these elements are described more fully below. Normally, the Offering Memorandum will attach as exhibits all of the documents a candidate is expected to sign in connection with the purchase of stock. (See the "Ownership Transition Program Documents" checklist on the facing page.)

Is an Offering Memorandum Necessary?

The law does not require that an Offering Memorandum be prepared in order to sell stock. Some founders may feel that it is unnecessary to provide detailed information to a candidate about the business of the firm where the candidate works and which the candidate may know quite well. However, preparation and distribution of an Offering Memorandum is strongly recommended to ensure that all material information about the firm issuing the stock has been communicated to a candidate, for two reasons: first, to enhance the candidate's ability to make an intelligent and informed decision about the candidate's investment of time and funds; and second, to protect the firm issuing the stock (and the founder, if the founder is selling the stock directly to the candidate) from later claims that material information was withheld. The Offering Memorandum is proof that the disclosures contained in it have been made to the buyer.

Common Topics in an Offering Memorandum

- Description of the offering—name of the firm or the seller of the stock, the number of shares of stock offered, and the price calculation
- Historical background of the firm
- Description of business, clients, and markets
- Financial information
- List of the firm's material liabilities
- Claims and litigation; insurance coverage
- Interested party transactions between founders or their families and affiliates and the firm
- Risk factors inherent in the firm's business as currently operated
- Description of Stock Purchase Agreement, Secured Promissory Note, Security Agreement, Indemnification Agreement, and any other agreements the buyer will be required to enter into
- Other information on stockholder role and responsibilities, benefits, compensation, and title

What Information Is Contained in an Offering Memorandum?

An Offering Memorandum describes the history, structure, business, and operations of a firm. While it is not possible to create a "one size fits all" form, there are nevertheless certain basic topics and types of information that will apply to almost all situations. (See "Common Topics in an Offering Memorandum," above.)

An Offering Memorandum should present a balanced view of the firm and its business, conveying factual information about the firm rather than acting as a sales document to encourage a candidate to buy stock. The warning language and disclaimers contained in an Offering Memorandum may sound discouraging and even alarming to a candidate, but the object of the document is to convey all material information, both good and bad, affirmative and cautionary, so that the candidate can make an informed decision about purchasing stock.

What Is Involved in Preparing an Offering Memorandum?

The time and effort required to collect information and to draft and revise the Offering Memorandum varies widely and depends on the complexity of the firm's history, financial structure, and operations. It is helpful to designate one person within the firm to coordinate collection and transmission of information to the attorney, who will edit and prepare the final version of the Offering Memorandum.

What Role Does the Firm Play in Preparing an Offering Memorandum?

The firm plays a critical role in collecting and transmitting information to the attorney about the firm's history, legal structure and documentation, financial matters, business and operational descriptions, and other matters. An attorney, no matter how familiar with the firm's business, must rely on the firm to provide all relevant information for the Offering Memorandum. The person designated to provide the information, to coordinate responses from within the firm, and to respond to the attorney's requests for clarification and additional information should have sufficient familiarity with the business and authority within the organization to provide the best information and contacts. The designated person may be the president, the president's assistant, the chief financial officer, the corporate secretary, or any other person with broad knowledge and contacts within the firm.

Stock Purchase Agreement

In an ownership transition program, the stock being offered may be issued and sold by either the firm or sold by an existing stockholder (often a founder of the business). Regardless of the identity of the seller, a Stock Purchase Agreement should be prepared to memorialize the transaction. A Stock Purchase

Principal Terms of a Stock Purchase Agreement

- Names of the seller and buyer
- Date of the agreement
- Name of the firm issuing the stock
- Number of shares and class of stock (common or preferred) being offered and sold
- Agreement to buy the stock and to sell the stock
- Price per share of stock
- Total price being paid
- Representations by buyer that:
  - Buyer is buying the stock for his or her own account and not for purposes of resale
  - The sale is made under an exemption from registration under applicable securities laws
  - Any later sale or transfer will be in accordance with applicable securities laws
  - Buyer is able to bear the total loss of the investment in the stock
  - Buyer has had adequate access to information about the business and finances of the firm
  - Buyer agrees to be bound by the Stockholder Agreement
- Representations by seller that:
  - The stock is free and clear of any encumbrances or liens
- Dispute resolution
- Recoverability of attorney's fees by prevailing party in a dispute
- Controlling law and other enabling provisions
- Spousal consent

Agreement is the contract by which a seller is contractually bound to sell stock to a buyer, and the buyer is contractually bound to pay for it, all on the terms and conditions stated in the Stock Purchase Agreement. The Stock Purchase Agreement specifies the number of shares of stock to be sold, the purchase price and the payment terms, if payment will be made in installments. Typically, a Stock Purchase Agreement also includes representations by the buyer, confirming his eligibility to purchase the stock and acknowledging restrictions that exist on the sale of the stock. (See "Principal Terms of a Stock Purchase Agreement," opposite.)

The Stock Purchase Agreement is an important agreement, because it explains the facts and circumstances of the purchase. However, the Stock Purchase Agreement does not normally contain provisions that govern the relationship of the buyer to his or her fellow stockholders in the future. Those provisions are found in the Stockholder Agreement, which is discussed below.

Secured Promissory Note

In an ownership transition program, the stock being bought by the buyer can usually be paid for either in cash or in installments. If payments will be made in installments, the buyer will sign a Secured Promissory Note, and payment will be secured by a pledge of the stock being purchased. A Secured Promissory Note is a promise to pay money. If the money is not paid as promised, then the lender can take certain property of the borrower in satisfaction of the debt. In this case, the property is the stock being purchased. The property that the borrower has agreed to use or pledge as collateral "secures" the debt. While

Principal Terms of a Secured Promissory Note

- Names of the seller (who is the lender) and the buyer (who is the borrower)
- Date of the promissory note
- Promise by borrower to pay the lender
- Principal amount borrowed
- Interest rate payable
- If interest is adjustable, how often and how much
- When payments are due
- Application of payments to interest first, then to principal
- Penalty for late payment
- No prepayment penalty
- Events of default, including failure to pay
- Recovery of attorneys' fees if needed to enforce note
- Waiver of notice of default
- Reference to the firm's stock as securing the debt
- Controlling law and other enabling provisions
- Spousal consent

there is no hard-and-fast rule, buyers often pay for the stock purchased over a period of one to three years. Once the stock has been paid for, the firm delivers the canceled promissory note to the buyer.

Security Agreement

A Security Agreement is the contract by which a borrower agrees to give up certain property to a lender if the borrower does not pay the debt as promised. The lender usually holds the property securing the debt, or the seller and buyer may agree that a third party may hold the property until the debt is paid, or, if the debt is not paid, until the lender claims the property. (See "Principal Terms of a Security Agreement," page 374.)

CASE STUDY

Problem: How Will the Candidate Pay for the Stock?

Barbara has received the Term Sheet offering her 10 percent ownership of the firm in exchange for $60,000. She wants to buy the stock, but finds that the purchase price of $60,000 is more than she can afford to pay now in one lump sum. The firm is willing to permit Barbara to purchase her stock in three annual installments. How should this transaction be documented? What protections can the firm have if Barbara defaults on her obligation to pay for the stock?

Solution

The firm's attorney prepares an Offering Memorandum and drafts of the documents needed for the ownership transition program. After reviewing the documents with her own attorney, Barbara signs the Stock Purchase Agreement, which documents the purchase and states the $60,000 purchase price for the stock. She pays one-third, or $20,000, in cash at the time she signs the Stock Purchase Agreement. She also signs a Secured Promissory Note in the principal amount of the balance owed, or $40,000, payable with interest at an agreed rate, in two annual installments timed to coincide with expected bonus payments by the firm. In addition, Barbara signs a Security Agreement, giving the seller (either Frank or the firm) the right to take back the stock if she does not pay the amounts due under the Secured Promissory Note.

In an ownership transition program, stock that is paid for with a promissory note is usually secured by a pledge of the stock itself. If the buyer does not pay fully for the stock, then the seller may recover the stock to satisfy the debt. Often the seller of the stock retains possession of the stock certificate until the buyer pays for the stock. Upon payment in full, the seller delivers the stock certificate to the buyer, and the stock is no longer subject to the Security Agreement.

Principal Terms of a Security Agreement

- Names of the seller and the buyer
- Name of the neutral party holding the stock (unless the seller holds the stock)
- Date of agreement
- Identification of the stock as security (how many shares, name of the issuing firm)
- Pledge of the security by the buyer to the seller
- Duties of neutral party holding the stock
- Procedure for seller to claim the security upon a default under the secured promissory note
- Procedure for buyer to dispute seller's claim
- Indemnification by seller and buyer of neutral party holding the stock
- Method for appointing new neutral party if resignation occurs
- Controlling law and other enabling provisions
- Spousal consent

Stockholder Agreement

What happens if an owner dies, becomes disabled, quits, is terminated, or retires? The answers to these questions are found in the Stockholder Agreement. The Stockholder Agreement establishes the "exit strategy" for ownership transition. It is an agreement among the owners that is intended to keep ownership of the firm within a limited group of employees who are active in the firm's business. The Stockholder Agreement preserves the employee-ownership sphere by limiting the situations in which an ownership interest may be transferred and by requiring an owner to sell his or her ownership interest to the firm or the other owners, if certain events occur. Although a Stockholder Agreement is not legally required, it is highly recommended, because it provides a framework within which ownership in the firm may be transferred with the least

CASE STUDY

Problem: What to Do When a Stockholder Leaves

After Barbara purchases a 10 percent ownership interest in the firm, Frank and Frances hire Charlie from a competing firm. In due course, Charlie also becomes a 10 percent stockholder of the firm, and Frank and Frances are considering offering Barbara and Charlie each an additional 10 percent ownership interest in the firm.

Unfortunately, due to health problems, Charlie is forced to resign his employment with the firm five years after becoming a stockholder and is deemed "disabled" under the terms of the Stockholder Agreement. What happens to Charlie's stock?

disruption to the firm, in accordance with procedures that all owners have agreed to in advance of the event that triggers the transfer.

In the absence of a Stockholder Agreement, if an owner dies, his or her ownership interest would usually pass to his or her heirs, who then become owners of the firm, subject to state law restrictions on ownership of design firms by nonlicensed owners. If an owner becomes disabled and is unable to contribute to the firm's business, then without a Stockholder Agreement there is no mechanism to provide for the orderly transfer of his or her ownership interest. Similarly, if an owner-employee quits or retires, in the absence of a Stockholder Agreement, the ex-employee would not be obligated to sell his or her ownership interest and could remain an owner of the firm, even after he or she became employed by a competitor. In a potentially more difficult case, if an owner's bad behavior results in termination of employment for cause, he or she cannot be forced to sell his or her ownership interest in the firm, unless a Stockholder Agreement is in effect.

By now, it should be apparent that a Stockholder Agreement is an important feature of an ownership transition program. The specifics of the agreement must be determined for each individual firm. The following is a summary of some of the principal issues that are typically addressed in a Stockholder Agreement. (See "Principal Terms of a Stockholder Agreement," page 382.) For ease of reference, this discussion assumes that the firm is a corporation and that the interests being transferred are shares of stock. If the firm were a partnership, or limited liability company (LLC), the stockholder provisions discussed below would be contained in the partnership agreement or the LLC operating agreement.

1. Restrictions on Transfers

The first question the Stockholder Agreement typically answers is: What happens if a stockholder wants to sell his or her stock? A stockholder might want to sell shares of stock to another stockholder of the firm, to a nonowner employee of the firm, or to an outside third party with no current ownership interest in the firm. The other stockholders have a vital interest in the identity of the party to whom the stock is sold, since they may not wish to be in business with someone they have not selected. In some states, an absolute prohibition on selling stock is unlawful. To address this problem, the Stockholder Agreement generally provides that before a stockholder may sell any of his or her stock, he or she must first offer to sell the stock to the firm and/or the other stockholders.

The Stockholder Agreement states the order in which the stock must be offered. Normally, the firm is given the first opportunity to purchase the offered stock on specified terms; it may purchase all or some of the stock, provided that it has sufficient funds to do so. If the firm does not purchase the stock, then the selling stockholder must offer the stock for sale to the other stockholders. Any stock not purchased by the firm and the other stockholders may be sold to the purchaser identified by the selling stockholder, on terms no better than those offered to the firm. Upon purchase of the stock, the purchaser must sign the Stockholder Agreement.

The time periods within which the firm and the other stockholders must purchase the stock vary widely among firms, depending upon a variety of factors, including the time necessary to arrange financing to purchase the stock. Normally, the purchase must occur within two to six months. Although owners want to restrict the transfer of stock, some Stockholder Agreements allow stockholders to transfer their stock to a trust for estate planning purposes, without complying with the transfer restrictions described above, provided that the trust agrees to be bound by the terms of the Stockholder Agreement.

2. Purchases of Stock on Certain Events

The most important feature of the Stockholder Agreement is that it identifies the events that will either require or permit the firm and/or the stockholders to purchase stock of another stockholder.

The purchase events can be broadly described as falling into two categories: personal hardship (death, disability, and bankruptcy) and termination of employment (voluntary and involuntary).

TIP

The most important purpose of a Stockholder Agreement is to identify events that permit or require the firm or the other stockholders to buy another stockholder's stock.

TIP

Certain events usually trigger the obligation of the firm and/or the other stockholders to purchase stock from a shareholder: death, total disability, bankruptcy, and termination of employment.

3. Purchase on Death

Without a Stockholder Agreement, a deceased stockholder's stock passes to his or her estate in the manner prescribed by will or by law; the deceased stockholder's heir(s) become stockholders of the firm. If a Stockholder Agreement is in effect, the provisions of the agreement alter this outcome, by requiring or permitting the firm or the remaining stockholders to purchase the stock of the deceased stockholder from his or her estate.

When a stockholder dies, there are several reasons why the remaining stockholders, and the deceased's heirs, will want the remaining stockholders to purchase the deceased stockholder's stock. By purchasing the stock: (a) the remaining stockholders are not forced to manage the firm in consultation with the deceased stockholder's heirs; (b) the deceased stockholder's estate receives liquidity for the stock; and (c) the firm retains the flexibility to sell additional equity to a new owner, whose services may be needed upon the death of a stockholder.

CASE STUDY

Solution: What to Do When a Stockholder Leaves

Charlie, a relatively new stockholder, is leaving the firm due to disability. Under the Stockholder Agreement, the firm and then the other stockholders are required to buy Charlie's stock, and Charlie is obligated to sell his stock to them. The Stockholder Agreement states the formula by which the value of the stock is determined and the manner in which the purchase price will be paid to Charlie. The firm's financial statements as of its most recent fiscal year-end are used to calculate the value of the stock under the formula in the Stockholder Agreement. The firm pays Charlie according to the payment provisions of the Stockholder Agreement, using any disability buyout insurance proceeds that may be available.

4. Purchase on Total Disability

Imagine that a stockholder becomes totally disabled due to illness or injury and that the stockholders have no agreement regarding the consequences of this disability to the firm. Without a Stockholder Agreement, a totally disabled stockholder remains an owner of the firm, despite the fact that he or she is unable to perform services for the firm. The disabled stockholder cannot force the firm or the stockholders to buy his or her stock, nor can the firm or other stockholders force him or her to sell. Such a situation can cause severe hardship on all parties, since the total disability of a working stockholder deprives the firm and the other stockholders of his or her services, and the disabled stockholder of a source of income.

To provide the disabled stockholder with liquidity and to permit the firm to sell additional equity to a new owner, the Stockholder Agreement often requires the firm and/or the other stockholders to purchase the stock of a totally disabled stockholder. Alternatively, as in the case of the death of a stockholder, this could be an event that triggers the optional purchase of stock.

TIP

Life and disability buyout insurance are sometimes available to fund stock purchases on death or total disability.

5. Funding Purchases on Death or Total Disability

The laws of many states require that a corporation meet certain financial solvency tests in order to purchase (or redeem) its own stock. Often a firm, particularly a new one, will be unable to meet such tests. Even if there are no statutorily prescribed tests, the corporation may not have sufficient resources to purchase the stock. If the purchase of a deceased or totally disabled stockholder's stock is mandatory, and the firm is unable to purchase the stock, the purchase price must be paid by the other stockholders, who may not be able to meet this financial obligation. To avoid this problem, the firm often purchases life and disability buyout insurance. The firm usually owns the insurance policies, pays the premiums, and is required to use the proceeds to purchase the deceased or disabled stockholder's stock. Insurance can be very expensive, especially disability buyout insurance, and some stockholders may be uninsurable. For this reason, some firms choose to make the repurchase provisions in the Stockholder Agreement optional, rather than mandatory. As the value of the firm changes over time, the amount of required insurance will vary from year to year and should be reviewed periodically.

6. Purchase on Bankruptcy and Termination of Employment

Often the firm and the other stockholders have the option to purchase the stock of a stockholder who is bankrupt. The rationale for this repurchase is that a person who has suffered severe financial hardship may not be able to bear the financial risk associated with ownership. Also, in bankruptcy, without a prior contractual agreement to sell the stock, stock could be sold by the bankruptcy trustee to an outsider.

If a stockholder voluntarily resigns as an employee or is terminated, his or her stock is usually subject to repurchase under the Stockholder Agreement to avoid a stockholder relationship with a person whose employment with the firm has been severed. If employment termination is "for cause" (for example, gross neglect of duties, dishonesty, or commission of a crime), the Stockholder Agreement may provide for a reduction in the purchase price paid to the terminated stockholder.

7. Purchase of Stock upon Dissolution of Marriage

If the marriage of a stockholder is dissolved, the court may award some or all of the firm's stock to the stockholder's former spouse as part of the settlement. This could lead to problems, as the former spouse would then become a stockholder of the firm in which the stockholder works. To avoid the uncertainties associated with this outcome, a Stockholder Agreement generally requires the stockholder whose marriage is being dissolved to purchase (and his or her spouse to sell) the former spouse's interest in the stock. In addition, if the stockholder fails to do so, the Stockholder Agreement would give the firm or the other stockholders the right to purchase the former spouse's interest. To ensure compliance with these procedures, at the time the Stockholder Agreement is executed, each stockholder's spouse must agree to these provisions by signing a spousal consent to the terms of the agreement. (See "Why Is Spousal Consent Required for Some Program Documents?" page 386.)

TIP

The Stockholder Agreement should provide that a spouse will be required to purchase any stock awarded to his or her former spouse in a marital dissolution, so that working stockholders do not have a former spouse as a stockholder of the firm.

8. Valuation of Stock

The Stockholder Agreement establishes the valuation method and purchase price for the stock purchased pursuant to its terms. In almost all cases, the valuation method in the Stockholder Agreement is the same as the valuation method that is used to establish the purchase price at the time of the initial purchase of stock by the candidates. Although the method of valuation is usually the same, the results may differ each time the firm is valued, since the purchase price for stock is determined at the time a buyout occurs, based on the financial condition of the firm at that time. The valuation method varies

Principal Terms of a Stockholder Agreement

- Names of the stockholders
- Date of agreement
- Restrictions on voluntary sales or transfers of the stock
- Rights of the firm and the other stockholders to buy the stock upon the occurrence of any of the following to a stockholder:
  - Death
  - Disability
  - Retirement
  - Termination of employment
  - Bankruptcy of stockholder
- Upon dissolution or divorce, a stockholder is required to acquire stock awarded to former spouse
- Valuation of stock to determine price for repurchase
- Terms of payment upon repurchase
- Annual limits on amounts available for payment to departing stockholders
- Priority of payments to departing stockholders
- Restrictions on solicitation of firm's clients and employees after leaving firm
- Cooperation between majority and minority stockholders if firm is sold: majority will include minority and minority will cooperate
- Confidentiality
- Voting requirements to add stockholders, issue more stock, and amend or terminate the agreement
- Dispute resolution
- Controlling law and other enabling provisions
- Spousal consent

widely from firm to firm and is unique to each firm. Usually, valuation begins with the accrued book value of the firm, as stated in the firm's financial statements; certain adjustments are then made to arrive at the final valuation, such as deductions for uncollectible accounts and insurance proceeds paid to the firm in the event of the death or disability of a stockholder. Valuation methods are more fully described in Chapter 16. The founder should discuss the valuation method with the firm's accountant in the early stages of developing the ownership transition program.

Indemnification Agreement

An Indemnification Agreement is a risk-spreading agreement among the firm's owners. Its principal objective is to ensure that if any one stockholder becomes obligated to pay a third party due to a debt of the firm, the other owners will reimburse the paying stockholder their respective pro-rata share of the amount paid. The Indemnification Agreement also usually obligates stockholders to sign personal guarantees for the firm's debt. By agreeing to do so, owners enhance the creditworthiness of the firm.

CASE STUDY

Problem: How to Share Risk among Stockholders

Frank and Frances were the sole stockholders of the firm for many years, and before Barbara bought her stock in the firm, they had established a $200,000 line of credit for the firm's use. The bank required that Frank and Frances personally guarantee the credit line.

A few years after Barbara became a 10 percent owner of the firm, and after the departure of the disabled stockholder Charlie, the outstanding balance under the credit line was $100,000. Then the economy entered a cyclical downturn, the firm was unable to make payments due to its bank under the credit line, and the bank canceled the credit line. The bank turned to Frank and Frances as guarantors, demanding that they pay the $100,000 outstanding under the credit line. Frank and Frances each pay the bank $50,000.

Frank and Frances own 90 percent of the firm, and Barbara owns 10 percent. Are Frank and Frances responsible for 100 percent of the amount they personally guaranteed?

Lenders, such as banks, landlords, and equipment lessors often request such personal guarantees from owners. Therefore, in addition to risk spreading, the Indemnification Agreement is also credit-enhancing for the firm.

In the case study above, the founders cannot require the other owner to reimburse them for the amount they pay, unless there is an Indemnification Agreement in effect. For this reason, all owners should sign an Indemnification Agreement at the time they purchase stock in the firm. Some candidates who have been offered a very small amount of stock may feel that they should not be required to personally guarantee obligations of the firm. To accommodate this viewpoint, some firms provide that no stockholder owning less than a certain percentage shall be obligated to sign personal guarantees in favor of the firm's lenders; however, all stockholders should be required to agree to indemnify one

CASE STUDY

Solution: How to Share Risk among Stockholders

At the time Barbara bought her 10 percent ownership interest in the firm, she also signed an Indemnification Agreement with Frank and Frances. Under the Indemnification Agreement, if the firm's board of directors requests that a stockholder guarantee an obligation of the firm, such as a credit line, and if the guarantor subsequently has to pay under his or her guaranty, then the stockholders will reimburse each other so that each pays a percentage of the guarantee equal to the stockholder's percentage ownership of the firm. Therefore, Barbara is obligated to reimburse Frank and Frances for 10 percent of the amount they paid the bank for the amount outstanding under the canceled credit line, or $10,000 ($100,000 × 10% = $10,000). Barbara must pay $5,000 to Frank and $5,000 to Frances.

Principal Terms of a Deferred Compensation Agreement

- Name of parties
- Amount of deferred compensation
- Payment period
- Interest rate
- Date payments commence

another in the event that a lender demands payment under a guaranty.

Deferred Compensation Agreement

In Chapter 17, we described the process by which a firm's value may be reduced and the purchase price for stock made more affordable by the use of deferred compensation. Most firms memorialize this firm obligation in a Deferred Compensation Agreement. The agreement establishes a commitment on the part of the firm to pay a certain sum to the founder over a prescribed time period. (See "Principal Terms of a Deferred Compensation Agreement," above.)

Employment Agreement

An Employment Agreement states the terms controlling employment, such as salary and benefits, title, and sometimes term of employment. Employment Agreements are optional, but if the firm enters into an Employment Agreement with a new owner, include terms of bonus participation, stock option grants, performance goals, and detailed nonsolicitation or noncompetition provisions upon the stockholder's departure from the firm, in addition to the usual provisions.

Principal Terms of an Employment Agreement

- Names of the firm and the employee
- Term of employment
- Position, title, duties, and responsibilities
- Performance goals
- Compensation and benefits, including bonus and options
- Termination and effects of termination on bonus and options
- Nonsolicitation and noncompetition after termination
- Confidentiality
- Controlling laws and enabling provisions

Employment Agreements vary widely in their terms and are often heavily negotiated between the parties. Although it is permissible for owners to place reasonable limits on a new owner's ability to compete with the firm if he or she leaves, such as restriction from pursuing the firm's clients or staff, the courts will generally not enforce provisions that completely restrict a person's ability to practice his or her profession. (See "Principal Terms of an Employment Agreement," above.)

Why Is Spousal Consent Required for Some Program Documents?

Some of the documents prepared for the program may require the consent of the buyer's spouse. These documents are the Stockholder Agreement and the Indemnification Agreement.

There are two reasons for requiring the spouse to agree to these documents. First, some states, such as California, are "community property" states. In community property states, any property acquired during a marriage becomes the joint property of the spouses. This means that the stock acquired by the buyer in an ownership transition program becomes marital property. To ensure that the stock is subject to the terms of certain agreements, the consent of the spouse is obtained. The second reason spousal consent is obtained is to facilitate the operation of the program. For example, if a stockholder were to leave the firm, the Stockholder Agreement would often require that the stockholder sell back his or her stock to the firm or the other stockholders. If the stockholder's spouse had a claim on those shares of stock—for example, because of divorce proceedings—the firm and the stockholders would have to negotiate with the divorcing spouse in what could be a difficult situation. By obtaining the spouse's consent in advance, such negotiations can be avoided.

Ownership Transition Documents for Organizations Other Than Corporations: Partnerships and Limited Liability Companies

For purposes of the above discussions, we have assumed that the entity involved in the ownership transition program is a corporation. There are some differences in the documents prepared for the ownership transition program if the entity is a partnership or an LLC. As explained above, a buyer will enter into a Stockholder Agreement and an Indemnification Agreement if buying stock of a corporation. For a partnership or LLC, there would not be separate agreements; rather, the partnership agreement or LLC operating agreement would be amended to include the same provisions contained in a Stockholder Agreement (such as restrictions on transfer of the ownership interest) and the Indemnification Agreement. For all entities, the buyer would receive an Offering Memorandum and would enter into a purchase agreement to purchase the ownership interest. For a discussion of the advantages and disadvantages of various entities, see Chapter 21, "Choosing the Form of Entity."

21 Choosing the Form of Entity

Many professional services firms are operated as sole proprietorships, or they begin as one. In a sole proprietorship, one person owns all the assets and does business without creating a legally separate business organization. For firms with more than one owner, the business can be organized as one of four legal entities: a *partnership*, a *general corporation*, a *professional corporation* (PC), or a *limited liability company* (LLC). An owner contemplating ownership transition should understand the advantages and disadvantages of these various legal forms because one of the initial questions to ask is whether the current form of business is appropriate for the transition program.

Before beginning an ownership transition program, the owner, together with his or her counsel and consultants, should evaluate whether the current form of the business is appropriate for such a program or whether it is advisable to reorganize the business into a new entity form. Each state has its own laws by which these entities organize and operate, so counsel in the firm's home state should be consulted for the particular legal requirements of that state. Consideration should also be given to the

Entity Categories and Descriptions

Form of Entity	Owner(s) Are Called	Ownership Interest Is Called	Formation Documents	Personal Liability of Owner(s)	Tax Effect
Sole Proprietorship	Owner	—	—	Unlimited	Income/loss flows through to owner.
General Corporation or Professional Corporation	Stockholders or shareholders	Stock or shares	Certificate (or Articles) of Incorporation; Bylaws	Limited	Corporation pays tax on its income, and stockholders pay tax on dividends. Corporation may elect to be taxed as an S- corporation, so that income/ loss flows through to stockholders.
Partnership	Partners	Partnership interest	Partnership Agreement	Unlimited (for general partnership)	Income/loss flows through to partners.
Limited Liability Company (LLC)	Members	Membership interest (also called units or stock)	Certificate (or Articles) of Organization (or Formation); Operating Agreement	Limited	Income/loss flows through to members.

laws of any other states in which the firm operates. The various forms of entity are discussed in the following sections.

Partnership

A partnership is a business conducted by at least two persons, who are the owners of the business. A partnership may be either a general partnership or limited partnership, but for reasons discussed below, professional services firms operating as partnerships are usually general partnerships rather than limited partnerships. This section focuses on general partnerships.

In a general partnership, each owner is a general partner, and there must be at least two general partners, although there may be more. A general partner may sign contracts, borrow money, and incur other obligations on behalf of the partnership without the approval of the other partners, as long as the obligations are within the scope of the partnership's business. A general partner has unlimited personal liability for the debts and obligations of the partnership, with certain exceptions, even if he or she did not personally approve the obligation.

The partnership is treated as a legal entity separate from its partners for many purposes. For example, a partnership can sue and be sued and can own property in the partnership name. Creditors can proceed against a partner's partnership interest, not just the assets of the partnership.

Owner Liability

General partners are subject to unlimited personal liability for debts and obligations of the partnership, with certain exceptions. A general partner is also liable for his or her own professional acts and omissions, as well as for those of the other general partners, including liability for projects and violation of the state regulations governing design professionals.

Management and Control

A general partnership is managed and controlled by the general partners in accordance with the partnership agreement. General partners must be chosen carefully, because each general partner may incur liability on behalf of the partnership, for which all partners are personally liable.

Formation and Maintenance

There are few legal formalities required to form a general partnership. A General Partnership Agreement, signed by all the partners, states the terms of the partnership, including the distribution of income and loss among the partners. A General Partnership Agreement may be oral, but it is strongly advised that it be put in writing to serve as proof of the terms to which the partners have agreed.

Because the partnership agreement governs the operation of all aspects of the partnership, including the distribution of income and loss among the partners, substantial time and effort can go into drafting the appropriate agreement. Once the agreement is completed, the costs of maintaining a general partnership are generally minimal; they include nominal filings with the state and preparation of informational tax returns for the partnership to be filed with the Internal Revenue Service and state taxing authorities.

Tax Aspects

A general partnership does not itself pay income tax; rather, income or loss flows through to each partner and is reported on each partner's personal tax return. Under the terms of the partnership agreement, income and loss may be allocated flexibly among the partners.

Why Not a Limited Partnership?

A limited partnership has one or more general partners, each with the same liability and power as a general partner in a general partnership, as discussed above. In addition, a limited partnership has one or more limited partners, whose liability is limited to the amount of each limited partner's invested capital.

A limited partnership may not be an appropriate form for a professional services firm, however, because limited partners are not permitted to participate in the management of the firm. Thus, a professional who is a limited partner would be excluded from management, or would have to assume unlimited personal liability for the debts and obligations of the partnership as a general partner in order to participate in management.

Other forms of organization, such as the general corporation, professional corporation, or limited liability company (LLC), which are discussed below, permit both involvement in management and protection from personal liability for debts of the firm, and are therefore preferred forms for professional services firms.

General Corporation

A general corporation is an entity owned by its stockholders, and is a separate legal identity from those stockholders. In some states, a corporation is permitted to have only one stockholder, but in all states a corporation may generally have an unlimited number of stockholders. The stockholders elect a board of directors to set policy for the corporation, and the directors appoint officers (such as a president and treasurer) to oversee the day-to-day operations of the business.

In their capacity as stockholders, the owners do not participate directly in management; but in professional services firms that are corporations, the stockholders often serve as directors and officers.

Owner Liability

Stockholders, who are the owners of a corporation, are personally liable for the corporation's debts and obligations only to the extent of their individual investments in the corporation, as long as the corporation observes certain formalities and is not used by the stockholders to perpetrate a fraud. Stockholders may become personally liable for the obligations of the corporation if a court finds one or more of the following factors, among others: the corporation was undercapitalized; corporate assets were used for personal reasons or commingled with personal assets; or corporate actions were not properly authorized by the board of directors or the stockholders.

A stockholder who is serving as a director or officer of the corporation may also be personally liable for his or her wrongdoing in that capacity. A stockholder may also be liable for his or her own professional acts or omissions, including liability for projects and violation of the state regulations governing design professionals; however, he or she would not generally be personally liable for the acts or omissions of other stockholders unless participating in management or design of a project.

Management and Control

The owners or stockholders elect a board of directors to set policy for the corporation, and the directors appoint officers (such as a president and treasurer) to fulfill legal requirements and oversee the day-to-day operations of the business. Stockholders have the right to vote on certain significant events in the corporation's life, such as a merger or liquidation. In general, however, the board of directors and officers are responsible for oversight and management of the corporation, and must exercise that management with care. A stockholder who owns the majority of stock of the corporation may be able to control the corporation through his or her stockholder vote to elect directors and to approve certain corporate actions. In a corporation with few stockholders, the stockholders often serve on the board of directors and as officers of the corporation.

Formation and Maintenance

The primary documents that must be prepared to form a corporation are the Certificate of Incorporation (called Articles of Incorporation or Charter in some states), which is filed with the state, and the corporation's bylaws. To form a corporation, standardized documents may be used because much of the governance of a corporation is established by state laws. This is especially true compared to partnerships and limited liability companies, whose partnership and operating agreements are open to much negotiation and are therefore more costly to prepare than formation documents for corporations.

Corporate formalities must be observed to avoid stockholder liability. These formalities include maintaining adequate capitalization, holding annual meetings of directors and stockholders, and maintaining minutes documenting authorization of certain corporate actions by the board or the stockholders. In addition, corporate tax returns must be filed, and there are ongoing annual filings with the corporation's home state. Therefore, corporations are considered to be more costly to maintain than partnerships or limited liability companies.

A corporation's existence can have a stated termination date or be perpetual. Upon the death or other departure of a stockholder, the stock owned by that stockholder is transferred to the stockholder's heirs, unless the stockholders have agreed in a Stockholder Agreement to give the corporation and the remaining stockholders a right to purchase the stock.

Tax Aspects

A corporation is generally taxed as a separate legal entity from its stockholders and pays taxes on its net income. Any money or property distributed by a corporation to its stockholders as dividends is subject to a second level of tax, as income to the individual stockholders. This "double taxation" is one of the principal disadvantages of the corporate form.

To avoid this double taxation, a corporation may elect to be taxed under Subchapter S of the Internal Revenue Code (a so-called *S corporation*). If a corporation elects to be an S corporation, taxes are levied only at the stockholder level, but all net income of the corporation is taxable to the stockholders, whether distributed to them or not. There are substantial limitations on a corporation's ability to elect S corporation status. For example, the corporation must have a limited number of stockholders and only one class of stock, and no stockholder may be a nonresident alien.

Most professional services firms seek to distribute net income to the owners currently instead of accumulating and reinvesting the earnings. A tax flow-through entity such as a partnership, LLC, or S corporation would be preferable for firms that intend to distribute net income currently because the net income can be distributed without incurring the second level of tax that would arise if a corporate form were used. However, if a general corporation (called a *C corporation*) is used, then taxes at the corporate level can be reduced or eliminated because earnings paid to stockholder/employees as salary, bonus, or other reasonable compensation can be deducted as expenses against the corporation's income.

Professional Corporation

A professional corporation (PC) is a special type of corporation that also must comply with state laws regarding certain professions. In many states, a professional services firm (usually established for architects, engineers, lawyers, accountants, and healthcare professionals) may be incorporated only as a professional corporation. In some states, a professional services firm may incorporate either as a professional corporation or as a general corporation.

Normally, a professional corporation is organized for the sole purpose of rendering the professional services, thus a majority of and sometimes all stockholders must be licensed in that profession. There may be other restrictions on professional corporations under state law, for example, specifying that all officers and directors must be licensed professionals and how the professional corporation may be named. Legal counsel in the states where the firm operates should be consulted to determine the applicable laws.

Limited Liability Company

A limited liability company (LLC) is a legal entity separate from its owners, who are called members. Members own units or membership interests in the LLC. Depending on state law, an LLC may have one member, or a minimum of two members may be required. The LLC may be managed by some or all of its members, or the LLC may be managed by an employee/manager who is not a member. LLCs are a relatively new form of entity, combining the management flexibility and tax advantages of a general partnership with the liability protection of a corporation.

Some states may not permit professional services firms to be operated as LLCs, but they may be operated as limited liability partnerships (LLPs). Legal counsel in the firm's home state and any other states in which the firm operates should be consulted.

Owner Liability

Members, who are the owners of an LLC, are personally liable for the LLC's debts and obligations only to the extent of their individual investments in the LLC, as long as the LLC observes certain formalities and is not used by its members to perpetrate a fraud. An owner who is also a managing member of the LLC may nevertheless be personally liable for his or her wrongdoing in that capacity. A member may also be liable for his or her own professional acts or omissions, including liability for projects and violation of the state regulations governing design professionals.

Management and Control

In an LLC, the members have great flexibility in determining how the LLC is managed, and their intentions are set forth in an Operating Agreement.

An Operating Agreement may be oral, but it is strongly advised that it be put in writing to serve as proof of the terms to which the members have agreed. The member or members who control the majority of interests in the LLC will generally control the LLC. The LLC may be managed by some or all of its members, or the LLC may be managed by a manager who is not a member. The LLC's management structure should be specifically set forth in the LLC's Operating Agreement.

Formation and Maintenance

An LLC is formed by filing a Certificate of Formation with the state. The main governing document is the Operating Agreement, which is similar to a General Partnership Agreement, setting forth, among other things, the management of the LLC and the distribution of profits and losses among the members. Each LLC Operating Agreement must be drafted to consider the particular needs of the members and the LLC. Because of the flexibility available to an LLC in its management and operating structures, considerable time and expense is usually expended to draft the Operating Agreement, especially compared to organizing a corporation. Once the organizational steps are completed, the costs of maintaining an LLC are generally minimal; they include nominal filings with the state and preparation of informational tax returns for the LLC to be filed with the Internal Revenue Service and state taxing authorities.

Tax Aspects

An LLC is an entity that provides the tax advantages of a partnership with the limited liability of a corporation. An LLC permits pass-through taxation to its owners or members with no entity-level tax. Since most professional services firms seek to distribute net income to the owners currently instead of accumulating and reinvesting earnings, a tax flow-through entity such as an LLC is preferable for such firms.

22 Developing Leadership in the Firm

Many, if not all, of the criteria for ownership described in Chapter 15 deal with leadership. What do we mean by that?

What Are Leaders?

Leaders have vision—the vision to see reality clearly and know where they are now; the vision to see the outline of where they want to be in the future; the capacity to see themselves and others accurately; and the vision to see how to mobilize resources—primarily people—to get to that future.

The ability to encourage others to mobilize toward a vision is the fundamental difference between leaders who can achieve outstanding professional work but may not need others to accomplish it and leaders who can move an organization. Much of the world believes in the existence of *whole* leaders, who are typically perceived to rely on natural skills and instincts, and who are believed to be singularly responsible for what is accomplished. Many so-called whole leaders create their firms and shape them in their own image. This is a contradiction for existing organizations which, when they insert a whole leader from outside, frequently discover that wholesale change by one or the other is required before the new leader and the existing organization reach a common vision.

Less understood is the role of *contextual* leaders who evolve and/or are developed within existing organizations. These leaders have the particular ability to lead within the context of that specific organization. Those who understand contextual leadership realize that leadership in established organizations is not a solitary act.

In reality, leadership is a set of discrete but interrelated functions:

- Creating a vision of tomorrow.
- Seeing the discrepancy between that vision and the reality of today.
- Understanding how the external world provides the ingredients for success.
- Tending to the human needs of those in the firm.
- Providing technical competence.
- Organizing individuals and groups effectively.
- Rewarding what most needs rewarding.

We call an individual who does one or more of these functions brilliantly a leader. In reality, most of these functions must be done well for a firm to have good leadership. Firms must concentrate not only on creating leaders, but on creating leadership. The dilemma in most professional design firms is that the type of leaders who founded the organization and performed one or more leadership functions brilliantly are not necessarily the best leaders to succeed in the next generation. The best successors will often have the capacity, collectively, to provide the full range of leadership as well as or better than the founder, while individually lacking brilliance in any one aspect of leadership. In considering the relationship and importance of leadership to ownership, especially to the next generation of ownership, the challenge is to increase in the next generation the collective capacity to provide the leadership that the firm will need to survive and thrive. Recognizing this as the real challenge is the essential first step to the successful development of leadership that will enable a successful transition of ownership.

What Attributes Do Leaders Have?*

Focus

Effective leaders pay close attention to the people with whom they are communicating. They "focus in" on the key issues under discussion and help others see those issues clearly. They have clear ideas about the relative importance, or priority, of different issues under discussion, concentrating only on the most important ones. Focus is demonstrated by the ability to manage one's attention and direct the attention of others.

Communication

Leaders have highly developed communication skills and so are able to communicate effectively. They can get the meaning of a message across, even if it means

*The discussion of these attributes is based on the work of Dr. Marshall Sashkin and is reprinted from *The Visionary Leader* by Marshall Sashkin, copyright 1995. Reprinted by permission of the publisher, HRD Press, Amherst, MA, (800) 822-2801, www.hrdpress.com

devising an innovative way to ensure that the idea is understood. They pay attention to, and have appreciation for, feelings, both their own and others', because feelings are an important part of the visionary leader's message.

Trust

Leaders are perceived as trustworthy. This is demonstrated by their willingness to take clear positions, avoid "flip-flop" shifts in position, and follow through on commitments. A leader's behavior illustrates that he or she is steady and reliable and can therefore be trusted to do as he or she promises.

Respect

The effective leader consistently and constantly expresses concern for others and their feelings, as well as taking care of his or her own feelings. In essence, this factor is what Carl Rogers called "unconditional positive regard" for self and others. Underlying this is the leader's sense of how he or she fits into the organization, now and in the future.

Risk

Effective leaders are deeply involved in what they do. They do not spend excessive amounts of time and energy on plans to protect themselves against failure. They are willing to take risks, not on a hit-or-miss basis, but after careful estimation of the odds of success or failure. All their energy is then invested in actions that will ensure success. Thus the risks that they take are not risks at all, because these leaders are confident that they can do what is required in order to make happen what they see as possible. In other words, effective leaders take risks that concern implementing parts of their vision. Finally, effective leaders design risks—really, challenging opportunities—that others can buy into, so that others can participate in realizing the leader's vision.

Bottom Line

Effective leaders have a basic sense of self-assurance—an underlying belief that they can personally make a difference and have an impact on people, events, and organizational achievements. They believe, in other words, that they can have an impact on final, bottom-line, outcomes in the organization. They know that people can make a difference, and they believe that they personally can do so.

Empowerment

Leaders have a strong need for power and influence; this should not be surprising. But effective visionary leaders want power and influence because they know that it is through power and influence that things get done in organizations. They realize that such power and influence must be widely shared, not just exerted at the top levels by a few. In effective organizations, everyone feels that he or she has a lot of influence, especially over the job for which one is personally responsible. Effective visionary leaders use power to empower others, who can then use their power and influence to carry out elements of the leader's vision.

Long-Term View

Visionary leaders are able to think clearly over relatively long spans of time, at least a few years. Their visions, and the more specific goals along the way, are not short-term to-do lists but are conditions that they are committed to creating over the long term. They know which actions to take to stay on the right track; they are able to clearly explain their long-range views to others (at least in basic outline); they see how their plans can be extended to take into consideration added elements of their organizations; and they can conceive how their visions might be expanded beyond their current views and plans.

Organizational Skills

All organizations must deal with change, achieve goals, coordinate the activities of organizational members, and maintain the system. This measure examines the degree to which the leader has a positive impact on these matters, helping the organization to adapt more effectively, to attain goals, to get members to work together effectively in teams and between teams, and to maintain a strong set of shared values and beliefs. To the extent that visionary leaders can do these things, they help to improve organizational functioning, thus laying the foundation for their visions.

Culture

An organization's culture is defined by the stable set of shared values and beliefs held by its members. Some values and beliefs are more likely than others to support effective functioning and the leader's vision. Leaders must develop and inculcate those values that will strengthen organizational functioning—adapting, achieving goals, teamwork, and maintaining the culture—and at the same time help build and support the leader's vision.

Questionnaire

Dr. Marshall Sashkin developed a self-scored Leader Behavior Questionnaire that describes characteristics of those seeking or being considered for leadership. Converted to question form, they include: Does the candidate . . .

- pay close attention to what others say?
- communicate clearly?
- demonstrate that he or she cares about others?
- consider how a specific action plan might be extended to benefit the entire organization?
- help the organization achieve its goals?
- encourage others to support their views and positions with concrete evidence?
- make points in clear and even unusual ways?
- follow through on commitments?
- accept taking risks?
- have a clear sense of priorities?
- recognize others' strengths and contributions?
- find ways to get others committed to new ideas and projects?
- help others develop a shared sense of what is important?
- communicate feelings as well as ideas?
- learn from mistakes?
- get complicated ideas across clearly?
- contribute to the organization's effective operation in terms of adapting to changes, attaining objectives and coordinating the work activities of individuals and groups?

Process of Leadership Development

Opening to Change

Leadership development in existing organizations requires both individual and organizational change. To separate the two and assume that those whom the founders see as having the potential to lead can be trained apart from the organization limits the likelihood of change by either the individual or the organization. An organization that is not currently developing all the future leaders it needs must change if it is to succeed in producing a new generation of leaders. Existing leaders cannot reasonably expect everything to continue as it always has while the emerging or rising future leaders are created, as if by magic.

The individuals who are not now moving toward realization of their potential must also change if they are to become successful organizational leaders. These people may be excellent technical leaders, but the skills that make them successful in project or unit roles are not the same as those that will enable them to lead in the context of the whole firm. The process of leadership development begins when the present and the future leaders agree that they both must change and that they share a common understanding of the changes their organization must undergo to allow the next generation to become leaders of the firm.

Differentiation

The second step, which is often the most difficult, is deciding who will be selected to be developed as the future leadership group. This means that both the present leaders and the next generation must make hard choices among colleagues. They must designate a smaller group within the whole as having the greatest potential for development. This requires having an honest conversation with those who are not to be included, at least initially. This step cannot be avoided. Postponing the inevitable by saying "let's develop everybody and later the real leaders will stand out" cripples the chance for meaningful development to occur. The act of singling out future potential in an organization only puts *on* the table what is already *under* the table. It forces the existing leaders to have conversations that need to happen. This is one of the very first steps of leadership development.

Embedding the Support Group

For the development of leadership to be successful organizationally, the process must be collective. This requires helping those selected for leadership development to see themselves as a group that can function both as a team with a common objective and as individuals who need to give and receive assistance from others if they are to achieve their goals. Structuring those selected as future leaders into a mutual support group, and then installing that group into the ongoing structure of the firm, assures that leadership development does not become separated and elite, but is fully integrated into, and supported by, the organization across the board.

Development Exercises

Once the context for leadership development is clearly established, the actual training can be accomplished by working through a series of problems in which trainees attempt to solve organizational challenges through simulated exercises that require leadership. Role-play and simulation can be used to create the dynamics of the real firm in developmental sessions. Case problems should be small group assignments that require trainees to experiment with different visions and observe who best fills which roles in a successful leadership team. Participants should also receive individual feedback on their styles and actions. Over the course of the development cycle, case problems can get closer to home until the group begins dealing with actual concerns of the firm.

Alternatively, leadership trainees can be brought into *actual* firm problems, as opposed to hypothetical case situations (as long as these are relatively low-risk situations), they receive a high degree of mentoring from the recognized leaders of the firm, and they are allowed to fail without personal retribution. High-level leaders in many organizations have stated that the most important factor that led to their development as successful leaders was being given the opportunity by their superiors to fail in noncritical situations.

Integration Interventions

The existing leaders of the firm should be brought into the development sessions at regular intervals. Their role is to observe the roles being taken by the trainees (whether in simulation teams or real-time problems) and to evaluate their approaches. The existing leaders should be encouraged to be themselves and to react openly, by expressing their comforts and discomforts with what they observe. Through this step, the foundation is laid for the existing and future leaders to become integrated in the day-to-day life of the firm after development training is concluded.

Conclusion and Recycling

In the optimum organization, leadership development is a continuous process, with progressively less formal training and more integrated development of potential future leaders occurring in the ordinary course of the firm's activities. The final formal exercise of the leadership development process should be a retreat of all the participants—both existing and potential leaders—to explore what further changes and steps can be taken within the firm to assure more internal development of leaders from within.

In *Leadership Is an Art*, Max dePree, the former CEO of Herman Miller, Inc., writes that current leaders owe a clear statement of the values to the organization. They need to identify, develop, and nurture future leaders. They owe the organization a reference point for what people can be in the organization. They owe maturity, as expressed in a sense of self-worth, a sense of belonging, a sense of expectancy, a sense of responsibility, a sense of accountability, and a sense of equality. They owe the organization rationality. Leaders are obliged to provide and maintain momentum, which comes from a clear vision of what the company ought to be, from a well-thought-out strategy to achieve that vision, and from carefully conceived and communicated directions and plans that enable everyone to participate and be publicly accountable in achieving those plans.

TIP

For additional information, see *Leadership Is an Art*, by Max DePree, Doubleday, New York, NY, 1987.

Leadership and Management

Telling "why" rather than "how" describes an essential difference between leadership and management. Leadership and management are different. Effective leaders understand management and management issues, whether or not they function as managers. Important differences are shown in the table titled "Characteristics of Leaders and Managers," page 412.

Characteristics of Leaders and Managers

	Leaders	Managers
Characteristics:	Imagination; ability to communicate; creativity; readiness to take risks; willingness to use power to influence the thoughts and actions of others.	Persistence; tough-mindedness; analytical ability; tolerance; goodwill
Goal attitudes:	Have personal, active goals; shape ideas; seek to change the way people think about what is desirable, possible, or necessary.	Have impersonal goals that arise from organizational necessities; respond to ideas.
Work conceptions:	Create excitement; develop fresh approaches to long-standing problems; open up issues; project ideas into images that excite people and only then develop choices that give substance to projected images.	Formulate strategies; make decisions; manage conflict; negotiate; bargain; compromise; balance; limit choices.
Relations with others:	Intuitive; empathetic; intense; concerned with what events and decisions mean to people; concerned with how to get things done.	Prefer working with others, with a low level of emotional involvement in them; role oriented.
Sense of self:	Feel separate; work in organizations but never belong inwardly.	Joiners; sense of belonging.

Generational Patterns

Ownership characteristics typically change from more entrepreneurial to less entrepreneurial in a repeating pattern. Entrepreneurial founders tend to surround themselves with others who will support, rather than contest, their vision and efforts to achieve it. Next-generation practitioners who stay tend to

Generational Characteristics

	Generation		
Characteristic	**First**	**Second**	**Third**
Entrepreneurisum	Yes	No	Yes
Risk Attitude	High	Low	High
Business Development Attitude	Get the work	Do the work	Get and do the work
Technical Focus	Conceptual	Implementational	Conceptual
Leadership Style	Transformational	Transactional	Transformational
Vision Focus	Long term	Short term	Long term
Patience Level	Low	High	Low

complement rather than duplicate the strengths of the preceding generation. The "Generational Characteristics" table above illustrates characteristics typical of first-, second-, and third-generation leaders.

If the firm continues in practice, it may bring in a third generation of professionals that is likely to be less supportive in nature and more like the founders. This generation of entrepreneurs may see those in the second generation as impeding their own elevation to leadership in the firm. The owners must stay aware that the goal is the overall success of the firm, even if success requires elevating junior entrepreneurial professionals above senior, more supportive ones. Even as early as the second generation there may well be owners who exhibit second-generation characteristics predominantly, and those who exhibit third-generation characteristics predominantly. The farther down the evolutionary path that the firm travels, the more frequently this occurs.

23 Preparing for Future Transition

Why Prepare for Future Transition?

Future transition of some kind is inevitable, even if the firm's owners cannot predict the specific nature of the transition. For any transition, except liquidation, the potential for successful transition is significantly enhanced if the owners begin planning for it, even before they embark on a formal transition program. Since the primary requisite for successful transition is having candidates who will be capable of operating the firm successfully, the nature of the planning should address the matter of identifying and then proactively developing those candidates who have such potential. Conversely, the firm's owners could begin practicing in a way that enables potential candidates to develop the capabilities and skills (rather than proactively develop them) that, if they are successful, will result in their being identified as prospective choices for ownership.

Start Early

There is no reason to wait until some definite or indefinite future time to: talk with the firm's staff

TIP

How to Prepare

- Start early.
- Recruit constantly.
- Share information routinely.
- Assign and delegate judiciously.
- Provide feedback and establish accountability.
- Communicate interest and intentions on a regular basis.
- Mentor continually.

about their careers; communicate information about the firm's strategic goals, including ownership; or identify and then train staff who have potential for developing the capabilities necessary to help the firm continue to thrive. Whether or not targeted candidates ultimately develop the characteristics and capabilities that would make them viable choices for future ownership, receiving the owners' attention can only encourage their professional progress in a way that will make them better employees.

In fact, the principle of educating and training the next generation of professionals is consistent with one important quality that distinguishes professionals from others: they are responsible for educating, training, and generally preparing the next generation, including even their future competitors, since no one except professionals has the necessary knowledge and experience to do so. Conscientiously executing this basic responsibility at every opportunity, not just when ownership transition is imminent, not only enhances the firm's ability to improve its practice, in general, but enhances the likelihood of having candidates on hand who can be considered as future owners.

Recruit Constantly

Recruiting does not necessarily imply hiring. Most firms recruit only when they have the need to add personnel—generally, to fill a specific new project's staffing needs. Constant recruiting enables the firm to keep abreast of changes in the marketplace regarding the education, experience, capabilities, quality, and cost of personnel at all levels. Then, if the firm chooses to manage staff aggressively—that is, replace low-performing staff with higher-performing staff—it will be able to do so. If the firm does not choose to manage staff aggressively, then it will be better informed and equipped to add staff when needed to fill available positions. The firm also will be better able to make decisions about whether prospective employees manifest the capabilities deemed necessary for (eventual) consideration for ownership, in addition to those necessary to fulfill specific project responsibilities.

Share Information Routinely

The owners should routinely communicate information about the firm to staff, especially to those they regard as prospective candidates for ownership. Since it may not initially be apparent who the candidates are, especially if the owners start early, they may be able to communicate to the prospective candidates only by communicating to everyone.

What should be communicated? There are two widely disparate attitudes regarding the kind and extent of information that should be shared. At one end is the "need to know" philosophy that says to only provide information that staff are deemed to require to do their jobs. At the project level, some firms that act on this philosophy provide little or no information at all, essentially keeping from the staff information that would enable them to function more efficiently and effectively. At the other extreme are firms that share virtually all information, believing that such openness fosters personal growth and firm success.

Experience indicates that providing information about the firm's vision for the future, and even about the strategies and tactics that have been adopted to achieve them, is highly energizing. This approach lets the staff know where the firm is going and how it intends to get there. It allows the staff to "buy into," support, and contribute to meeting the objectives of the firm and its practices. Owners who share this firmwide level of information communicate a clear sense of what their firm is about. Doing so also conveys that they are thoughtful, forward-looking, and proactive about the firm's future success. Owners choosing to take this tack may report overall financial objectives and indicators (if not finite dollar amounts) that convey the firm's (and sometimes individuals') progress in reaching these objectives. Conscientious owners communicate information to staff about short-term future assignments as well as long-term career paths. At the project level, such owners communicate information about project objectives, client needs, conceptual approaches, schedules, milestones, budgets, deliverables, and key roles and responsibilities.

Even in firms in which information is shared broadly, however, most owners are understandably reluctant to share certain kinds of information beyond the ownership group, particularly regarding firmwide financial operations and status, personal compensation, and owner-specific data.

Assign and Delegate Judiciously

Delegation is essential to a firm's success. The owners should assign junior staff to projects based upon their skill level, and delegate as much project responsibility as possible, as soon as possible. Assigning appropriate tasks to those at lower levels and salaries ensures they will gain necessary experience and knowledge for their professional growth; moreover, this practice ensures that everyone in the firm, but especially the delegators, can operate most effectively, both professionally and personally—that is, at their highest and best use. It is a widely established and accepted fact that the farther down in the hierarchy a task can be assigned, and accomplished successfully, the better managed the firm will be.

Professionals frequently believe that they cannot delegate tasks to junior staff members who they view as not having as much experience as they have. This is, of course, true. Each year that the junior professional acquires an additional year of experience, the senior does as well, so the junior cannot catch up. The point is, however, that junior professionals gradually develop experience and capability sufficient to assume increasingly greater responsibilities. It is to the owners' advantage to recognize those advanced capabilities and to apply them in the firm's interest.

It is important to note that delegating is different from "dumping." Dumping, which doesn't work, is characterized by the superior who assigns a task to a lower-level staff person, and then completely relinquishes any responsibility for its accomplishment. The superior who "dumps" does not provide the information, guidance, oversight, supervision, and counseling necessary for the staff person to develop the skills necessary to accomplish the task properly or to grow professionally. Conversely, a superior who delegates well assigns a set of overall responsibilities and specific tasks; establishes expectations for their successful fulfillment; provides, or directs the assignee as to how he or she can obtain, the information and support required to accomplish the task; oversees progress; and is available to answer questions and provide advice and counseling, as required.

Provide Feedback and Establish Accountability

The only way junior professionals (in fact, anyone) can know whether they are performing to expectations is for their superiors (in small to midsized firms, the owners) to tell them—to provide direct and honest feedback about their performance on the general responsibilities and specific tasks to which they have been assigned. Such feedback should be offered frequently, and be specific and constructive. The feedback can be given during informal conversations, or written in memo form or other instruments designed for that purpose. Feedback should focus on the candidate's progress in achieving the goals and objectives established for him or her by the candidate and his or her superior.

Regarding accountability, professionals typically understand, and can confirm, the responsibilities to which they have been assigned (although they may be less clear about who is responsible for decision-making on those assignments). When asked, for example, "What happened when you successfully executed that assignment?" the most frequent answer is, "Nothing." If asked, "What happened when you failed to execute an assignment successfully?" the most frequent answer is again "Nothing." This response is a clear indication of a system of responsibility without accountability. Above all, accountability implies consequences; without consequences, there is no accountability. Contrary to popular belief, consequences need not be monetary. On the positive side, they can include personal compliments, public recognition, greater responsibility, growth in status, additional benefits, and other options. At the very least, the consequence of less than satisfactory performance should include specific, direct feedback about that performance and how to improve it in the future.

Communicate Interest and Intentions on a Regular Basis

Prospective candidates for ownership should be made aware of the owners' interest in them. This is particularly important for candidates who can most easily be identified as "rising stars." Rising stars are passionate about, and devote energy to, what they do; generally they have a high level of self-esteem, and often have begun to manifest that charismatic quality typically evident in leaders.

As stated previously in this book, entrepreneurial owners frequently surround themselves with supporters: key staff who assist in achieving the owners' objectives. The members of this supportive group are often the first to be identified as having achieved a higher status in the firm; frequently they are called "associates." As the firm grows, junior professionals who are hired later may regard those in that esteemed group as an impediment to their own rise to the top. If a "rising star" emerges from among the junior professionals—someone whose knowledge, ability, interest, and personality signal future potential—he or she will not remain content to be on a slow track to the top. If that person is, or becomes, capable of acting at an ownership level, he or she is more likely to leave the firm than stay and wait, especially if he or she sees another staff member as being an impediment to his or her personal growth.

Rising stars should be viewed as the future potential of the firm. The owners should express their interest in, and intentions for, them regarding their candidacy for ownership in the firm. Probably this should be done long before the owners might ordinarily think about expressing such intentions. Furthermore, once candidates have been targeted for promotion, the owners should begin positioning them, signaling their intention before the promotions are announced.

Mentor Continually

Mentoring is different from direct supervising and from coaching. The term *mentoring* derives from classical mythology. Mentor was the friend and advisor to Odysseus, and for 10 years was the guardian and teacher of his son, Telemachus. Mentor served as what today would be considered a quasi-coach, guru, and role model. The current practice of mentoring has similar significance. Successful mentors understand the importance of the role they play to a "student," and do not underestimate their responsibility. Being a mentor means more than saying, "My door is always open." Open or shut, junior professionals frequently find it difficult to pass through what can seem to them to be invisible, psychological barriers between owners and staff.

Being a mentor requires taking a proactive stance and establishing a one-on-one relationship between oneself and one's mentee. A mentor acts as counselor/adviser on a wide range of issues that go well beyond day-to-day project matters, extending to all manner of professional and personal issues revolving around the individual questions and needs of the mentee. Specifically, successful mentoring requires staying in regular contact, establishing camaraderie, being available, welcoming questions and expressions of concern, suggesting training and educational opportunities, and providing guidance for personal and professional development.

Most leaders report that having a role model was a key ingredient to their own success; in short, mentors are role models.

Glossary

Following is a listing of terms and their definitions as they are used in this book. Although all are consistent with conventional definitions, a few of the terms have multiple meanings, not all of which are employed herein.

Accrual accounting. Accounting method that recognizes revenue as having been earned when services are performed, and that recognizes expenses when they are incurred, without regard to when cash is received or disbursed.

Accrual basis. See *Accrual accounting*.

Acquisition. Purchase of one firm by another.

Adjusted net income. Reported net income revised to take into account profits that were distributed and expensed as bonuses, profit-sharing, and so on.

Asset. Resource owned by the firm on which a monetary value can be placed.

Backlog. Value of services contracted for but not yet earned.

Book value. The owners' equity accounts representing the net worth of the firm; the firm's assets less its liabilities.

Capital. In the broadest sense, the value of the total assets of the firm carried on the balance sheet; in the narrowest sense, the net worth or value of the owners' equity accounts; more typically and informally, the funding needed to operate the firm.

Cash accounting. Accounting method that recognizes revenue when payment is received in cash, and that recognizes expense when cash payment is disbursed.

Cash basis. See *Cash accounting.*

Corporation. Legal entity organized under the laws of a particular state for the purpose of conducting a business.

Deferred income tax. The liability carried on the books of a corporation to record the federal income tax that the firm would pay if it reported taxable income on the accrual basis of accounting, less the amount actually paid on the cash basis. Since most firms of the kind discussed herein are ongoing concerns, and since any such positive balances that might be produced in liquidation would likely be distributed as compensation, the liability for deferred income tax is more theoretical than real.

Employee Stock Ownership Plan (ESOP). A tax-qualified plan in which the firm's employees become participating owners, in proportion to their compensation, of that portion of the firm owned by the ESOP.

Equity. Value of the firm's assets in excess of its liabilities; the total claims the owners would have to the value of the business if all assets were liquidated and all liabilities paid, as reflected on the firm's balance sheet. See also *Net worth.*

Founder(s). The person or persons initiating the firm. In this text "founder" is sometimes used in place of "selling owner" or "current owner."

Gross revenues. Total value earned by the firm as a result of providing services, or from aspects of the business not central to the primary purpose such as rents or royalties, including value provided by the firm's consultants and owed to them.

Income. Profits remaining after expenses have been subtracted from revenue. See also *Operating income* and *Net income*.

Liabilities. Debts or obligations of the firm owed to others.

Limited liability company. Business entity created by statute to enable professionals to enjoy the tax advantages of a partnership and the limited liability of a corporation while maintaining personal responsibility for individual professional acts.

Liquidation. Dissolution of a company, generally accompanied by collection of its assets and payment of its liabilities.

Memorandum of Understanding. See *Term Sheet.*

Merger. Joining of two businesses to create a new business, generally by combining the assets and liabilities of both.

Net income. Profit after corporate income taxes.

Net revenues. Value generated by the firm's employees, excluding value attributable to consultants or to nonlabor project expenses for reproductions, travel, and so on.

Net worth. The value of the owners' equity in the firm, basically assets less liabilities. In a proprietorship, the proprietor's capital account; in a partnership, the total of the partners' capital accounts; in a corporation, the total of capital stock, plus paid-in capital, plus retained earnings.

Offering letter. See *Term Sheet.*

Offering Memorandum. Document presenting all material information about a firm and its business to a prospective buyer.

Operating income. Revenue remaining after direct and indirect expenses.

Operating profit. See *Operating income.*

Owner. Anyone who has a financial investment in a firm, whether as a sole proprietor, partner, corporate shareholder, or member of a limited liability company.

Partnership. Form of organization in which two or more persons share in the ownership, risks, and rewards of the business.

Principal. Generally, any individual with an equity position in a firm, but sometimes expanded to include anyone with a significant leadership role.

Professional corporation. Legal entity organized under the incorporation laws of a particular state, created to allow professionals to enjoy the financial benefits inherent in corporate forms of business while maintaining personal responsibility for professional acts.

Proprietorship. Business organization owned entirely by one person and in which the profits and losses are the individual's, as are the legal, business, and financial obligations.

Revenue. Primarily, value received from clients as a result of the firm providing its services.

Share. See *Stock*.

Shareholders' equity. See *Equity*.

Stock. Certificate evidencing ownership in a corporation.

Stockholders' equity. See *Equity*.

Term Sheet. Document that embodies conditions (terms) agreed upon by buyer and seller before proceeding to document a transaction; sometimes called a Memorandum of Understanding.

Working capital. Current assets less current liabilities.

Bibliography

The Architect's Handbook of Professional Practice. Joseph A. Demkin, ed., The American Institute of Architects, Washington, DC, 2008.

Financial Management for Architects. Robert F. Mattox, The American Institute of Architects, Washington, DC, 1980.

Leadership Is an Art. Max DuPree, Doubleday, New York, 1989.

Managing Architectural and Engineering Practice. Weld Coxe, Van Nostrand Reinhold, New York, 1980.

The Visionary Leader. Marshall Sashkin, HRD Press, Amherst, MA, 1995.

Index

A

B

C

D

E

F

K

L

M

N

O

P

Q

R

S

T

V

W

Z